The Holy Trinity of American Sports

MERCER
UNIVERSITY PRESS

Endowed by
TOM WATSON BROWN
and
THE WATSON-BROWN FOUNDATION, INC.

The Holy Trinity of American Sports

Civil Religion in

Football,

Baseball, and Basketball

Craig A. Forney

MERCER UNIVERSITY PRESS
MACON, GEORGIA

MUP/P401

Books published by Mercer University Press are printed on acid free paper that
meets the requirements of American National Standard for Information Sciences—
Permanence of Paper for Printed Library Materials.

Forney, Craig A.
The holy trinity of American sports : civil religion in football, baseball, and basketball /
Craig A. Forney. -- 1st ed.
p. cm.
Includes bibliographical references and index.
ISBN-13: 978-0-88146-173-2
1. The sports of American civil religion — 2. Holy rites of football, baseball, and
basketball — 3. Football : American myth of history —4. Baseball : sacred story of
American aspirations — 5. Basketball : American story of irreversible progress — 6.
Doctrines of the sports trinity —7. The ethical dimension of football, baseball, and
basketball — 8. Social tenets of the sports trinity — 9. Experience of football, baseball,
and basketball — 10. Revelations of the sports trinity. I. Title.

GV706.5 .F66 2007
306.483—dc22

2007012035

Contents

For Roy Y. Forney, Jr.

Acknowledgments

Decades ago, I began the journey to write this manuscript as a boy with glove, a wall, and a baseball. Roy and Arlene Forney encouraged my growing concern by providing me with balls for three sports. My sister Linda tolerated frequent use of the car and television for pursuit of sport. Over the next two decades, many coaches, teammates, and opponents helped shape my understanding of games in the United States. At Fresno Pacific College, I came to recognize the near impossibility of playing in the National Basketball Association or Major League Baseball, and shifted more complete attention to academics. Professors Delbert Wiens, Paul Toews, and Devon Wiens inspired me to more disciplined and thoughtful study, a way of life that eventually led to analysis of the sports once played.

Graduate school at the University of Chicago provided much training for the identification of "religion" in unconventional places. Martin Marty shaped and guided my understanding of American religion, particularly the civil religion evident in football, baseball, and basketball. Early in my teaching career, colleagues at Carleton College in Northfield, Minnesota, enlisted me to teach a course on "Religion and Sports," leading to original ideas for this text. Students at Arizona State University helped me clarify and expand pivotal concepts. Joseph Price provided a sense of direction in addition to detailed feedback. My in-laws, Pierre and Janine Gilles, have always been ready to offer support. Pierre-Allen Forney endured my determination to teach him football, baseball, and basketball, while putting up with incessant game-watching at home. Most of all, my wife, Marlene Forney, encouraged me year after year to integrate my academic vocation and sports knowledge, leading to this manuscript.

Sports and Religion

A SERIES EDITED
BY JOSEPH L. PRICE

Books in the series:

Eric Bain-Selbo, *Game Day and God: Football, Religion, and Politics in the South*

Arlynda Boyer, *Buddha on the Backstretch: The Spiritual Wisdom of Driving 200 MPH*

Robert J. Higgs and Michael C. Braswell, *An Unholy Alliance: The Sacred and Modern Sports* (2004)

Allen E. Hye, *The Great God Baseball: Religion in Modern Baseball Fiction* (2004)

Craig A. Forney, *The Holy Trinity of American Sports: Civil Religion in Football, Baseball, and Basketball*

Marc A. Jolley, *Safe at Home: A Memoir on God, Baseball, and Family* (2005)

Joseph L. Price, ed., *From Season to Season: Sports as American Religion* (2001; 2004)

Joseph L. Price, *Rounding the Bases: Baseball and Religion in America* (2006)

Chapter One

The Sports of American Civil Religion

In the United States, sports inspire frequent association with religion. Beyond explicit references to "God," fans "follow" a team like religious disciples of history and speak of "mixed marriages" between supporters of rival teams, considering such unions an interfaith effort. Movies portray the "church of baseball" and "angels in the outfield" while many football fanatics claim that "my religion is football."[1] Slogans of winning teams sound like religious campaigns: "Do you believe? Team of destiny! Year of miracles!" Notorious losers, the Chicago Cubs and Boston Red Sox, generate belief in a "curse" at work to cause their chronic losing, convinced of a determining influence by some diabolical and greater force. Football fans remember the "immaculate reception" by Franco Harris and a "hail Mary" pass from Doug Flutie, apparently evidence of the miraculous.[2] Recently, ESPN advertised games in the National Basketball Association (NBA) as "revelation of the Truth." Nike shoe commercials depict the "congregation of basketball," expectant of

---

[1] *Bull Durham* depicted the "church of baseball," while other films like *Field of Dreams* developed a similar sense of religion-like devotion to the game. See Stephen C. Woodward and David A. Pineus, *Reel Baseball: Essays and Interviews on the National Pastime, Hollywood and American Culture* (Jefferson, North Carolina: McFarland and Co., 2003).

[2] Harris caught the famed pass in 1972 for the Pittsburgh Steelers, while Flutie threw the most famous college passes for Boston College in 1984.

wondrous achievements by "the One," LeBron James, apparently the savior of play on the hardwood.[3] Perception of much similarity between sports and religion pervades American culture.

Historically, sporting games have an intimate relationship with religion. Some tribes of Native Americans played a ball game to mark an especially sacred time of year, while others linked the running of long distances with knowledge of the spirit world.[4] Zen Buddhists performed archery and sword fighting as pivotal forms of meditation, and Taoism produced acrobatic exercises for priestly rites along with the practice of martial arts. Like many indigenous groups, tribes from New Guinea made sport of warfare, then embraced cricket in the twentieth century, transforming the game to fit faith of the people.[5] The ancient Greeks and Romans organized spectacles of sporting competition to honor a pantheon of gods.[6] Enthusiasm for games remained during the Middle Ages, though in a more Christian and localized manner. With the Enlightenment and modernity, sports appeared to separate from religion like church from the state. Nonetheless, they increasingly grew in status, producing mega-industries of professional games and the reestablishment of the Olympics. Athletic contests achieved an unprecedented position of social importance in the twentieth century very personal in meaning for masses of individuals. Sports reached a level of public significance well beyond its historical place. Today, Americans give incredible

---

[3] Currently, Nike promotes the "we are witnesses" campaign about the career of "King" James, asserting similarity between events on the basketball court and those associated with religious faith.

[4] Alice C. Fletcher, *Indian Games and Dances with Native Songs* (Boston: Birchard Press, 1915); James Mooney, *Cherokee Ball Game* (Washington: Judd and Detweiler, 1890). Recently, ESPN covered traditional games of Inuit people in Alaska.

[5] Gary Kildea, dir., *Trobriand Cricket: An Ingenious Response to Colonialism*, video (Berkeley: University of California, 1975).

[6] Stephen G. Miller, *Arete: Greek Sports from Ancient Sources* (Berkeley: University of California Press, 1991); David J. Phillips and David Pritchard, *Sport and Festival in the Ancient Greek World* (Swansea: Classic Press of Wales, 2003); Mark Golden, *Sport in the Ancient World from A to Z* (London: Routledge, 2003).

amounts of time, energy, effort, and money in dedication to play on a field or court, disclosing a quality and quantity of devotion that demands investigation for "the religious."

Scholars of religion help explain the exalted place of sports in the United States. Michael Novak presents abundant examples of how spectators gain far-reaching purpose from sporting events, a sense of direction much like that produced by religions.[7] Joseph Price provides a more systematic investigation, delineating seasonal and mythological meaning.[8] Christopher Evans and William Herzog contribute focus to the discussion through connection of baseball to American civil religion, the national worldview.[9] Michael Mandelbaum explores the "meaning of football, baseball, and basketball," highlighting close association of each sport with one particular era of history.[10] Though giving depth and breadth to the study, current scholarship lacks investigation of how three major sports (football, baseball, basketball) interact to provide a comprehensive and in-depth illustration of civil religion, the belief system of the nation.

Examination of the religious in American sports pivots on the definition of "religion." Too often, definitions focus on beliefs too narrowly defined, so particular as to exclude many historical religions. For example, emphasis on devotion to a personal God fails to include Confucianism and forms of Buddhism. After a century of

---

[7] Michael Novak, *The Joy of Sports: Endzones, Bases, Baskets, Balls, and Consecration of the American Spirit* (New York: Basic Books, 1976).

[8] Joseph L. Price, ed., *From Season to Season: Sports as American Religion* (Macon GA: Mercer University Press, 2001).

[9] Christopher H. Evans and William R. Herzog II, eds., *The Faith of Fifty Million: Baseball, Religion, and American Culture* (Louisville: Westminster John Knox Press, 2002). Evans and Herzog present baseball as an illustration of postmillennial optimism by liberal Protestants, wielders of much socio-political power in the early twentieth century.

[10] Michael Mandelbaum, *The Meaning of Sports: Why Americans watch Baseball, Football, and Basketball and What They See When They Do* (New York: Public Affairs, 2004).

academic research, scholars highlight broad-reaching characteristics and concepts to define religion. Rudolph Otto underscores experience of "numinous" awe, awareness of someone or something far superior, while Paul Tillich stresses the element of ultimate concern, whoever or whatever is of supreme importance.[11] Victor Turner concentrates on "liminality" and "communitas," life-shaping moments of liberating change and unifying purpose that direct a person's "return" to everyday living. Disclosing a set of foundational qualities in religions, scholarship reveals religion to be a complete way of life based upon belief in someone or something sacred, a supreme person or force of controlling influence.[12]

The Six Dimensions of Religion

Most helpful for identification of core features in a religion, Ninian Smart delineates the element of "worldview," marked by six "dimensions" of meaning.[13] First, the dimension of ritual features prescribed actions to guide believers through each facet of time. Second, sacred stories provide the basis for a belief system by way of narratives about key events (e.g., regarding the distant past and future to come). Third, the dimension of doctrine offers concise beliefs about issues of truth, giving well-defined precepts for understanding the source of knowledge, where to find information about truths, and how to solve problems. Fourth, the ethical aspect of a religion defines guidelines for the conduct of daily life. Fifth, the social dimension

---

[11] Rudolph Otto, *The Idea of the Holy: An Inquiry into the Non-rational Factor in the Idea of the Divine and its Relation to the Rational* (London: Oxford University Press, 1955); Victor Turner, *The Ritual Process: Structure and Anti-structure* (Chicago: University of Chicago, 1969) 94–130; Paul Tillich, *The Protestant Era*, trans. James L. Adams (Chicago: University of Chicago, 1948) 59, 273.

[12] In addition to those named above, Mircae Eliade has much influence on my understanding of religion, especially by way of writing about the sacred and profane, the distinction in religion between the extraordinary and the commonplace in religions. See Eliade, *The Sacred and the Profane* (New York: Harcourt Brace, 1959).

[13] Ninian Smart, *Worldviews: Cross-cultural Explorations of Human Beliefs* (Englewood Cliffs NJ: Prentice Hall Publishers, 2000).

reveals modes of interaction with other human beings, specifically in relation to people outside and inside the religion. Sixth, religions generate feelings and thoughts inside the individual in a dimension of experience. Six dimensions of significance express the all-encompassing character of religion, revealing constellation of characteristics to guide investigation of the religious in sports.

Easiest to identify, the ritual dimension presents beliefs of a religion through prescribed actions.[14] Muslims pray five times a day while facing the holy city of Mecca. Christians eat a sacred meal of bread and wine or grape juice, while Buddhists practice some form of sitting meditation. These acts of obligation guide the believer through every facet of time, ranging from daily situations to the once in a lifetime. Ritual actions, such as prayer and meditation, help move the faithful through daily affairs, intended to give an ongoing sense of direction. Less frequent, weekly or monthly activities gather the devoted in a show of dedication to shared faith. Jews congregate as a synagogue, Muslims at a mosque, and Christians in the formation of a church. In a yearly manner, religions demand special actions in observation of holidays and seasons, annual practices to preserve pivotal convictions. Rituals of the lifecycle offer greatly anticipated "rites of passage" to mark maturation of an individual through a lifetime, especially at extraordinary moments of birth, adolescence, mid-life, and death. Religion generates a comprehensive set of ritual activities, providing directive influence during each element of time.[15]

Illustrated by rituals, sacred stories characterize religions of the world. They present select narratives about extraordinary events.[16] Myths of origin give an account of beginnings, particularly regarding the start of life in general and origins of the religion, considered the

---

[14] Ibid.

[15] Arnold van Lenepp, *The Rites of Passage* (Chicago: University of Chicago, 1960).

[16] Smart, *Worldviews*, 71–86. Contrary to popular opinion, myth is not by definition something false, but a story, a narrative of events to uphold characters and ideas. The story can be false, true, or some combination of the two.

way to knowledge of truth. On the other hand, ending stories reveal the conception of things to come. The mythology of a religion depicts the future, providing understanding of how things will change or remain the same. Third in the mythic equation, stories of history underscore a distinctive set of heroes, villains, and events.[17] They highlight who and what is most important in between the beginnings and ends. Religion offers a worldview based upon core stories of origins, endings, and history.

Developed from myths, the dimension of doctrine upholds concise beliefs for guidance on key issues of truth.[18] Most importantly, it gives directives about the source for truth (i.e., theology), where to find knowledge of truths (i.e., cosmology), and how to solve problems (i.e., soteriology). In theology, religions inform believers through belief in a supernatural person, persons, force, or forces.[19] For cosmology, they direct attention to certain locations within the surrounding world for information about ultimate truth.[20] Historically, Judaism, Christianity, and Islam stress the unique status of one book and a special group of people—looking well beyond or transcendent to ordinary aspects of life—while indigenous religions encourage study of more commonplace settings—immanent revelation to be discovered inside the natural. In soteriology, a religion defines how to solve problems and achieve the truths revealed. It presents thinking about the self-help capability of human beings and the aid of someone or something greater. Religion features a set of core doctrines that present broad directives for understanding of truth.

---

[17] Joseph Campbell, *The Hero with a Thousand Faces* (New York: Pantheon Books, 1949). Also, see the distinction of myth from legend by Richard E. Wentz, *American Religious Traditions: The Shaping of Religion in the United States* (Minneapolis: Fortress Press, 2003) 9–10.

[18] Smart, *Worldviews*, 87–103.

[19] Ibid.

[20] Mircae Eliade, *Myth of the Eternal Return* (Princeton: Princeton University Press, 1971); Mary Douglas, *Natural Symbols: Explorations in Cosmology* (New York: Pantheon Books, 1970).

Besides abstract concepts of doctrine, the ethical dimension provides guidelines for topics of daily living.[21] First and foremost, religions offer a method for moral decision-making, offering the guidance of commands, motives, and dedication to relationships. Some prescribe many commandments, strict rules of conduct. Others focus more on motivation of the individual who acts. Indigenous traditions concentrate on responsibility to and interaction with other beings. Beyond a methodology, religious traditions give directives on particular issues of moral concern (e.g., wealth, diet, personal appearance, sexuality, violence, and many other topics).[22] Ethical convictions mark religion everywhere, directing the conduct of everyday behavior.

Often in contrast to ethical ideals, social life involves observable conditions of human relations.[23] First, it includes certain modes of interaction with people outside the faith, approaches ranging from assimilation to separation from the world of outsiders. Secondly, religions generate relationships with other believers (i.e., insiders). Explicitly, they give authority to a special group of people (e.g., priests, prayer leaders, monks, rabbis). Within religious communities, general groups (e.g., the elderly, a gender, an ethnicity, a race) have supreme status. Religion exhibits far-reaching influence, shaping societal relations of the faithful.

Like their strong impact on life external to the believers, religions have great power on thoughts and feelings inside the person of faith in the dimension of experience.[24] Religious experiences vary from intense discomfort and sense of much personal distance from the ultimate truth to comforting awareness of closeness to the source

---

[21] A. D. Hunt, *Ethics of World Religions* (San Diego: Greenhaven Press, 1991).

[22] Nancy Martin and Joseph Runzo, *Ethics in the World Religions* (Oxford: Oxford University, 2001); S. Cromwell Crawford, *World Religions and Global Ethics* (New York: Paragon House Publishers, 1989).

[23] Smart, *Worldviews*, 131–44; Phil Zuckerman, *Invitation to Sociology of Religion* (New York: Rutledge, 2003).

[24] Smart, *Worldviews*, 55–70.

of faith.[25] Much more than a force of fleeting emotions, a religion generates long-lasting changes in individuals. At times, it produces dramatic transformation of an individual (i.e., rebirth), while bringing more subtle shifts in at other situations.[26] The experiences of individual believers reveal the internal and life-changing force of religion.

Reaching into every facet of life, religion features the dimensions of ritual, sacred story, doctrine, ethics, social life, and experience.[27] Of comprehensive influence, it discloses belief in someone or something sacred, a greater power of ultimate importance and all-encompassing consequence. After close examination, sports in the United States exhibit the multi-dimensional character of religions, revealing a national sense of the sacred source of truth. More specifically, the games of football, baseball, and basketball show much evidence of providing a religious orientation, a worldview of far-reaching influence. Working together in a yearly cycle, they portray key ingredients for belief system of the nation, American civil religion.

Civil Religion of the United States

After the revolution against England, founding fathers of the country envisioned creation of a "civil religion," hoping to replace the historical role of the church as provider of a worldview for government.[28] They conceived a "religion of the Republic," a

---

[25] See William James, *Varieties of Religious Experience* (Cambridge: Harvard University Press, 1986) 110–12, 167–69, 371–72. For the classic description of numinous experiences, see Otto, *Idea of the Holy.*

[26] William James describes the contrast between these two types of experiences as that of the "twice born" in contrast to the "once born." See James, *Varieties of Religious Experience,* 173, 356–57, 470. Also see Mircae Eliade, *Rites and Symbols of Initiation: The Mysteries of Birth and Rebirth* (New York: Harper and Row, 1965).

[27] Religion is not something manipulated by the believing individual. It is much more of a directing than a directed force.

[28] See Robert H. Horwitz, *The Moral Foundations of the American Republic* (Charlottesville: University of Virginia Press, 1986); Janet Podell, *Religion in American Life* (New York: H. W. Wilson, 1987).

national set of beliefs to unify the otherwise divided states. A century later, sociologist Emile Durkheim delineated the existence of such faith tenets throughout Europe and North America. He disclosed emergence of "the society sacred in modern nations," illuminating how nationalistic values took on the character of religious absolutes, especially by way of "moral" convictions.[29] Regarding the American form of this civil faith, Sydney Mead described the "nation with the soul of a church," while Robert Bellah underscored the country's trust in "covenant" responsibility to supreme truths preserved in constitutional documents.[30] Historically, the United States has generated a belief system of religion-like function, providing a worldview of great directive power.

Like conventional religions, American civil religion produces dedication to ritual actions. Daily, it inspires acts of devotion to beliefs of the nation, which are formally expressed in pledges of allegiance to the flag and playing of the national anthem at public events. Informally, individuals display flags or other objects to convey patriotic faith. On a weekly schedule, worldview of the country generates public gatherings. Before mass communications existed, citizens would gather in town meetings of political parties to show common civil faith. Recently, gathering occurs around television or radio broadcasts, during "talk to the nation" by the president each week and less formal messages on talk radio or the internet, each venue conveying much devotion to the spoken word. Federal holidays mark passage of each year. Memorial Day, Fourth of July, and Thanksgiving bring special activities for annual reflection on events, people, and beliefs of pivotal importance.[31] Similar to a

---

[29] Emile Durkheim, *Elementary Forms of Religious Life* (London: Allen and Unwin, 1976) 243, 250.

[30] Sidney E. Mead, *The Nation with the Soul of a Church* (New York: Harper and Row, 1975); Robert N. Bellah, *The Broken Covenant: American Civil Religion in Time of Trial* (New York: Seabury Press, 1975).

[31] The Martin Luther King, Jr. holiday encourages mindfulness of the civil rights movement as pivotal time in the nation's history, whereas, Presidents Day draws veneration for exemplary leaders during diverse moments of past adversity.

traditional religion, the belief system of the United States produces rites of passage to define movement through a lifetime. Reception of a birth certificate represents initiation into nationwide community of eminent significance. Action to obtain a driver's license results in dramatic shift to adult level of freedom and responsibility, while the granting of a marriage license or public recognition for vocational achievement marks further maturation according to the nation's way of life. At end to the life-long process, individuals are not officially dead until formal act of declaration by civil official.

Alongside the comprehensive set of rituals, civil religion of the United States upholds sacred stories, narratives best articulated by legendary orators like Abraham Lincoln and Martin Luther King, Jr. Lincoln spoke of a time "four score and seven years ago," recounting story of national origin to declare how founding fathers "set slavery in the course of extinction."[32] One hundred years later, King exalted "marvelous words" of constitutional documents. He took the country back to beginnings by way of storytelling for recovery of original devotion to "freedom, justice, and democracy."[33] Beyond myths about origins, stories of a much better future have been foundational for the nation. For Lincoln, freedom and equality remained "the great work undone," futuristic goals still to be achieved, while King helped inspire sweeping reform by way of a "dream," an account of things to come. Complements to mythology of origins and future ends, stories of history depict national trust in irreversible progress toward ideal conditions. King narrated historical events of exalted importance, "beacons of light" like the "Emancipation Proclamation" of Lincoln revealing destined advancement to a much better future. Stories of beginnings, the future, and history provide the basis for the American worldview.

---

[32] Abraham Lincoln, "The Emancipation Proclamation," 1 January 1863, record group 11, General Records of the United States, National Archives and Records Administration, Washington DC.

[33] His "Dream" derived from the larger "American dream." See Martin Luther King, Jr. *The Speeches of Martin Luther King*, video (MPI Video, 1990).

Derived from national mythology, doctrines mark civil religion of the United States, giving a sense of direction on broad matters of truth. First, the belief system of the nation upholds trust in a higher power, intimately associated with historical progress toward greater "freedom and justice." After more than two centuries, the public faith remains theistic, asserting a supreme being (i.e., "God") as the source of truth. Second, the worldview of the country asserts the transcendence of ultimate truths, knowledge discerned from study of three extraordinary documents (i.e., the Declaration of Independence, Constitution, and Bill of Rights) and the events of a peculiar people, the United States. Third, civil doctrine encourages trust in the works of human beings and in reception of much aid from external forces of divinity, promoting a balance of faith in self-help and other help for resolution of problems. Doctrinal convictions provide structure of belief for many millions from Maine to Hawaii.

Beyond more abstract precepts of doctrine, American civil religion provides directives in ethical matters. Most importantly, it gives supreme importance to concept of civil rights, the governing principle for behavior in the United States. The founding fathers established devotion to "inalienable rights," a source of inspiration for later reforms of the nation. Martin Luther King, Jr. focused on "sacred obligation" to constitutional ideals, a moral responsibility that demanded compliance "now."[34] Commitment to rights of the individual upholds an ethic of individuality, competition, and equality. Opposed to the extreme freedom of individualism, the belief system of the country generates dedication to individuality, much liberty for the individual but with limitation of preserving freedoms for others. National belief in competition supplements the virtue of individuality, asserting trust in struggle against other individuals to best facilitate personal and social improvements. Ideals of individuality and competiveness express civil devotion to pursuit of equality between each citizen, not giving special privileges to special

---

[34] Ibid.

groups. Faith in the absolute authority of civil rights produces an ultimate concern with individuality, competition, and equality, informing moral decision-making throughout the nation.

Of far-reaching influence, civil religion of the United States shapes social life through prescribed modes of interaction for relations with people outside and inside the country. Especially during times of crisis (e.g., war), it promotes separation from outsiders and periods of isolation from others. In more common circumstances, the national worldview generates aspiration for integration with countries across the globe, creating push for a more international life and sphere of influence. For domestic matters, the belief system of the nation expresses measure of belief in a hierarchy of power. It inspires much trust in the federal government, which is deemed to be the special guardian and agent of the public faith.[35] Therefore, historical moments of renewed dedication to constitutional ideals bring greater power to institutions in Washington DC.[36] While generating support for sovereign power of federal institutions, civil faith also nurtures aspiration for equality in society, the inspirational for institutional checks and balances to offset inequities of power. The national worldview promotes a commitment to a combination of separation from and integration with outsiders, supplemented by balanced concern for leadership by way of hierarchy and a quest for equality in domestic affairs.

Like conventional forms of religion, American civil religion produces life-shaping experiences inside of individuals, showing much power in the private realm of feelings and sensibilities. Most of the time, it generates numinous experiences, dissatisfying moments of

---

[35] As a result, Washington DC possesses sacred meaning for the country. Dr. King spoke of the capital city as "this hallowed place," most famously during the "March on Washington" in 1963. See Martin Luther King, Jr. *I Have a Dream* (San Francisco: Harper and Row, 1993).

[36] Recently, the civil rights movement fostered increased authority for Congress, the Presidency, and Supreme Court. See Juan Williams, *Eyes on the Prize: America's Civil Rights Years, 1954–1965* (New York: Viking Press, 1987) 61–62, 142–47, 195–98.

guilt and fear about distance from constitutional goals. Symbolizing faith of the nation, the flag evokes an uncomfortable sense of reverence in the individual and an anxiety about the possibility of taking the country for granted. Times of reform (e.g., the civil rights movement) cause similar discomfort within and evoke a strong sense of guiltiness about great disparity from ideals of the nation.[37] Periodically on a holiday or moment of exceptional achievement (e.g., landing on the moon), Americans enjoy more comfortable experiences, mystical times of feeling close to the ideal life. Much more than a source of feelings, the national belief system inspires dramatic changes in individuals and moments of rebirth. The culture of the nation promotes rich expectations for sudden transformation of fate, anticipating "rags to riches" swings of personal revolution.[38] The United States is the source of beliefs with wide-ranging significance, external and internal to a person.

American civil religion generates many dimensions of meaning, offering comprehensive and in-depth guidance. Like traditional religion, it prescribes rituals for directive influence during every phase of time (i.e., daily, weekly, yearly, and life-cycle moments). Ritual actions of the nation illustrate sacred stories of national origins, future ends, and historical progress. In a set of doctrines, the worldview of the country asserts trust in a supreme being of transcendent truth, supplemented by confidence in self-help abilities of human beings and the aid of someone greater. Ethically, public faith centers on devotion to constitutional rights, which are dedicated to individuality and competition in pursuit of equality. In social matters, it upholds a commitment to a balance of separation from and integration with other countries along with hierarchical authority and

---

[37] King, *Speeches of Martin Luther King, Jr.*

[38] Such expectation drives the gambling industry, offering the promise of overnight change through the lottery or visits to Las Vegas. See James Haley, *Gambling: Examining Popular Culture* (San Diego: Greenhaven Press, 2004); Richard O. Davies and Richard G. Abram, *Betting the Line: Sports Wagering in American Life* (Columbus: Ohio State University , 2001).

push for equity in domestic concerns. Finally, in the dimension of experience, national beliefs generate a strong sense of dissatisfying distance from ideals inside individuals alongside aspiration for personal change of dramatic proportions. Reaching across the country and deep inside the individual citizen, the worldview of the United States inspires prolific cultural expressions, highlighted by three sports of supreme significance.

The Trinity of American Sports

American civil religion exerts much influence on people inside the nation, a reality evident in diverse areas of popular culture. Fast food, drive-through Starbucks, cellular phones, Disney World, and Hollywood movies convey core convictions of the nation. Emerging in the nineteenth century, the sports of football, baseball, and basketball express beliefs distinctive to the country. Key shaper of baseball and a former officer at West Point Academy, Abner Doubleday upheld strong devotion to national values.[39] The "father of American football," Walter Camp was a staunch Republican and passionately patriotic, while the creator of basketball, James Naismith, emigrated from Canada to embrace life in fifty states to the south.[40] Originating in the United States, the three games formulated from pivotal beliefs of the nation, convictions which were inspirational for inventors and shapers of each sport.

Though influenced by civil religion of the United States, early contests of football, baseball, and basketball were highly local events, yet empowered by national institutions. In the late nineteenth century, a game of baseball represented one among many features of popular culture alongside the circus, rodeo, orchestral concert, or

---

[39] Abner Doubleday, *My Life in the Old Army: The Reminiscences of Abner Doubleday* (Ft. Worth: Texas Christian University, 1998).

[40] Harfold Powell, *Walter Camp, the Father of American Football* (Boston: Little, Brown, and Company, 1926); Richard P. Borkowski, *The Life and Contributions of Walter Camp to American Football* (Philadelphia: SN, 1979); Bernice Webb, *The Basketball Man, James Naismith* (Lawrence: University Press of Kansas, 1973).

match of horseshoes. Thousands of small towns and villages sponsored teams, making the game something like the fire department or general store, quite parochial in significance.[41] Similarly, early basketball generated intimate association with the nearby high school, while football inspired close ties to a neighboring college or university. Into the twentieth century, the three sports remained strongly connected to provincial perspectives and were guided by civil beliefs of a heavily local flavor. They resembled the county fair or family-owned business on Main Street, localized manifestations of the nation's worldview, distant to Washington DC.

During World War I, sporting activities achieved more nationalized importance. In particular, Major League Baseball took on weightier meaning as a prominent symbol of the American lifestyle, seemingly threatened by hostilities in Europe.[42] President Woodrow Wilson consecrated the game with great significance, throwing out "first pitch" for the 1917 season.[43] In the subsequent decade, radio communications produced an increasingly nationwide culture, further elevating baseball to featured status. The World Series drew special attention like the Fourth of July, while Babe Ruth, Lou Gehrig, and Kenesaw "Mountain" Landis became prominent personalities across the states.[44] Supported by expanding agencies of news, radio also carried football and basketball to a more advanced position, prompting establishment of the National Football

---

[41] Dale Taylor, *Simpler Times: Baseball Stories from a Small Town* (Waverly OH:, 1997); Taylor, *Baseball through Small Town Eyes* (Portsmouth OH: Shawnee Press, 1996); Robert F. Gayman, *History of Dillsburg, PA., 1901–1950* (Dillsburg PA: Northern York County Historical and Preservation Society, 2001).

[42] Charles C. Alexander, *Our Game: An American Baseball History* (New York: Holt Publishing, 1991) 107–12; Joseph Lawler, *1915 World Series was the First to Attract a U.S. President* (Philadelphia: Philadelphia Phillies, 1987); Benjamin G. Rader, *Baseball: A History of America's Game* (Urbana: University of Illinois, 2002) 119–142.

[43] Ibid.

[44] Thomas W. Gilbert, *The Soaring Twenties: Babe Ruth and the Home Run Decade* (New York: Franklin Watts, 1996); Alexander, *Our Game* 130–55.

League and National Basketball Association, professional organizations of nationwide value. Though not equal with Ruth or Gehrig, football stars like Red Grange, Bronco Nagurski, and Knute Rockne attained important places in the consciousness of the country. More than a decade later, George Mikan and Dolph Shayes of basketball gained similar recognition. Throughout the twentieth century, football, baseball, and basketball grew increasingly associated with way of life in the United States. No longer three among many expressions of the civil religion, they formed a trinity of "major sports," working together each year in portrayal of the national worldview.

Developments in mass communications beyond radio strengthened and expanded exalted position for the sports trinity. Television brought increased attention to events on a "gridiron," "diamond," or "court" of play. Major networks designated time each week to coverage of football, baseball, and basketball, enhancing distinction from other sports. Bowl games of college football and the NFL Super Bowl became inseparable from the holiday schedule of the country, while concern for Major League Baseball grew with increasing number of televised contests. Broadcasts also lifted the NBA and basketball to higher place in national life, presenting dramatic struggles between Larry Bird, Magic Johnson, and Michael Jordan. Advancements in cable television, the internet, and satellite communications brought nonstop coverage to the three sports. Though not the only forms of culture empowered by coast-to-coast forces, football, baseball, and basketball are part of a select group of institutions at the center of attention in the nation. Like activities in Washington, DC, Hollywood, and on Wall Street, they generate actions and thoughts considered distinctively American.

Disclosing special connection to civil religion of the United States, the sports trinity possesses intimate relations with federal institutions. Ceremonially, the president throws the first ball to begin each season of Major League Baseball (MLB) and frequently addresses fans at start of play in the NFL. Congress and the Supreme

Court give privileged status to the three sports, especially to MLB through exemption from "antitrust laws."[45] Stoppage or corruption of games in football, baseball, and basketball draws the intervention of Congress, revealing close association of game action with the "public trust." Like the federal government, armed forces of the nation have remarkably familiar relationship with the trinity of sports. Military personnel are often present at games, many times for presentation of the flag to begin a college or professional contest. Air Force jets fly overhead to punctuate a particularly meaningful game, revealing the strong tie between the play and the national sense of mission. Beyond the federal connections, Wall Street and the largest corporations generate attachment to the three major sports. They pay many billions in advertising costs for affiliation with the competition on a gridiron, diamond, or court of hardwood. The strong bond with national institutions of government, the military, and business express the exalted significance of football, baseball, and basketball.

Though of diverse sporting interests, people in the United States give unparalleled importance to three types of sports. Tens of millions invest large amounts of time, energy, and money in dedication to games of the three, especially to college and professional competition. For better or worse, football, baseball, and basketball command incredible power in the lives of Americans, producing a presence throughout culture of the country. Nationally renowned stars of movies, television, and the musical stage frequent the game action, while phrases and concepts from the sports shape thinking in everyday affairs. Social commentators often describe how a public official "hit a home run" or "dropped the ball" on an issue of civic importance. Corporate executives speak of "punting" and "going deep" on business deals. Sales personnel pursue a "full court press" and sometimes an "all out blitz" to overcome aggressive

---

[45] *Baseball's Antitrust Exemption: Hearing before the Subcommittee on Economic and Commercial Law of the Committee on the Judiciary, House of Representatives* (Washington DC: United States Government, 1993).

actions by a competitor.[46] With informal ties to almost every area of society, the sports trinity conveys intimate association with worldview of the nation.

Federal officials and people of prominence did not orchestrate privileged position for football, baseball, and basketball. Rather public interest pushed the three games ever more to the forefront, motivated by recognition of distinctively American characteristics. Taking place over many decades, movement to center of attention refined the game action to further fit features of national culture. The three sports began as local and even individualistic expressions of civil religion. They later developed into more nationalistic forms. In Major League Baseball, the players union grew strong alongside advancing conditions for workers of the country, while teams organized like centralizing efforts of corporations. Basketball became fast-paced and high-flying similar to the ever faster, more elevated life of the nation. Football developed with increasing coordination of team activities, resembling systemization of society. In each sport, players utilize new equipment and training techniques that produce quicker movements, faster running, and harder hitting, parallel to evolving capabilities of the public by way of technology. Highly organized and powerful forces of the twentieth century groomed the trinity of sports into finely-tuned connection to American beliefs, a close relationship revealed by playing of the national anthem to start each game.

Why Not the Other Sports?

Many games and sports express elements of civil religion in the United States, drawing interest from sizeable segment of the population. Poker, bull riding, surfing, skateboarding, and numerous other activities are very American, each with dedication to certain aspects of the nation's belief system. Poker conveys national expectations for dramatic improvements in personal fate, especially

---

[46] Recently, commercials for Federal Express feature prevalence of sports language in business life.

for the risk-takers.[47] Card-playing for high stakes possesses mythic significance across the states, closely associated with entrepreneurial efforts in "the wild west," believed to have produced more advanced conditions today.[48] Bull riding and the rodeo also preserve meaning from legendary life of the past, illustrating much devotion to conquering nature's adversities.[49] Similarly, surfing portrays American imagination for close yet domineering relations with nature through triumphant human effort on top of the majestic ocean. Surfers exemplify the aspiration of the nation for great harmony with natural forces in the synergistic moment of riding a wave.[50] Skateboarders translated the surfing culture to movement on land in like-minded pursuit of propelled and elevated conditions over nature below.[51] They represent the fast-paced lifestyle of the country, committed to quick departure from the present location in search for greater enjoyment elsewhere.[52] Numerous sporting activities inspire extensive interest in the country, featuring diverse parts of the national worldview.

Though many sports originated from American civil religion, three remain set apart by the quantity and quality of public concern from coast to coast. The president does not initiate a season of poker or rodeo action, while the national anthem and flag are distant from surfing competition. Lacking federal pomp and circumstance,

---

[47] See W Arens and Susan P Montague, *The American Dimension: Cultural Myths and Social Realities* (Sherman Oaks CA: Alfred Publishing Company, 1981).

[48] Wayne Swanson, *Why the West was Wild* (Toronto: Arnick Press, 2004); Nolie Murney, *Poker Alice: Alice Ivers Duffield Tubbs Huckert, 1851–1930; History of a Woman Gambler in the West* (Denver: Artcraft Press, 1951).

[49] See Jeff Coplon, *Gold Bucket: The Grand Obsession of Rodeo Bull Riders* (San Francisco: Harper Collins, 1995); Ty Murray and Kendra Santos, *Roughstock: The Mud, the Blood, and the Beer* (Austin TX: Equimedia, 2001).

[50] Leonard Lueras, *Surfing, the Ultimate Pleasure* (Honolulu: Emphasis International, 1984).

[51] Ben Marcos and Jeff Divine, *Surfing USA: An Illustrated History of the Coolest Sport of all Time* (Stillwater MN: Voyageur Press, 2005).

[52] Rhyn Noll, *Skateboarding: Past-Present-Future* (Atglen PA: Schiffer Publications, 2003).

"extreme sports," such as skateboarding and snowboarding, occur devoid of military personnel. Poker matches may be popular for a time, drawing television coverage, but not year after year. Currently growing in popularity, it attracts viewers on only a few channels of cable systems and for just a few hours per week. From Massachusetts to Hawaii, nonstop discussion on "talk radio" rarely mentions card playing, the rodeo, surfing, or any other sport not from the trinity. Likewise, corporations give little attention to athletes outside the three major sports. Distinct from other types of games, football, baseball, and basketball provide comprehensive portrayal of national beliefs, far surpassing the "niche" following for poker, rodeo, and surfing.

A sport does not have to originate in the United States to generate widespread support in the country. Tennis and golf command extensive interest across the states, though from English origins. Tennis gives expression to the American concern for individuality, dedication to independent efforts by individuals in competition of equal opportunity with others. The finely made court and rackets symbolize national trust in great capabilities of human beings by way of technology, even when without shelter under the open sky. Golf also arrived from across "the big pond" to gather much attention. Like tennis, it fits the individualistic ethic of the nation, giving concentrated importance to personal struggle against other people and nature. A golf course illustrates national devotion to transcendence of the natural. It features prime spaces set apart by meticulous human effort, while nature's provisions present "hazards" to keep distant.[53] The "rough" grass grows naturally and ominously in contrast to the "fairway," an area manicured for optimal conditions of play. Tennis and golf hold positions of much significance as a result of compatibility with pivotal elements of the country's belief system. Conversely, they lack example of group relations (i.e., team

---

[53] For example, golf courses in Scottsdale, Arizona, provide sharp distinction from the surrounding desert, especially visible from the air. Conversely, British courses are more naturalistic, providing "links" much less defined boundaries.

action) and originate overseas, resembling the Episcopal Church or Roman Catholicism, acculturated but not indigenous enough to inspire the majority of the population.

More directly American than tennis or golf, NASCAR grows steadily in civil importance. Increasingly, major networks televise races, while ESPN provides consistent coverage each week. President George W. Bush recently attended a NASCAR event, seemingly to bestow greater status on the sport.[54] Popular for many decades, stock car racing expresses foundational beliefs of the United States. Traveling at high speeds, the everyday-looking automobiles portray grandiose expectations for remarkable feats by common citizens, people who drive mass produced cars.[55] Drivers race in ever faster competitions like the increasingly frantic pace of life on the nation's roads, exemplifying a "get ahead" philosophy and dogged competitiveness. Like successful people across the country, racers benefit from a group of supporters who work out of the spotlight. NASCAR offers more team-oriented action than tennis or golf, appearing truer to life. Compared to the sports trinity, however, it gives too much significance to one individual, the driver, moreover featuring individuals from too limited portion of the country. The vast majority are young men of European descent from the South, contrasted to a more diverse group of participants in football, baseball, and basketball.[56] NASCAR possesses expansive though restricted potential like Protestant revivalism, distinctively American and qualities of great appeal, yet too narrowly defined to motivate most of the nation.

---

[54] CNN News, The President at NASCAR, February 16, 2004 http://www.cnn.com/.

[55] Jeff MacGregor and Olya Evanitsky, *Sunday Money: Speed! Lust! Madness! Death!: A Hot Lap around America with NASCAR* (New York: Harper Collins, 2005); Patrick B. Miller, *The Sporting World of the Modern South* (Urbana: University of Illinois Press, 2002).

[56] Ibid.

The world's most popular sport, soccer, generates growing interest in the United States. Today, millions play the game, while national teams receive an unprecedented level of fan support and media coverage. World Cup matches produce increasing concern, giving stars of the international competition a place in consciousness of the nation.[57] Though advancing in popularity, soccer remains in decidedly secondary position within the country. It receives marginal attention, no primetime broadcasts on television, rare mention by news agencies, and small endorsements from corporations. Worldwide "football" is absent from daily conversations on sports talk radio across the states. Primarily, it functions as a youth activity in national life, a rite of passage into more adult responsibilities and sporting interests.

Similar to ice hockey, soccer provides team action of much international appeal, providing greater potential for growth than NASCAR, golf, or tennis. On the other hand, the game is not particularly American, undoubtedly an obstacle to future expansion in the United States. Unlike the sports trinity, global "football" originated in Europe, the location of things to keep distant according to national mythology. Sacred story of the country's origin highlights independence from England and things European.[58] Consequently, the nation consistently believed evils emerged from somewhere in Europe, generating passionate opposition to the Roman Church in the nineteenth century and Soviet Communists of the twentieth.[59] In all likelihood, soccer is too European to gain exalted status in the states.

---

[57] Much of the country recognizes Mia Hamm, Landon Donovan, and Freddie Adieu.

[58] For example, Daniel Webster admonished the nation to be a "new man," distinct from parent Europe. See Ellen Hovde and Muffie Meyer, dir., *Liberty: The American Revolution*, video (Hollywood CA) PBS Video, 2004).

[59] Marc Stephen Masta, *Anti-Catholicism in America: The Last Acceptable Prejudice* (New York: Crossroad Publishers, 2003); Karen Zeinert, *McCarthy and the Fear of Communism in American History* (Springfield NJ: Enslow Publishers, 1998).

Developed from beginnings in Europe, international "football" exhibits "un-American" characteristics. First and foremost, it prohibits use of the hands. According to mythology of the nation, heroic pioneers possessed little other than their hands to build "civilization" from the "wilderness," while legendary inventors hand sketched visionary ideas to guide the creation of life improving technology. Alongside the exaltation of the hands, the nation upholds strong belief in historical progress and faith in the ability of human beings to produce dramatic advancement of conditions. Football, baseball, and especially basketball generate much scoring, illustrating abundant capability for productive change by the people who play. Routinely, soccer matches end in scores of one to zero, one to one, or two to one, difficult for audiences in the states to reconcile with expectations of grandiose accomplishments.

American civil religion promotes aspiration for success by way of elevation from the earth, symbolized by the airplane and skyscraper. In all probability, soccer plays too close to the ground compared to more airborne action of the sports trinity. As a portrayal of social relations, it seems to preserve European veneration for aristocracy since the goalie remains almost exempt from physical contact, set apart from the mass of teammates. Football, baseball, and basketball encourage equal opportunity to "attack" everyone on the rival team, particularly the most valuable player.[60] Though of great appeal worldwide, soccer grows within limited boundaries in the United States, similar to the United Nations, representing convictions that can be embraced by the nation yet on the whole considered distant to distinctively American beliefs.

Set apart from many other types of games and intimately associated with the national worldview, the trinity of sports maintains an extraordinary position from Maine to Alaska and Hawaii. Each of the three originated in the United States, inspired by the belief

---

[60] In American football, rules offset excessive violence against quarterbacks because of abundant opportunities to "smash" and "sack" the quarterback with much violence.

system of the country, an association refined to greater symmetry through historical development to place of public prominence. As team activities, football, baseball, and basketball illustrate relations of the individual to the larger nation, offering example of individuals from diverse groups inside the states and beyond. Most importantly, the three sports work together to provide a comprehensive and in-depth portrayal of civil beliefs. In isolation, each sport conveys only a certain facet of the nationwide culture. As a unit, however, the three games give an all-encompassing illustration of convictions from American civil religion, expressing pivotal elements of ritual, myth, doctrine, ethics, social life, and experience.

Chapter Two

Holy Rites of the Sports Trinity

Football, baseball, and basketball are yearly rituals of American civil religion, highly expected activities that identify seasons of the year. Football signals beginning of fall and the approach of winter, while baseball announces spring's arrival in a much anticipated movement to summer. Present between football and baseball, basketball marks advancement from winter to the spring. Together, the three sports produce a daily way of life and provide acts of nonstop guidance, particularly by way of devotion to spoken and written words. Beyond the everyday, game action inspires gatherings of fans at certain times in the week, congregating actions in expression of common faith. At special points in a lifetime, the sports trinity produces rites of passage to mark maturation during pivotal moments of birth, adolescence, mid-life, and death. From daily life to the once in a life, three types of games provide ritual activities of directing influence in the United States.

The Seasons of Football, Baseball, and Basketball

American civil religion generates a special concern for holidays, supremely meaningful times of year. The Martin Luther King, Jr. holiday, President's Day, Mother's Day, Labor Day, and Thanksgiving highlight movement through one year, each day with devotion to extraordinary people and historical events.[1] Memorial Day and the Fourth of July particularly define annual time in the United States. Like high holy days of conventional religions, they offer two foundational times of year, one to show dedication and seriousness, while the other produces much celebration.[2] Memorial Day brings yearly remembrance of individuals who died in military service of the country and serves as a moment for display of solemn respect.[3] Conversely, the Fourth of July prompts festivity and activities of exuberance in joyful recognition of many benefits received from national life.[4] On special days of the year, Americans express devotion to beliefs of the nation.

Football, baseball, and basketball give further definition to seasonal rhythms of the United States, providing acts of dedication to civil convictions for extended periods of the year. Football declares the gearing up for winter, particularly difficult months for most of the country. It initiates a season of serious self-sacrifice, a time for the expression of personal commitment to greater good of the nation. Baseball reveals the coming of summer, the ideal season for majority of the states. Games on a "diamond" bring a long-lasting time of festive celebration, a prolonged period each year for activities of enjoyment. Well-situated between football and baseball each year, basketball discloses the advancement from winter's hardships to life-giving renewal of spring. It produces a season of transition and a mindset of dramatic progress from difficult conditions of sacrifice to

---

[1] Like conventional forms of religion, civil religion provides a yearly calendar to preserve a particular understanding of history, highlighting a distinctive set of characters and events.

[2] For example, Judaism encourages solemnity on Yom Kippur and more festivity at Passover, while Islam upholds much seriousness during Ramadan and celebration at breaking of the fast (i.e., the Eid).

[3] See Robert Haven Schauffler, *Memorial Day, Its Celebration, Spirit, and Significance as Related in Prose and Verse* (Detroit: Omnigraphics, 1990); Lynn Hamilton, *Memorial Day* (New York: Weigl Publishers, 2004).

[4] Andrew Burnstein, *America's Jubilee* (New York: Vintage Books, 2002); Tom Schactman, *America's Birthday: the Fourth of July* (New York: Macmillan, 1986).

a more festive future. Based on the seasonal significance of each sport, Americans associate football with the harsh realities of life, baseball with ideal conditions, and basketball with advancement to the ideal.[5]

Football generates a season of serious self-sacrifice, inspiring the endurance of much hardship for a display of commitment to the good of society. Games begin near Labor Day, a time of reflection on sacrificial works by citizens to better the country. Like the honored laborers, teams exhibit strenuous effort for the welfare of the larger group, illustrating dedication to the well-being of the nation. They "leave it all on the field" in exemplary acts of devotion, often despite much pain. Players endure many bumps, bruises, and sometimes broken bones, giving up personal comfort to pursue a greater purpose. The fierce action brings intensely serious time of year, an annual period to marshal capacities of self-denial for service of a higher purpose (i.e., the national good).

Sacrificial acts of football begin with preparation for the next season. Players leave the comforts of home for the austere conditions of a training camp, enduring much suffering in anticipation of severe circumstances to come.[6] To prepare for a game, teams depart a relaxed environment with family or friends for a restricted situation at a hotel, even when at "home." In the secluded environment of the pre-game, a team follows strict rules, demanding extensive self-restraint to deny late-night fun. Close to game time, they escalate concern for sacrifice by taking off comfortable clothing to put on burdensome equipment. To achieve a serious "game-face," teammates pound each other on the side of the head for familiarity with pain and reject personal peace in shouts of commitment. During the game, players refrain from cleaning off after soiled from contact

---

[5] The seasonal meaning remains even where the weather follows a different pattern (e.g., Florida, California) since natural conditions of the eastern and midwestern United States shaped the original character of each sport.

[6] Gerhard Falk, *Football and American Identity* (New York: Hayworth Press, 2005).

with the earth, preserving evidence of self-effacing effort. Displayed on a gridiron of play, prolific actions of self-sacrifice exemplify the American devotion to service of the nation.

Like the players, fans exhibit the sacrificial message of football. They avoid eating much during game action, intensely focused on the field of play. The most fanatical go shirtless in freezing temperatures, and they pierce or paint the body in individual sacrifice to inspire a team.[7] Many stand for much, if not all, of a contest, showing their self-disciplined dedication through straight-ahead looking, intensive concentration on the game. Similar to the sacrifices on the field, he or she stomps and screams without regard for personal enjoyment, creating the most intense of sports environments in the United States. Football generates a season for expression of commitment, time to develop concern for self-sacrifice.

Each year, the abundant acts of self-denial in football lead to a festive end, expressing the American belief in a celebrated life to result from sacrificial actions. At Thanksgiving, games take on festivity. NFL contests in Detroit and Dallas provide part of the holiday feast, associated with thankful celebration quality of life given by the country. Weeks later, college bowl games and the NFL playoffs enhance the festiveness in a time of good cheer for the conclusion to the difficult season of play. Ritualistically, winning teams leave harsh conditions of winter to enjoy the ideal warmth in Florida, Arizona, and California for one postseason contest. Fans join in the celebration, devoting much time to eating, drinking, and site-seeing in a fun-loving time away from home. On New Year's Day, a feast of games produces a festive end to college competition, while the nation gives undivided attention to one final game in late January. Consecrating "the world champion" of professional play, Super Bowl Sunday draws the feasting and fanfare to a yearly peak, a celebrated

---

[7] Frank Wenzel and Rita C. Wenzel, *The Fanatic's Guide to SEC Football* (Pensacola FL: Light Side, 1993).

conclusion to months of sacrifices on gridirons of every state.[8] Football generates an American season of renewed dedication to sacrifice for the good of the nation, commitment inspired by the expectation of much enjoyment to come.

The pomp and circumstance of the Super Bowl signals the approach of longer lasting festivity. Only two weeks away, the start of baseball season announces the arrival of spring and the approach of ideal conditions. "Hope springs eternal" with the beginning of play in the near perfect climates of Florida and Arizona.[9] Highly expectant, fans make pilgrimages from cold surroundings to warm sites of spring training. After the holiday-like preparations of Major League Baseball, opening day for the "regular season" generates abundant celebration, highlighted by "first pitch" from president of the country.[10] Even on the solemn occasion of Memorial Day, games provides a celebrative element, showing gratitude for individuals who died in military service through performance of the "national pastime." Games gain a festive feel with the Fourth of July, the most enjoyable of civil holidays, inspiring play from morning to night and the soon-to-follow All-Star Game.[11] In September, the competition takes on greater significance, as the best teams push for postseason life, while others pursue much anticipated "next year." October brings an escalation of the fanfare, a holiday-like time of the playoffs

---

[8] See Joseph L. Price, ed., *From Season to Season: Sports as American Religion* (Macon GA: Mercer University Press, 2001) 61–76.

[9] Mike Schatzkin and James Carleton, *The Baseball Fan's Guide to Spring Training* (Reading MA: Addison-Wesely, 1988); David Falkner, *The Short Season: The Hard Game* (New York: DK Publishers, 2001).

[10] Thomas Boswell, *Why Time Begins on Opening Day* (Garden City NY: Doubleday, 1984); Lyle Spatz, *New York Yankee Openers: An Opening Day History of Baseball's Most Famous Team, 1903–1996* (Jefferson NC: Macfarland and Company, 1997); John G. Erardi and Gregory L. Rhodes, *Opening Day: Celebrating Cincinnati's Baseball Holiday* (Cincinnati OH: Road West Publishers, 2004).

[11] Nicholas Dawidoff, *Baseball: A Literary Anthology* (New York: Library of America, 2002); David Vincent, Lyle Spatz, and David W. Smith, *The Mid-Summer Classic: The Complete History of Baseball's All-Star Game* (Lincoln: University of Nebraska Press, 2001).

in the Major Leagues, motivating the display of red, white, and blue banners. Ultimately, thousands of games lead to a dramatic conclusion with a two-week festival of the "best baseball on earth," the World Series.[12] Baseball guides people of the United States through a prolonged season to celebrate the national way of life.

Players exhibit the festivity of baseball, particularly in the Major Leagues. They remain in comfortable setting for many "home games," enjoying weeks of closeness to family and family-like supporters at the ball park. Even when "away," teams stay for days in the luxury of a five-star hotel, free to make leisurely trips to local attractions. Before a game, individual players arrive at the park to put on a comfortable uniform, free of bulky equipment. Unburdened, they prepare in a relaxed manner, starting with the easy-going swings of batting practice and other not-so-strenuous "warm-ups." As game time approaches, team officials announce the starting line-ups in carnival-like tone, while the home team "takes the field" in fun-loving jogs like performers at the circus. Furthering the festive feel, they normally throw, hit, and field without painful consequences, engaged in comfortable manner of play. Moments of suffering are highly unusual, stopping the action for medical attention. Routinely, players chew, drink, and sometimes eat in self-indulgence, often engaging in relaxed conversation. At times, one team jumps out to a big lead, making the contest a "laugher" of especially light-hearted experience, true even for the opponent who is delivered from pressure to win. Enjoyable actions of the baseball game generate a season of celebration, expressing American pursuit of long-lasting "happiness."

Like the teams, fans express baseball's festive atmosphere. For extended time, they sit comfortably within supportive chairs and enjoy abundant refreshments in a picnic-like setting. Symbolic of the feasting mood, many foods (e.g., hot dogs, pizza, Cracker Jack,

---

[12] Thomas Boswell, *How the World Series Imitates Life* (Garden City NY: Penguin Books, 1983).

peanuts, cotton candy) possess intimate association with the game. Inspired by the exuberant feel, fans spend money in buying celebration. They receive gifts, compete for prizes, and collect foul balls as souvenirs, while carnival style music extends the happy tone in between plays on the field. Enamored by the playful surroundings, spectators wear fielder's gloves to join in the action, often taking pictures to commemorate the enjoyable time. Teams employ mascots who add humor to the fun-loving setting. They stage musical concerts and display of fireworks to complete the merriment. The festivity of baseball produces yearly time of celebration, a long-lasting season to enjoy the legacy of accomplishment associated with the United States.

In a complementary role, basketball brings an annual transition from the sacrifices of football to baseball's festivities, months of dedication to self-sacrifice in advancement to celebrated achievements. Illustrating a commitment to progressive change, it produces a season without clear distinction from the other two sports. Games begin when football gains significance in November and end during trumpeted beginning to Major League Baseball. After the relatively quiet start, the competition gains a tinge of fanfare at Christmas by way of one or two highly watched contests in the NBA and soon-to-come tournaments of college action.[13] Three weeks later, the Martin Luther King, Jr. holiday carries awareness of something great to celebrate, a legacy of social progress represented by the many African Americans in game action for the day. In two months, college basketball generates carnival-like weeks of March Madness, motivating masses of fans to stay home from work or school, immersed in the fun of nonstop game-watching for four days. Similarly, the NBA playoffs bring enhanced enjoyment of games in May and June, increasing the excitement with each contest. Every year, hoops action leads to the NBA Finals, a seven-game celebration

---

[13] Though nondescript, the annual start of basketball generates "midnight madness," an opening night of fanfare to initiate practice by college teams.

of the sport's very best. Basketball guides the country in a prolonged season to commemorate the advancement toward festive conditions to come.

Upholding American faith in progress from sacrificial effort to celebrated accomplishments, basketball encourages much dedication to acts of self-sacrifice. For training, coaches demand exercises requiring endurance of much personal difficulty, ascetical actions like passing a ten pound medicine ball or scrimmaging with lids on the two field goals. During a game, players exert strenuous effort, resulting in frequent pain. Oftentimes, they hobble off the court, injured in self-sacrificial output. Teams wear slight uniforms, demanding sacrifice of the body in periodic dives for a loose ball. Influenced by the giving tone, fans remain in serious and straight ahead watching for extended time, not much concerned with self-indulgence. Displayed on courts of hardwood, denial of comforts for a greater purpose illustrates devotion in the United States to personal sacrifice for achievement of national betterment of the nation.

The self-sacrifices of basketball express American pursuit of more enjoyable conditions, aspiration for a future of much celebration. After enduring difficulty to "push" the ball "upcourt," teams often achieve moments of celebration as a result of prolific scoring, many times of joy to offset the hardships. Though periodically in pain, players remain mostly free of suffering, able to enjoy post-game activities in relative comfort. Similar to the players, fans frequently transit from sacrificial sitting in focused restraint to exuberant shouting and celebration on their feet. NBA franchises give many gifts and special acts of entertainment to spectators, furthering the sense of festivity. By way of celebrative events to supplement acts of self-denial, basketball produces season of commitment to sacrifice for the generation of festival-like results.

The playing of football, baseball, and basketball marks the passage through one year in the United States. A fourth sport (e.g., hockey, soccer) never quite achieved major status, unable to provide a season distinct from the big three.[14] Together, the sports trinity generates an American alternative to the natural cycle of yearly time, highlighted by three rather than four or more annual periods. Three seasons of sports illustrate the human-centered philosophy of the country, pivoting on faith in the ability of humanity to achieve triune modes of prescribed action regardless of natural circumstances.[15] Like the sacred places for the nation (e.g., Mount Rushmore, Gettysburg Cemetery, the Washington Monument), the games exalt accomplishments by a special group of human beings, not much concerned with following nature. Football depicts sacrificial effort by heroic people (i.e., the United States) to overcome much adversity, oftentimes the result of natural forces, while baseball portrays national expectation of celebrated achievements by people, well beyond nature's provisions. As the third element to the equation, basketball expresses dedication to acts of sacrifice to foster dramatic progress into a more festive time, upholding faith in human capabilities. Functioning as a unit, the trinity of sports generates man-made seasons of sacrifice, festivity, and progressive change.

Daily Acts of Devotion

The convergence of football, baseball, and basketball produces a daily way of life.[16] Aided by talk radio and the internet, fans meditate on and debate the significance of games each day of the year.[17] Showing great dedication, a fan awakens to read, hear, and reflect on

---

[14] Michael L. LeBlanc and Mary K. Ruby, *Hockey* (Detroit: Gale Research, 1994); Randy Martin and Toby Miller, *SportCult* (Minneapolis: University of Minnesota Press, 1999).

[15] The national faith pivots on three modes of operation in every major area of society (e.g., politics, sports, law, business) and is distinct from the fourness of institutions in more naturalistic societies like those of Native Americans.

[16] See Joe Queenan, *True Believers: The Tragic Inner Life of Sports Fans* (New York: H. Holt, 2003).

[17] ESPN exemplifies the never-ending character of the American sports calendar, broadcasting "twenty-four hours a day, seven days a week, 52 weeks a year, year after year" (Game Night, ESPN Radio, 7 November 2005).

commentary about yesterday's action, ritualistically leading to intense discussion with others of common faith through a website or radio program. He or she gives supreme concentration to preparation for watching a game to come, daydreaming about fantastic success by the favored team and clearing the personal schedule for the day in a fasting-like pursuit of pure focus. Post-game, devotees of sports shift to studied reflection on the concluded events and search for greater understanding from a "guru," reached through click of a computer mouse or television remote. Despite many experiences of painful disappointment, fans remain ultimately concerned with the actions of a team or player. Day after day, the sports trinity inspires acts of passionate devotion in the United States, drawing the undivided attention of millions to a field or court of play.

Commitment to football, baseball, and basketball provides the American fan with the daily ability to balance emotions and thoughts, a capability historically associated with religion.[18] The beloved franchise in baseball can give hope when frustration comes from following the local basketball team.[19] If the heroes of football inspire overwhelming exuberance, poor play by baseball players brings a sobering dose of anguish. Similarly, the three branches of federal government offer opportunity for balanced exchange of ideas in politics. Hoped for legislation from Congress can modify disdain for the president, while rulings by the Supreme Court may be cause for comfort to offset troubling debates of senators. Like other pivotal institutions of the United States, the three major sports produce ongoing capacity to check and balance influences by way of triune devotion. Collectively, they provide an uninterruptible flow of events

---

[18] For balance in Buddhism, see Will Johnson, *Balance of Body, Balance of Mind: A Golfer's Vision of Buddhist Practice in the West* (Atlanta: Humanics Paperbacks, 2003). On Islam, see David P. Brewster, *The Just Balance: Al-quistas Al-mustaqim* (Jakarta: Dar al-ilm, 2000). Related to Christianity, belief in the virtue of moderation expresses aspiration for balance of influences.

[19] Recently, Philadelphia fans began a "lets go Eagles" chant while witnessing another loss by the Phillies.

that is foundational to the nation's heartbeat. Even the outbreak of war stops the sports calendar only for a brief moment, as recommitment to playing the games generates a revived purpose for the country.[20] After the devastation of 11 September 2001, football and baseball contests immediately took on even weightier meaning, quite naturally the source of inspiration for renewed faith in civil beliefs. The constant presence of the sports trinity guarantees the potential for national regeneration regardless of when disaster might strike.

Daily rhythms of American life pivot on devotion to the spoken word, dedication to verbal communication as prime means of truth.[21] From its early years, the nation gave unparalleled significance to public proclamation of guiding words, mythologizing declarations of Paul Revere and George Washington. Delivered at Gettysburg, legendary speaking by Abraham Lincoln helped revitalize the Union from growing despair regarding the Civil War.[22] Providing a verbal sense of direction, Franklin Roosevelt instituted weekly "talk to the nation" by the president, while the country expects comforting words from voice of the "commander in chief" in times of tragedy.[23] Beyond political life, American comedians deliver spoken monologue to start a performance, not much concerned with silent miming. Musical tastes encourage "jacking up the amps" for lead singers in heightened focus on mouthed words of meaning. Talk radio and cellular phones thrive in the United States, revealing abundant faith in talkative ways to truth.[24]

---

[20] Jere Longman, *If Football's a Religion, Why Don't We have a Prayer?: Philadelphia, It's Faithful, and the Eternal Quest for Sports Salvation* (New York: Harper and Row, 2005).

[21] Undoubtedly, Protestants had much influence on the American reverence for the spoken work, giving supreme importance to the sermon of a worship service.

[22] Abraham Lincoln, *The Gettysburg Address* (Boston: Houghton Mifflin, 1995).

[23] President George W. Bush delivered such a message in 2003 after the loss of the Columbia Space Shuttle with crew of astronauts on board.

[24] In dedication to the spoken word, popular figures like Rush Limbaugh and Howard Stern exemplify the national faith.

With daily frequency, the sports trinity expresses American dedication to the spoken word. Led by "talking heads" of television and voices on the radio, the media and fans release a never-ending sound of devotion to the games. Players generate much chatter, prolific voicing of words to aid teammates. Good teams "talk it up" in vocal support of each other.[25] At key moments in a game, coaches shout directions and support. They are strong believers in dramatic acts of the mouth. If ineffective, they call "timeout" to verbalize their guidance more clearly. Verbal statements of "play ball" and "here we go gentlemen" initiate the action. Announcers speak words of majestic and enthusiastic tone to introduce "play-by-play" detail of the game, perpetual talking in show of great concern. Post-game, the public anticipates words of explanation, expecting players and coaches to talk to the media. In prolific ways, football, baseball, and basketball display overflowing trust in verbal expression of words as the daily means to meaning.[26]

Increasingly surpassed by devotion to talk, reading written words remains pivotal for the American worldview. Historically, the nation looked to sacred sentences in constitutional documents for understanding of ultimate truth. Legendary leaders (e.g., Abraham Lincoln, Martin Luther King, Jr.) are often quoted from founding texts, inspiring sweeping changes in society.[27] Presidents read prepared speeches, today by teleprompter, to provide guidance for the public in facing adversities. National monuments feature written letters of memorial, present for reverential recitation. From coast to

---

[25] The sacredness of talking in the United States contrasts with the more meditative cultures of countries like Japan where tradition informs teammates by way of silence. See Robert Whiting, *You Gotta Have Wa* (New York: Macmillan Press, 1989) 84, 94–100.

[26] Like devotion to the spoken word, civil faith in the written word expresses Protestant influence on the country. Daily reading of scripture is foundational to American Protestantism. For illustration, see William H. Lazareth, *Reading the Bible in Faith* (Grand Rapids MI: Eerdmans, 2001).

[27] Abraham Lincoln, *The Speeches and Addresses of Abraham Lincoln* (New York: Little Leather Library Company, 1911).

coast, reading a verdict makes jury decisions final, while police read arrested individuals "their rights" to consecrate the act with legality.

Football, baseball, and basketball illustrate daily devotion in the United States to the pursuit of truth through the reading of extraordinary words. For preparation, players read the supremely important playbook, while readings from the inerrant book of rules direct game action. During play, teams follow directions written in public display by a coach. Baseball managers write out a line up of participants for reverential viewing by every team member. In football and basketball, coaches draw designs of plays in commanding marks on a board or tablet. Especially in baseball, fans keep score to record the memory of highly significant events on the field. Regardless of the sport, participants and spectators look to written-like figures on the scoreboard for final word on a contest. Post-game, "scribes" write for newspapers and web sites to help explain the weighty meaning of the competition. Ultimately, the games direct national attention to written words of recognition at a Hall of Fame, giving "immortal" status to a player through honored marks on walls for public reading. The sports trinity conveys American reverence for the written and spoken word.

Weekly Gatherings of the Faithful

Beyond daily acts of devotion, the trinity of sports inspires much anticipated gatherings at particular moments in the week, expressing strong dedication in the United States to weekly cycle of ritual actions.[28] Early in the nation's history, Protestant faith produced commitment to special activities on Sunday each week.[29] During the nineteenth century, town meetings became pivotal to culture of the country with weekly congregations of much significance. Labor

---

[28] The Protestant influence is evident in special concern for weekly time and by way of great importance given to the Sabbath each week.

[29] For Sabbatarian beliefs in early America, see Winton U. Solberg, *Redeem the Time: The Puritan Sabbath in Early America* (Cambridge: Harvard University Press, 1977).

reforms of the twentieth century brought reduction of the work schedule, creating the "weekend," extended time for "recreation." Currently, the "thank God it's Friday" philosophy upholds sacred significance for the end of the week, while proliferation of venues for leisure expands weekend culture into evenings and other nonworking hours. The American way of life promotes the supreme importance of weekly gatherings with a community of common belief, distinct from more routine acts of work.

Expressing devotion in the United States to weekly acts of shared faith, fans gather to watch football, baseball, and basketball, often traveling many miles in show of exceptional commitment. Motivated by the playing of a game, they congregate at select times of the week. Ritualistically, and highly inspired, a fan leaves home to attend games, moved by much dedication to a team. Attendance of football is most directly a weekly effort since most give extraordinary concentration to one game per week, played by the favorite professional or college team.[30] Similarly, certain times of the week demand heightened attention in baseball and basketball, as even the most devout attend select contests circled on the calendar, not a game every day. Set apart from more commonplace watching at home on television, game attendance obligates the fan to wear clothes and other objects of devotion to a particular team or player. To witness live action, sports devotees give hundreds of dollars for parking, food, drink, tickets, and souvenirs in a generous offering displaying much faith. Game attendance highlights the passage of weeks for a fan, disclosing great trust in the importance of activities at a stadium, park, or arena.

If not present at a game, fans gather in a sports bar or in front of a home television to declare common dedication. Each year, the interplay of football, baseball, and basketball ensures such a time of obligation sometime soon, at least once and often several times a week. As though present at the competition, individuals display

---

[30] He or she watches other games with much less intensity.

clothes or other objects of unified veneration for a team, shared belief further disclosed by eating, chanting, cheering, and booing in congregational unity. Sports gatherings pivot on ultimate concern for watching game action, conveying the sense of ultimate significance by search for a big screen to portray the competition. The supremely important watching generates abundant chanting, cheering, and booing in congregational unity. Devoted to the watching of a game, a fan strives to clear obstacles before the television image, demanding an ever better, if not perfect, picture to match the lofty expectations. Giving every capacity to the viewing effort, he or she finds meaning in small details of the competition, often fully engaged in running commentary with others. Problems arise when an individual arrives who is not so concerned with the team of special interest, causing intolerable disturbance from less than total concentration. Faithful followers of a team seek the company of like-minded individuals, gathering at special times of the week in illustration of extraordinary devotion.

By way of congregational acts of weekly sequence, sports fans renew and develop ties with a local community of faith, expressing a parochial version of civil religion in the United States. Each denomination of team devotion possesses a distinctive set of representative colors, objects, foods, heroes, and villains in a unique presentation of the national worldview.[31] In the NFL, Philadelphia fanatics wear dark green, eat cheesesteaks, chant "let's go Eagles," venerate Donovan McNabb, and hate the Dallas Cowboys. Conversely, the "Raider's Nation" features individuals who don black with silver, display shocking items (e.g, decapitated dolls and skulls) to intimidate opponents, yearn for a return to past glory, exalt owner Al Davis, and despise all outsiders. Related to Major League Baseball,

---

[31] For illustrations of the local character to fan culture, see Longman, *If Football's a Religion?*; Dan Schaughnessy, *Ever Green: Boston Celtics: A History in the Words of Coaches, Players, Fans, and Foes from 1946 to the Present* (New York: St. Martin's Press, 1990); Gene Wojciechowski, *Cubs Nation: 162 Games, 162 Stories, 1 Addiction* (New York: Doubleday, 2005).

the Yankees faithful wear a black and white "NY" on the forehead, demand a "world title" every year, gobble down Hebrew National Hot Dogs, trust in a constellation of star players, and nurture great animosity for the Red Sox of Boston. In contrast, members of the "Red Sox Nation" don caps of red and silver, pray for "curse of the Babe" never to return, slurp down clam chowder, reveres hard-working players like Jason Varitek, and harbor much contempt for the Yankees. Supporters of the Los Angeles Lakers from the NBA appear in gold-striped gear of beloved individuals (i.e., Jabbar, Johnson, West, Bailor, Bryant), fly team flags from speeding vehicles on the freeway, arrive late, leave early, and remain not too concerned with anything beyond "SoCal." Gatherings of the faithful followers of a team produce provincial expression of belief system for the United States.

Through weekly acts of team devotion, fans of the sports trinity convey faith in a combination of local and national convictions. Week after week, they gather with parochial motivation, yet are inspired by broader concepts of the nation. Most fans uphold quite personal thoughts and feelings closely associated with the United States, integrating the most intimate convictions with coast-to-coast values. To start each game, singing of the national anthem produces reflection on weighty meaning of the country at least once a week, while the ever-present flag provides a constant reminder to balance local allegiances with dedication to the nation. Gatherings for the watching of football, basketball, and baseball encourage connection to both local and nationwide tenets of faith, resembling congregations of a religious denomination expressive of a larger tradition of religion (e.g., the Methodist Church of Christianity).

Life-Cycle Rituals

Offering a complete set of rituals for guidance of the public, American civil religion generates activities to direct movement through a lifetime, rites of passage that mark maturation for individuals at key moments of birth, adolescence, mid-life, and death.[32] Prime agent of the national worldview, the federal government demands purposeful interaction at pivotal points in the life cycle. After a birth, parents give money and personal information to obtain a birth certificate from civil authorities, representing possession of a future opportunity and responsibility. At age sixteen, young people endure governmental examination to receive a driver's license, a public event to mark the dramatic shift to adult status by way of ability to freely travel. Later moments of marriage, divorce, and retirement require formal recognition from officials of government, bringing marked changes in the lifestyle of the individual.[33] At death, the deceased remains on list of the living until declaration by civil authority, not quite passed on without the public action. Providing a sense of direction throughout every phase of time, the belief system of United States upholds devotion to ritual acts of obligation at pivotal moments in a lifetime.

Originating from distinctively American beliefs, the sports trinity is very much part of the life cycle in the nation. After birth, the gift of a football, basketball, or baseball encourages parental dedication to raise the baby in ways of the games, commitment closely associated with the teaching of national convictions. Gift-giving inspires the vow by the parents to play one or more of the three sports with the child sometime soon. Motivated by this sense of responsibility, fans take infants to a game in an initiation to sports devotion.[34] Whether the parent of a baby or not, they gain awareness of infant stage to life through ritual watching of games, at some point

---

[32] See Fiona Bowie, *The Anthropology of Religion: An Introduction* (Malden MA: Blackwell Publishing, 2000); Victor Turner, *The Ritual Process: Structure and Anti-structure* (Chicago: University of Chicago, 1969) 168–72.

[33] Jane R. Chapman and Margaret J. Gates, *Women into Wives: The Legal and Economic Impact of Marriage* (Beverly Hill: Sage Publications, 1977); Lynne M. Casper and Suzanne M. Bianchi, *Continuity and Change in the American Family* (Thousand Oaks CA: Sage Publications, 2002).

[34] Such acts of initiation are especially characteristic of baseball fans. See Wayne Stewart, *Fathers, Sons, and Baseball: Our National Pastime and the Ties that Bind* (Guilford: Lyons Press, 2002).

cognizant of a player who misses action for birth of a son or daughter. Knowledgeable of birth information for players, a fan may grow more appreciative of infants everywhere, the result of recognition that even the greatest players were once babies too.

Initiated by birth, Americans play football, baseball, and basketball as rites of passage into adulthood. Coast to coast, dedication to the sports trinity nearly guarantees that an individual will find maturing direction in at least one of the three games.[35] Most citizens identify with one of the sports trinity to participate during childhood and often into adolescence, gaining exposure to beliefs and values of the national worldview like a civil catechism. Frequently, attendance of a professional football, baseball, or basketball contest provides public activity to highlight special birthdays for teenagers (e.g., the sixteenth), while attending at a game by personal choice for the first time marks a key moment in the development of a fan, establishing voluntary participation in devotion to the games.[36] Through ritual watching of games, fans become mindful that heroic figures were somewhat confused and awkward teenagers not so long ago, creating potential for ongoing respect for the young.

Sometime after teenage years, the change from player to spectator of the sports trinity represents maturity to a more senior position in the United States, a guardianship role with overseeing responsibilities.[37] Perception of elevated status fuels the popularity of talk radio and chatting online, as many thousands make public pronouncements about state of the games, motivated by self-concept of advanced position.[38] Fans declare seemingly authoritative

---

[35] Other sports like soccer grow in popularity for this stage in life but not so much into more adult years.

[36] See below, chapters 2–10 discuss the ingredients of this worldview.

[37] Many individuals continue to play as "weekend warriors" while in transition to full time fans.

[38] For an overview of sports talk radio, see Alan Eisenstock, *Sports Talk: A Journey inside the World of Sports Talk Radio* (New York: Pocket Books, 2001); John M. Dempsey, *Sports-talk Radio in America: Its Context and Culture* (Binghampton NY: Haworth Half-court Press, 2006).

statements, often with assumption of knowing more than the coaches or professional analysts. Inspired by the self-concept of much maturity, they predict outcomes in the role of the seer. When not pontificating, a fan helps conduct "fantasy leagues," exercising the imagined ability to run a team better than the real officials of teams.[39] The annual convergence of football, baseball, and basketball makes permanent a fan's sense of eldership, without end, year after year. Ultimately, visit to the Hall of Fame in Cooperstown, Canton, or Spring-field completes the maturation process, sealing the intimate relationship with the game honored there.

Pivotal for fans, memorable events of the sports trinity highlight passage through a lifetime. Individuals remember seasons of life based on extraordinary moments on a field or court of play. Bostonians associate years around 1986 with the catastrophic error by Bill Buckner, turning the joy of an apparent championship into a difficult defeat to accept. In Boston, painful memories seem distant now in a more enjoyable time after 2004, the year of World Series victory by the Red Sox. Philadelphians are mindful of hard years during the 1960s, illustrated by the Phillies' collapse of 1964 and frequent loses to teams of Celtic greats by the Seventy-Sixers. Today, they yearn for happier times like the 1980s when city franchises won championships. Until 2005, Chicago fans expected disappointment in baseball, influenced by nearly a century of defeats for the Cubs and White Sox. Chicagoans maintained more hopeful sensibilities, however, as a result of excellence by the Bulls and Bears not so long ago. Unforgettable moments in football, baseball, and basketball mark the lifespan of millions in the United States, making a game as a prime setting for key steps in life such as an engagement or wedding.[40]

---

[39] Convinced of their advanced knowledge, fans frequently submit applications for open positions of head coach in the NFL. See Robert Ley, *Outside the Lines*, ESPN Television, 16 October 2005).

[40] On Valentines Day, Feburary 2006, five couples married at halftime of a Miami Heat game, while the "Mike and Mike Show" on ESPN Radio promoted

Of great significance throughout the life of a fan, the sports trinity provides rites of passage at times of death. Particularly zealous individuals request that their cremated remains be spread at or near a beloved field or court.[41] In 2006, MLB granted permission to Eternal Images Corporation to produce caskets and cremation urns with team logos and colors, providing opportunity to make a final statement of devotion. Others mark completion of the life cycle by leaving their season tickets to posterity, passing on inheritance of dedication to the games.[42] Most fans leave behind a less dramatic yet inspirational legacy, a life-long example of devotion to football, baseball, and basketball. Then, game watching takes on weighty meaning to children of the deceased, becoming an act of memorial to a departed loved one. Similarly, players point skyward to express motivation from passed loved ones who motivate their efforts. In the public eye, they face the death of parents, spouses, or children, exemplars of how to confront inevitable demise of beloved persons. Every spectator watches the unstoppable aging of players, a witness to the mortality of even the greatest stars. Though seventy years ago, the shocking revelation of Lou Gehrig's cancer still shapes national

---

"March Marriage" for couples to tie the knot as part of festivities for the NCAA tournament of basketball.

[41] Recently, a son spread the ashes of his mother, a die-hard Eagles fan, while a Pittsburgh Steelers fanatic was buried with his seat from Three Rivers Stadium.

[42] E.g., Chicago Cubs great Ernie Banks frequently speaks of a special purpose in playing at Wrigley Field because "generation after generation follow the Cubs." Ernie Banks, interview by Carl Ravich, *Baseball Tonight*, ESPN, 5 August 2005.

sense of human finitude.[43] From transitional moments in the life cycle to acts of devotion, the three major sports produce a never-ending way of life, offering the guidance of distinctively American beliefs from birth to death.

---

[43] Later events furthered the understanding of human mortality, like the sudden retirement of Magic Johnson in 1991.

Chapter Three

Football:
American Myth of History

Football is more than a game. It is life marked by one hundred yards. Football is where men become myths and moments legend.[1]

Three sports mark the passage through one year in the United States, expressing three sacred stories of the national worldview. Football depicts the mythology about the realities of life inside history. Baseball portrays an eschatological myth, a narrative of existence to come at the end of time. Third element to the mythic equation, basketball illustrates the mythology about irreversible progress from difficulties of the past to a much better future. Collectively, the sports trinity presents American stories of history, the future, and rapid advancement to an ideal end.

Football demonstrates the narrative of historical realities. A clock governs the action, communicating perception of life inside of time, common conditions within history.[2] The playing field is a rectangle, filled with smaller rectangles like the setting of ordinary

---

[1] NFL Films (Bristol CT: ESPN Broadcast, 12 September 2004).

[2] For a discussion on the significance of time in rituals, see Richard K. Fenn, *The End of Time: Ritual and the Forging of the Soul* (London: SPCK, 1997); Goran Aijmur, *Symbolic Textures: Studies in Cultural Meaning* (Goteburg, Sweden: Acta Universitatis Gothoburgesis, 1998).

living.[3] Everyday, similarly shaped cars move people through rectangular intersections on the way to a rectangle of office space at work. Players too present rectangular look as a result of the shoulder and hip pads that cover more round features of the body. To start each play, teams line up in rectangular fashion, forming "the box" of most intense action near the line of scrimmage. Representing objectives of the game, the end zones offer rectangles of scoring sanctuary, while goalposts form an open-ended rectangle that extends the four-sided imagery into eternity. Pervasive rectangles convey association of the game with ordinary circumstances in the United States.

Like the vast array of figures that clutter everyday affairs, numbers permeate a football field like the overwhelming figures that clutter everyday affairs. Players move past number after number similar to the addresses, phone numbers, and identification digits of the daily grind. Ever-present numbers give a specific location to each movement in a game, resembling the overanalyzed activities of the typical day. Ball carriers run to very particular places like drivers across the country who move past clearly defined street positions. A running back receives the hand-off at the ten yard line, runs to the fifteen, twenty, twenty-five, thirty, thirty-five, forty, and goes out of bounds at the forty-three, a well located trip. Numbers situate play in relation to width of the field. For offensive performance, odd numbers designate space to left of center and even numbers represent areas on the right. Prescribed plays from the sidelines call for running through the "three hole" left or "four hole" right, giving specific directions for travel like prescribed errands of work life in the nation. Displayed on the gridiron, familiar looking numbers express American perception of everyday realities.

---

[3] Barbara Rose, *Ellsworth Kelley: Curves/Rectangles* (New York: Blum Helmun, 1989); Mircea Eliade, Joseph M. Kitagawa, and Charles H. Long, ed., *Myths and Symbols: Studies in Honor of Mircea Eliade* (Chicago: University of Chicago Press, 1969); Tim Imgold, *Encyclopedia of Anthropology* (London: Routledge, 1997).

Among the vast array of numbers, the number four pervades football, enhancing the connection to four-sided conditions of daily life. Teams receive set of four downs to move forward ten yards, while four quarters of time complete one game. A multiple of four, twenty four-sided shapes make up a football field, covering four times thirty yards in length and four times forty feet wide. Goals of the game, two end zones are four times one hundred-seventy square feet. Every line on the field is four inches wide, except for the goal line of four plus four inches.[4] The regular season of play occurs during four months, while twelve or sixteen games, multiples of four, routinely characterize the schedule for college and NFL games respectively. The abundant use of the number four illustrates association of the game with ordinary existence.

The football is a flawed shape, an oblong representing American perception of decidedly imperfect conditions. It never bounces the same way twice in portrayal of far from ideal settings where players cannot fully anticipate. Oftentimes, coaches and fans believe "the ball is simply not bouncing our way," communicating a sense of the problematic state of affairs that cause much adversity without just cause. If not thrown just right, the ball "wobbles" and "flutters" in an unsightly manner. Even when flung properly, it produces a "spiral," movement linked to situations of impending loss of control and disaster. In flight, the ball resembles a "bullet," boring in on the receiver with an intensity that makes the catch difficult. Flights of the football express civil mindset of highly flawed and adverse realities.

A football is brown, associated with the earth, considered crude and "dirty" in the United States and is covered by much concrete.[5] Nicknamed "the pigskin," it draws association with an animal deemed

---

[4], *NCAA Football Rules and Interpretations: ISSN 0735-5144* (Shawnee Mission KS: NCAA Publication, 2004).

[5] Traditionally, Native Americans have a very different view of the earth, symbolized by prayer places dug down into the earth. See Joseph Bruchac, *The Native American Sweat Lodge: History and Legends* (Freedom CA: Freedom Press, 1993).

unclean, ever close to the ground.[6] Currently played on a grass-covered field, a game leads inevitably to closeness with the brown ground. Games occur in fall and winter when the grass turns earthy brown, while incessant contact with the turf causes emergence of brown soil by the end of a contest. Invariably, "chewed up" conditions on the field bring a brownish setting, resembling earthly color of the ball. Football conveys the American understanding of much difficulty lived near the ground.

Civil religion of the United States upholds belief in the adverse nature of life close to the earth. According to national stories, heroic pioneers faced great hardships living on "wild" lands of the West. Frequently, they became "stuck in the mud," only to find suffocating dust at the end of long journeys.[7] Decades later, dusty ground on the Plains drove many thousands to California, home of destructive mudslides and earthquakes.[8] Despite the wonderful inventions of the twentieth century, masses of American troops still encountered harsh and primitive conditions in the icy, muddy, and bloody trenches of warfare on the ground. Recently, the space program generated imagination for high reaching progress, yet the situation on earth remained under the plague of ancient problems like poverty, ignorance, and war.

Football expresses the American mythology of historical hardships in life near the ground. Each play begins from a point of contact with the earth, creating the awkward situation of bending low in a vulnerable position to "snap" the ball up to the quarterback. Grounded start to the action results in struggle with the opponent to

---

[6] Richard P. Horwitz, *Hog Ties: Pigs, Manure, and Mortality in American Culture* (New York: St. Martin's Press, 1998).

[7] Richard White, *The Frontier in American Culture* (Berkeley: University of California Press, 1994); Frank Triplett, *Conquering the Wilderness: the Life and Times of Pioneer Heroes* (Minneapolis: Northwestern Press, 1888); John P. Hale, *Trans-Allegheny Pioneers* (Cincinnati: The Graphic Press, 1886).

[8] Brad Lookingbill, *Dustbowl, USA: Depression American and the Ecological Imagination, 1929–1941* (Athens: Ohio University Press, 2001); Caroline A. Henderson, *Letters from the Dust Bowl* (Norman: Oklahoma University Press, 2001).

protect the quarterback for completion of the difficult ball exchange. If not able to score a touchdown, teams record points by placing the ball on earth for a field goal kick. The difficulty of effort requires a holder to catch and place the football for the kicker, leaving just nine players to block eleven defenders in compounded hardship for the kicking team. Grounded situations in a game illustrate a sense of great adversity in life, depicting the daily struggle to advance from low points of vulnerability and unproductivity to more elevated accomplishments.

Most dramatically, kicking the football portrays the American perception of far from perfect realties in the present existence. National stories exalt the pioneers for the use of their hands, not feet, to expand the country on the frontier. They feature inventors who sketched out heady ideas to create technology of remarkable advancements.[9] Similarly, the sports trinity of the nation gives supreme significance to hands with much less attention to the feet or legs.[10] Even "football" draws little concern with foot efforts, overwhelmingly focused on hand-eye coordination. The center snaps the ball with outstretched hand into the hands of the quarterback. Subsequently, quarterbacks "hand-off" to a running back or throw the ball from his strong hand to a receiver with "soft hands." On defense, players use hands to push away blocking efforts by opponents and work to "strip the ball away" from a ball carrier with hand pressure. Like baseball and basketball, football expresses American veneration of the hands, upholding conviction that use of the feet lacks the control, power, and sophistication of hand action. Unlike the other two sports, however, it tolerates kicking the ball as a

---

[9] Jeffrey Young, *Forbes Greatest Technology Stories: Inspiring Tales of Entrepreneurs and Inventors who Revolutionized Modern Business* (New York: John Wiley and Sons, 1998); Russell Doubleday, *Stories of Inventors* (New York: Doubleday, Page and Company, 1904).

[10] Baseball and basketball strictly oppose "kicking" as a play-killing violation or a "cardinal sin," conveying foot action as unaccomplished activity in contrast to highly acclaimed use of the hands.

result of more adverse and grounded conditions of play. Football illustrates the natural story of life's harsh realities.

The kicker on a football team remains a marginal figure, representing the American association of foot action with "lowly" conditions. He performs an important specialty, the only person who is able to score by kicking the ball from the ground.[11] Kickers stay distant from the other players, not in possession of more nationally recognized talents to block, throw, catch, and tackle with the hands. Frequently, he is a "foreigner," a former soccer player from Europe or Latin America (e.g., Jon Stenerud from Sweden, Garo Yepremian of Cyprus, Sabastian Janikowski from Poland). Players and fans become outraged when loss of a game results after failed kick by the one player uninvolved in the ongoing action. Then, they experience a sense of great injustice that such a marginal part of the competition decides the outcome. Buffalo Bills fans still lament the inequity of a 1991 miss by Scott Norwood to end Super Bowl XXV. Kicking action on the gridiron displays the story of adverse and unaccomplished realities, believed to demand every human capacity for overcoming hardships, sometimes the use of the feet but especially generating concern for the highly skilled and powerful work of the hands.

The Severe Limits of Life

In its mythic account of life's realities, football depicts the American understanding of severe restrictions that afflict human beings, particularly the limiting factor of time. Players defer to the authority of timed conditions during each play of a game, as the clock dictates hurried choice and execution of a play. Failure to meet the demands of time results in a "delay of game penalty." Inevitably, the clock becomes the "greatest enemy" of teams who trail in the score, Relentlessly, it moves the action to an irreversible end, forcing ever

---

[11]Dan Herbst, ed., *The Art of Placekicking and Punting* (New York: Simon and Schuster, 1987); George Sullivan, *Pro Football's Kicking Game* (New York: Dodd, Mead, 1973).

more desperate efforts from the players. Timed conditions push quarterbacks to throw the "Hail Mary pass" in a last ditch appeal for a miracle, while causing others to lateral the ball wildly to teammates in hope of keeping the final play alive. The all-powerful clock of football portrays perception in the United States of unstoppable movement to historical events, greatly restricting the possibilities for human beings.

Beyond the dynamics of a game, time has much power in the playing season and career of a football player. It dictates absolute end to the games each year. If they survive the timed conclusion to the annual schedule, a team faces a "do or die" situation of one game opportunity in the postseason, a fixed moment for determination of success or failure. As the clock ticks, the pressure mounts with each snap of the ball, pushing players into uncharacteristic mistakes or overly conservative play.[12] Ultimately, the end to a championship game forces everyone into off-season activities of rest and preparation, the result of the clock's power to determine the dramatic change. Similarly, "Father Time takes over" in the lifespan of a player.[13] In the NFL, most players fail to complete four years, while only 1 percent of Division I college players continue to play a down of professional football. After retirement, greats of the game quickly fade from public consciousness, powerless before the passage of time. Bronco Nagurski, Red Grange, and Ray Nitzchke remain quite distant today. The power of time in football expresses the American perception of severe restrictions on human efforts within the timed conditions of history.

Football portrays a highly limited humanity by way of impassable boundaries. Movement out of bounds is completely out of play, abruptly halting the advancement of the ball carrier.[14] Touching the boundary kills a play, producing many moments of instant replay

---

[12] Samuel L. Jackson, *NFL Game Day*, ESPN, 8 January 2005.

[13] Boomer Esiason, *Monday Night Football*, Westwood One, 11 November 2004.

[14] David M. Nelson, *Illustrated Football Rules* (Garden City NY: Dolphin Books, 1976);, *NCAA Football Rules and Interpretations*.

to monitor enforcement of the restriction. Offensive lineman and the quarterback cannot move beyond the line of scrimmage during a pass attempt. On defense, rules prohibit players from crossing the scrimmage line until the opponent snaps the ball and constrains defenders to pull up from assault on a ball carrier who moves out of bounds. Even the ultimate achievement, a touchdown, stops the advancement of the successful team since the referees demand unceremonious departure to the sidelines or suffer a penalty. Displayed on a gridiron, severe limitations on players illustrate the American faith in legal restrictions to maintain order, clear boundaries to offset the potential for chaos.

Civil religion in the United States encourages the acknowledgement of quite restricted conditions for human beings at present. According to national mythology, heroic pioneers faced harsh limitations of nature, isolation, and lack of resources, while legendary immigrants confronted obstacles of poverty and ignorance.[15] Mass destruction, the burden of heavy equipment, scarce food, and physical exhaustion hampered war veterans of the twentieth century, highly restricted like soldiers of old. Storied reformers of society (e.g., Lincoln, King) encountered prejudice, low morale, and violent opposition.

Football portrays the American story of severe restrictions today like generations of the past. Opponents impede every attempt to move down the field. Teams zigzag across the field with stops, starts, and regressions, typically anything but smooth progress, while gladiatorial-like equipment hampers the movements of each player. Protective helmets block peripheral vision, inhibiting the ability to see incoming rivals in a "blind side" attack. Individuals become much slower in the pads of the game, especially those who ran an eye-popping 4.4 second dash of forty yards in shorts and T-shirt. Frequently, athletic players look quite awkward and limited in agility.

---

[15] June Namias, *First Generation: In the Words of Twentieth-Century American Immigrants* (Urbana IL: University of Illinois Press, 1992); John Higham, *Send These to Me: Immigrants in Urban America* (Baltimore: John Hopkins Press, 1984).

The greatest players succeed in restricted fashion, running run one step at a time down the field to score. Though super fast, Randy Moss takes at least seven to eight full ticks of the clock to run length of the field for reception of a touchdown. Similarly, a team typically scores after an extended "drive" that requires much time "to develop," rarely in quick strike manner. Restricted advancements in game action display national perception of quite limited accomplishments at present.

Harsh conditions of football demand rest for recuperation, displaying the finitude of the human beings who play a game. Even the stars play less than half of a contest, while good strategy calls for long-term possession of the ball to give defensive players time to regain physical capabilities. Because of restricted ability to play, games occur only once a week.[16] Over the course of a season, few endure the punishing action without missing at least one game. The best teams rarely have everyone available in postseason action, disclosing the tenuous and finite potential for any seemingly great collection of humanity. Limited ability to play the game conveys American recognition of human finitude.

Football illustrates the restrictive nature of humanity through highly the constrained use of the ball. First and foremost, it restricts exchanges with team members. Repeated violation of this absolute restriction with a "fumble" or "interception" of the football will eventually result in a player's dismissal from game action by the head coach. Quarterbacks "eat the ball" and accept a painful "sack" for loss of yardage rather than give up possession to the opponent. Running backs carry the football in a restrictive manner, tight to the body and covered at three points by hand, arm, and elbow in avoidance of free use by opposing tacklers. Teams strictly limit ball exchanges to minimize the possibility for a turnover, seeking limited movement from center to quarterback to running back or receiver. When

---

[16] After playing in the Monday night contest, NFL teams have a poor record on the following Sunday, just six days later rather than the normal seven between games.

involving an additional exchange or two, plays become "tricks" or "gadgets," too dangerous and not restrictive enough for frequent use.

The rules of football further limit ball handling to the "skill players" (i.e., quarterback, running backs and receivers), expressing dedication in the United States to restricted roles for members of the nation to best meet the demands of adverse conditions. Prestigious awards like the Most Valuable Player or Heisman Trophy almost never go to a player beyond the limited group of ball handlers.[17] Defensive players rarely touch the all-important football, often generating humor when they do. A defensive lineman with the ball is highly unusual and a funny sight. Even stranger are times when kickers, specialists in use of the feet, carry or throw the ball. Fans still remember the surreal image of Yaro Yepremian fumbling the football during a botched play in Super Bowl VII. Displayed on a gridiron, severe restrictions in use of the ball portray American trust in very limited roles for citizens, specialized efforts in response to limitations imposed during situations of national crisis.

Illustrative of life's limiting power, football dramatically restricts handling of the ball especially to one individual. Only the quarterback controls the pigskin on every offensive play since game action begins with his reception of the snap. Because of highly limited concern with quarterbacks, teams exert great effort to find one person for this position of focused interest. Far more than any other player, the quarterback receives praise or condemnation for the fate of the group, despite being just one person on a team of dozens. Fans often blame a quarterback for loses and expect one new "signal caller" to turn around a professional franchise or college program. Frequently, the backup quarterback is most popular team member because of unique promise given to the position. Restricted attention to one player among many expresses American faith in a special individual (i.e., the president), believed best able to respond to highly

---

[17] Bill Pennington, *The Heisman: Great American Stories of the Men Who Won* (New York: Regan Books, 2004); *Official NFL Statistics and Records* (St. Louis: The Sporting News Publication Company, 2004).

restrictive situations of emergency. The game discloses civil belief in severely limiting conditions and the need for much restriction in national activities.

The Hostile World

Beyond the limits of life, football illustrates the perception of hostile forces at work in history. Civil religion of the United States upholds an understanding of the struggle against enemies of great hostility. According to national mythology, Americans early faced the tyranny of English rule and European opposition to push for greater freedom.[18] Decades later, the country divided into two warring factions in the Civil War, each side viewing the other as the enemy of American values. Similarly, legendary pioneers encountered strong resistance of native tribes and aggressions from powerful gangs of outlaws.[19] In the twentieth century, the nation confronted war machines of Germany and Japan, then the communist "menace" during forty years of "Cold War," seemingly ever opposed by an anti-America. Recently, President George W. Bush initiated the "War against Terror," continuing persistent conflict with "evil empires."[20]

Football portrays the American stories of chronic opposition from hostile enemies like the communists of old and present-day Muslim fundamentalists. The violence of a game depicts the struggle against belligerent human beings who are dedicated to destruction of

---

[18] Claude H. Van Tyne, *England and America, Rivals in the American Revolution* (New York: Macmillan Publishers, 1927); Lewis B. Namier, *England in the Age of the American Revolution* (London: Macmillan Press, 1961).

[19] This information is myth, not simple truth or fallacy, but the story line of narratives about history in the United States, stories still foundational for much of the nation. Most accept taking of the land from Native Americans, as they do not give much justification to native hostility about current consequences of this conquest, at least not enough to change the situation. See Vine Deloria, *God Is Red: A Native View of Religion* (Golden CO: Fulcrum Publishers, 2003).

[20] Former President Ronald Reagan gathered support for a fight against "the Evil Empire" (i.e., the Soviet Union), while George W. Bush leads opposition to "the axis of evil."

the enemy. Games are "battles," "wars" between two fiercely opposed groups. Each team encounters "combat in the trenches," the area of heightened aggressions along the line of scrimmage similar to the frontlines in warfare. On offense, players face "head-hunters," "assassins," "missiles," and "monsters" who "attack" in efforts to "smash," "hurt," "punish," and "bury" them. Similarly, defensive personnel confront attacking opponents devoted to "run the ball down their throats" and "smash mouth action," coordinated with an "air assault." Frantically, coaches work to outthink an opposing group of experts plotting their demise. Violent conflict on a field of play illustrates the perception in the United States of great enmity in human relations.

The mythic hostilities of football include a sense of destructive forces from nature like those broadcast on the Weather Channel. Teams "fight the elements," natural hardships of ice, snow, cold, wind, rain, and heat. Hostile weather does not delay or cancel games, encouraging recognition that nature will frequently bring harsh conditions.[21] As the season advances, nature's forces "rattle the bones," transform human breath into hazy fog, and "muck up" a field with mud. Each year, fans witness how nature often works against human beings. They observe players "mired" in muddied situations or blinded by near whiteout conditions of a blizzard. Games of natural adversity, the "Ice Bowl" of 1967 and the "fog game" of 1988 live on in public memory.[22] The game of football brings to mind dramatic images of brutally cold temperatures, "frozen tundra," and difficult wind or rain, illustrating the American belief in chronic struggle against nature's provisions.

---

[21] Situations of extreme danger like a hurricane or severe thunderstorm once in awhile postpone a football contest.

[22] The Dallas Cowboys played the Green Bay Packers in the "Ice Bowl" for the 1967 championship of the National Football Conference, while the "fog game" occurred during the 1988 playoffs in Chicago, involving the Philadelphia Eagles against the Chicago Bears.

In the United States, civil religion upholds stories of great conflict with a wild and hostile nature. According to national mythology, early settlers of Puritan faith landed on the cold and harsh coastland of present-day Massachusetts, while legendary pioneers encountered deadly cold on the Plains, then the devastating heat of Western deserts.[23] Storied veterans of war fought nature's difficulties in addition to the human enemy, facing frigid temperatures at Valley Forge, debilitating snow in the Civil War, and foggy drizzle on D-day of World War II.[24] Today, the nation's news features earthquakes, wildfires, tornadoes, blizzards, and hurricanes, expressing mindfulness of natural hostilities.

Most dramatically, football portrays the natural land as a great oppositional force. Contact with the earth immediately kills the action, causing an abrupt stoppage of forward progress by a team on the offensive. Putting the ball on the ground in a fumble represents the worst sin of the game, sure to draw outrage from coaches and fans. Quarterbacks strive to hand-off or pass the ball cleanly without touching the turf, while receivers work to keep the football from falling incomplete to earth below. Punt and kick returners follow a "cardinal rule" not to let the ball hit the ground in prevention of much difficulty. On defense, players oppose efforts by the opponent to put them incapacitated on the turf. The highly negative role of the earth illustrates the American belief in the struggle against nature's landscape, a battle that started with westward clearing of the land and continues today through the daily moving of bulldozers.

According to football, nature above is perilous like the land below: "Three things can happen in throwing the ball [through the

---

[23] Triplett, *Conquering the Wilderness*; Hale, *Trans-Alleghany Pioneers*.

[24] Kristiana Gregory, *The Winter of Red Snow: The Revolutionary War Diary of Abigail Jane Stewart* (New York: Scholastic Incorporated, 1996); Martin Bowman, ed., *Remembering D-Day: Personal Histories of Everyday Heroes* (London: Harper Collings, 2004).

air] and two are bad."[25] Over the years, the game became less deterred but not free from this basic truth. Because of the danger, passes through airspace occur at sporadic and infrequent rate, measurable by attempts that can almost be counted with fingers and toes.[26] Most pass plays involve short "dink and dunk" tosses of ten yards or less downfield to minimize the risk, while nearly every throw features just one simple connection between passer and receiver. To avoid the dangers of throwing, teams frequently run the ball in a much safer ground game, also offsetting the ability of the opponent to anticipate when the football will enter vulnerable position in the air. To make a pass, the quarterback avoids putting "too much air under the ball" for quick movement through the dangerous world above. Routinely, he "throws the ball away," out of bounds, rather than risk an airborne situation in play. Receivers "snatch the football out of the air" to end flight of the pass quickly. Teams utilize the air but with much caution, portraying the American perception of the promise yet also the peril of conditions above the earth. A sense of grave danger is represented by disappearance of Amelia Earhart and more recent catastrophes with space shuttles.

In its illustration of hostile forces at work, football communicates the belief in the United States that harsh conditions hamper the benefits of technology, inhibiting productivity of inventive ability by human beings. Symbolizing technological items, equipment does not directly aid scoring efforts. Players use helmets and pads for protection from injury but not to help them propel or catch the ball, depicting the inability to fulfill the productive promise of tools. In the attempt to produce points, the quarterback throws without aid, even hindered by the shoulder pads that make passing difficult. Running backs "run to daylight" amid a mass of humanity without the benefit of a paved pathway. Receivers catch the ball

---

[25] Legendary coach of Ohio State University, Woody Hayes is most often associated with this famous precept, revealing the great potential for an interception or incomplete pass.

[26] Baseball and basketball make more prolific use of the air.

without the help of easy to trap gloves. On defense, players launch into the ball carrier by way of self-generated energy alone. Highly limited use of tools in the game conveys the national understanding of obstructed advancement in employment of technology, hindered by hostilities that demand equipment for protective purpose.

Beyond the many pads, tools are distant in football. Players benefit from the latest weight-training facilities, but these are far from the field of play. They ride bicycles to stay loose during a game, yet outside the boundaries of game action. Kickers practice with a tee, but they kick a finger-held ball for points during a contest. Coaches benefit from advanced systems of communication, however, on the sidelines and without direct impact on a pass, kick, block, or tackle. Ever connected to technological gadgets, they resemble commanders on the hostile battlefield, too concerned with survival for the use of equipment to improve the quality of life. The game depicts American mythology of much enmity, pushing achievement of technology's promise into the distance, to the future well-removed from the current struggles.

Sacred Departures

In response to the hostile world, football illustrates dedication in the United States to a sharp departure away from present circumstances for pursuit of fulfillment elsewhere. According to national stories, legendary pioneers and immigrants exemplify departures of great consequence.[27] From the beginning of the nation, people of pioneering spirit departed situations in eastern locations to seek a much better life somewhere west. Near turn of the twentieth century, families like the Gehrigs left hardship in a European homeland in

---

[27] National stories of immigrants resemble biblical narratives of exemplary individuals like Abraham who moved far from ancestral home to an unknown destination. Similarly, American mythology features rags-to-riches stories about dramatic departures from dire conditions inside the United States (e.g., Elvis Presley, Ray Charles, and many others).

search of betterment in the United States.[28] Christina and Heinrich Gehrig moved far from Germany to find advancement through success by their son Lou, a longtime star for the New York Yankees. Similarly, Andrew Carnegie departed poverty in Scotland to become a steel tycoon in a rags-to-riches story of nationwide significance.[29] More recently, the narrative of Orlando Hernandez moved the nation, detailing dramatic account of late-night departure from Cuba for fame and fortune as pitcher for the Yankees.[30] Resembling immigrants of old and new, Americans frequently move to distant locations within the states in search for achievement elsewhere.

Like mythic pioneers and immigrants, football players sharply depart the current location to pursue advancement somewhere else. Good ball carriers are "downhill runners," ever moving forward and away from the starting point. "Shifty" individuals move side to side, seeking an opening to cut directly up field and leave the line of scrimmage well behind.[31] Expressing national devotion to movement of departure, running backs often inspire nicknames associated with vehicles of departing transportation. "Cadillac Williams" and Jerome "the Bus" Bettis carry the football in drives to distant destinations like daily departures of drivers across the country. Quarterbacks throw the ball directly downfield in a dramatic advancement into the distance similar to the across-the-sky departure of an airplane. On defense, players rush ahead to leave behind blocked circumstances in pursuit of the ball carrier. Departing action of a game portrays

---

[28] Richard Bak, *Lou Gehrig* (Dallas: Taylor Publishing Company, 1995). The story of the Gehrigs became well established in national culture with the film *Pride of the Yankees* in 1942.

[29] Zachary Kent, *Andrew Carnegie: Steel King and Friend to the Libraries* (Springfield NJ: Enslow Publishers, 1999); Burton J. Hendrick, *The Life of Andrew Carnegie* (Garden City NY: Doubleday, Doran, and Company, 1932).

[30] Hernandez left in the middle of the night on a flimsy boat to cross many miles of ocean water to seek great expectations in the United States.

[31] For examples, see video of Gayle Sayers in the 1960s and Barry Sanders not so long ago.

American trust in forward progress, direct movement away from the present location to pursue a new and better situation.

Football illustrates the civil faith of the United States in a sharp departure from the people associated with difficult conditions of the present. On offense, teams push to leave the opponent in a "cloud of dust," while speedy carriers of the ball "blow past" the other team in a burst of acceleration like the nation's fast departing cars. Good receivers possess "breakaway speed" for separation from defenders to catch a pass. They have explosive power to leave crowded conditions for open space. Similarly, defensive players exhibit departure by dramatic movement away from a blocker in a "shedding" action.[32] As a result of multiple points awarded for scores (i.e., two, three, or six), a team builds up high numbers of achievement in a "blow out," leaving the rival in the low-numbered distance. Dramatic departures on the gridiron express American dedication to abrupt movement away from groups and individuals opposed to present efforts for advancement.

Civil stories of the United States exalt heroes who quickly depart the present time in movement to a better future. According to the mythology, legendary reformers like Abraham Lincoln and Martin Luther King, Jr. pushed to leave behind injustices now for greater justice to come.[33] War veterans fought to depart current destruction for a coming peace, anxious to someday focus on life close to family and friends. Likewise, sacred departures of football feature an exodus from the present time in search of a more productive future. Teams line up in crisp fashion to leave the current moment rapidly, conducting a "hurry up" offense late in a game for departure from the losing situation. Striving to depart things at present, quarterbacks ready teammates through frenzied pointing and barking of directions. Sometimes overwhelmed by the hurriedness, offensive linemen move

---

[32] For illustration, watch a video of Lawrence Taylor from the New York Giants during the 1980s.

[33] Abraham Lincoln, *The Speeches and Addresses of Abraham Lincoln* (New York: Little Leather Library Corporation, 1911); Martin Luther King, Jr. *The Speeches of Martin Luther King*, video (: MPI Video, 1990).

too quickly in a "false start," while defenders anxiously "jump off-sides." Before start to a play, linebackers pace and jump around with eyes bulging in intense readiness, focused on rapidly departing the unsatisfactory now for a coming moment of impact with the ball carrier. Defensive linemen surge forward in a rush of motion, quite similar to the rushed drive home each day by workers in the nation. Football portrays American devotion to a fast departure from the present time, a hurried way of life in frenzied pursuit of future fulfillment.[34]

In the United States, dedication to dramatic departures produces great concern with movement away from established or old methods of accomplishment, ever in search for a better way. National stories venerate inventors of technology, exalting individuals like Alexander Graham Bell and Bill Gates, creators who initiated remarkable improvements. According to mythology, Bell helped propel the country beyond almost ancient forms of communication through invention of the telephone, while Gates facilitated legendary shift away from archaic life before computers.[35] Depicting the nation's trust in inventiveness, football teams aspire to depart existing styles of play, searching for more advanced ways to attack opponents. Coaches stay up late and arise early in pursuit of a novel strategy. They spend much time "in the laboratory" to discover "gadget" or "trick" plays. Like revered inventors of technology, great coaches are geniuses, mad scientists, and masterminds who invent revolutionary strategies.

---

[34] It conveys the "thank God it's Friday" mindset of the country, ever concerned with the next weekend and ultimately with retirement to come. According to Native American mythology, leaders had visions of dramatic changes that came with hurried life of "the white man." See, *Paha Sapa: The Struggle for the Black Hills*, video (New York: Mystic Fire Video, 1994);, *Hopi: Songs of the Fourth World*, video (New York: New Day Films, 1983).

[35] Dorothy Eber, *Genius at Work: Alexander Graham Bell* (New York: Viking Press, 1982); Elizabeth MacLeod, *Alexander Graham Bell: An Inventive Life* (Toronto: Kids Can Press, 1999); Paul Andrews, *How the Web Was Won: How Bill Gates and His Internet Idealists Transformed the Microsoft Empire* (New York: Broadway Books, 2000).

Football generates a passionate search for new and better ways to achieve success, conveying the American faith in sharp departures from old methods in inventive pursuit.

Most dramatically, flight up and away from the earth expresses devotion in the United States to departure from present conditions. Civil stories give great importance to Orville and Wilbur Wright, famous brothers who initiated beloved practice of flight above natural situation on the ground.[36] Decades later, Charles Lindbergh flew across the Atlantic Ocean, enhancing the country's commitment to advance ever further beyond established limits of travel.[37] During World War II, fighter pilots inspired greater trust in departing movement up with celebrated success against Germany and Japan. Soon, the explosive growth of airline companies and the space program brought nearly boundless belief in national ability to depart grounded limitations for remarkable achievement somewhere higher.

A game of departures, football depicts dedication in the United States to crisp departure from natural conditions on earth. Like the mythic Wright brothers, players follow a rising pattern from the ground with each play of a game. Offensive and defensive linemen rise on every snap of the ball from "four point" stance in contact with the turf to upright and prime position. Receiving the football in a hike up from the land below, quarterbacks extend the lifting action by launching the ball into flight, while receivers work to keep the ball above the play killing earth. Ball carriers fight to stay elevated and reach the end zone without falling down. After a score, a signal of the referee declares the ultimate importance of distance from the earth, pointing straight up into the air like the trajectory of a NASA rocket.

---

[36] See James Tobin, *To Conquer the Air: The Wright Brothers and the Great Race for Flight* (New York: Free Press, 2003); Caryn Jenner, *First Flight: The Story of the Wright Brothers* (New York: DK Publishers, 2003).

[37] Charles Demarest, *Charles Lindbergh* (New York: Crown Publishers, 1993).

The game of football illustrates American faith in pursuit of unprecedented accomplishments by way of intensive movement away from the ground, devotion to departure symbolized by the airplane and skyscraper, icons of the country.

Chapter Four

Baseball
Sacred Story of American Eschatology

Baseball is like a church. Many attend. Few understand.[1]

Alongside the mythology of overcoming historical adversities, American civil religion upholds stories of an ideal life to come. The nation early embraced the Puritan aspiration to be a "city on a hill," adopting a vision for becoming a model society for the world.[2] During the Civil War, Abraham Lincoln inspired national commitment to "the great work undone," a storied account of greater freedom and equality not yet achieved.[3] Victories in two world wars of the twentieth century produced increased anticipation of better conditions ahead. More recently, Martin Luther King, Jr. revitalized imagination for the future through a "Dream," a story about a coming someday when the nation will fulfill constitutional ideals.[4] Historically, the belief system of the United States generates great expectations for futuristic advancements.

---

[1] Quotations by Leo Durocher, BrainyQuote, http://www.brainyquote.com/quotes/authors/leo_durocher.html.

[2] Perry Miller, *Errand into the Wilderness* (Cambridge MA: Belknap Press of Harvard University, 1956) 1–15.

[3] Abraham Lincoln, *The Speeches and Addresses of Abraham Lincoln* (New York: Little Leather Library Company, 1911) 38–41.

[4] Martin Luther King, Jr. *The Speeches of Martin Luther King*, video (: MPI Video, 1990).

Baseball portrays the American mythology of a perfect world to come.[5] Players aspire to the perfect game, accomplished by recording the twenty-seven outs of a game without the blemish of one opponent reaching first base.[6] Otherwise unspectacular pitchers like Don Larsen and David Cone became "immortal" for one moment of perfection. More frequently, teams achieve the putouts of a contest with no errors, a perfect defensive effort, highly publicized by the ever-present line score. On offense, individuals accomplish a perfect day by hitting safely during each official plate appearance (e.g., three hits in three at bats) or even more so through "hitting for the cycle" (i.e., single, double, triple, and home run) in perfect symmetry.[7] Quite often, a batter hits the ball in the perfect spot between fielders, creating impression that the baseball "has eyes" like in an ideal world where situations perfectly follow personal wishes. Displayed on a diamond of play, aspiration for perfection expresses hope in the United States for a much more perfect future.

The baseball is round, a perfect circle.[8] It bounces in a predictable fashion, routinely with a perfect hop, enabling players to use their powers of anticipation perfectly. A bad bounce of the ball rarely occurs, the cause of special commentary from the announcer and inspection of the field to find the cause of such imperfection.

---

[5] The game conveys the country's millennialism, a belief in a future perfection. For an overview of the topic, see Darrol Bryant and Donald Dayton, eds., *The Coming Kingdom: Essays in American Millennialism and Eschatology* (Barrytown NY: International Religious Foundation, 1983); Gardiner B. Moment and Otto F. Kraushaar, *Utopias: The American Experience* (Metuchen, New Jersey: Scarecrow Press, 1980).

[6] The concept of a "perfect game" is foreign to football and basketball. A football team is "undefeated" after winning every game in a season and is considered more the survivor of great adversity than perfect.

[7] As a Baltimore Orioles fan, I most remember attending a "perfect day" by Don Baylor at Tiger Stadium in 1974. Baylor went six for six with three home runs, a double, and a triple.

[8] See Barbara Rose, *Ellsworth Kelley: Curves/Rectangles* (New York: Blum Helmun, 1989); Dorling Kindersely, *My First Look at Shapes* (New York: Random House, 1999).

Because of its perfect shape and size, a baseball can be thrown with incredible velocity, routinely at speeds of over ninety miles an hour. Oftentimes, it travels too fast for the naked eye to follow, bringing vision of a world to come when objects will travel instantaneously. Coaches and fans expect a near-perfect ability by the pitcher to control the fast propelled ball. Balls thrown outside the small strike zone award first base to the opponent and draw outrage, especially from the manager who will soon dismiss the too imperfect pitcher. Summoned relievers inherit the perfectionist standards along with runners on base, often able to stay on the mound for just one or two batters. Pursuit of perfection in the game conveys aspiration in the United States for a future of perfect accomplishments.

A baseball is white, furthering the association with the American imagination for the ideal. It resembles the White House, whiteness of the Washington Monument, white paper for constitutional documents, and other icons of the nation.[9] Umpires watch for a defaced ball and are intolerant of discoloration or disfigurement similar to special concern about "desecration" of a national monument.[10] Players also expect perfection in a baseball, frequently demanding a brand new and very white ball. On average, 120 or so unblemished balls enter play in one major league game, as demarcation brings permanent banishment to practice only. Perfectionist expectations for the ball communicate a mythic anticipation for perfect way of life.

Commentators, fans, and players see perfection in the flight of the baseball. They marvel at a "frozen rope" hit in a perfectly straight line or in response to a home run of majestic and perfect-looking arc into the distance. "Bloop" hits appear less spectacular but follow

---

[9] William Seale, *The White House: The History of an American Idea* (Washington DC: American Institute of Architects Press, 1992); John W. Ward, *Red, White, and Blue: Men, Books, and Ideas in American Culture* (New York: Oxford University Press, 1969). Regarding the exalted significance of whiteness, national history reveals the special and unequal significance given to "white people."

[10] Football and basketball do not generate concern for an unblemished ball.

circular trajectory to be admired, falling in ideal placement onto the outfield grass, just beyond the reach of defenders. Pitchers throw "fastballs" in almost perfect directness, while "curve balls" rotate in circular motion, perfectly complementing straight fastballs. Perceptions of ball movements illustrate the American perception of ideal events to come.

Baseball takes place on a diamond, a form deemed near perfect in the United States, set apart from the common-looking and rectangular field for football.[11] Extraordinary moments of marriage call for gift of a stone in the shape of a baseball park. The diamond highlights circles of round perfection to match the cyclical rotations of the ball. [12] Persistently, a game draws attention to the circular mount for cyclical flights of the baseball toward the roundish glove of the catcher, while hitters prepare in the on-deck circle. Resembling the restrictive quality of everyday life, straight lines are difficult to find and the object of efforts by players to erase or avoid in superstitious behavior. The center of the action, home plate lies at the vortex of an open-ended triangle, extending the field into infinity. The setting for baseball is the American imagination for the eternal, expressing vision for everlasting existence to come.

Baseball parks portray the American aspiration for ideal conditions of environment. Routinely, games stop when a foreign object comes to rest on the pristine field. Umpires halt the action to remove the invading item and restore a perfect look like the officials who worry about the White House lawn. In Major League Baseball, teams employ fulltime groundskeepers to protect and care for the all-important playing surface, resembling caretakers for sites of great national meaning. Beyond the nearly perfect appearance, a ballpark features unique dimensions and characteristics, set apart from the

---

[11] Ordinary life is full of rectangular images like those of the football field. In the United States, everyday living involves driving similarly shaped cars through rectangular intersections on the way to a rectangle of office space.

[12] Joseph L. Price, ed., *From Season to Season: Sports as American Religion* (Macon GA: Mercer University Press, 2001) 61–76.

mass produced quality of ordinary life. Yankee Stadium possesses a "short porch" in right field and "death valley" in left center with monuments to "immortals" from the past, while Fenway Park in Boston houses the famed "Green Monster," a thirty foot high wall in nearby left field, contrasted to the distant fence of right center. The distinctiveness of each playing space brings unpredictability and novelty to the game action, similar to sense of the remarkable produced by visitation to places of spectacular beauty under federal protection (e.g., the Grand Canyon). Like national parks, baseball parks represent places of immeasurable wonders, conveying the American perception of life's boundless potential yet to be fully realized.[13]

Depicting the expectation of an ideal future, baseball exalts the number three, a number of supreme significance in the United States. The nation has three branches of federal government, three constitutional documents, and three primary forces of the military. Three parties (i.e., Democrats, Republicans, and Independents) decide elections, while three-way interaction between jury, judge, and the lawyers determines judicial truth. Not coincidentally, the country features three major sports, one of which—baseball— expresses its highest aspirations, idealistic thinking closely associated with three-fold manifestation of truth. Three strikes create an out, and three outs complete an inning. Three times three players make up one team of active players, whereas the same number of innings culminates a game. The bases are three times thirty feet apart, and the pitcher's mound resides sixty feet and six inches from home plate, multiples of three. Most legendary of players, Base Ruth wore number three. Like other pivotal elements of the nation, the game highlights trinitarian mindset, expressing a story about the future perfection of national institutions already established.

---

[13] Alfred Runte, *National Parks: The American Experience* (Lincoln: University of Nebraska Press, 1997); Richard L. Saunders, ed., *A Yellowstone Reader: The National Park in Popular Fiction, Folklore, and Verse* (Salt Lake City: University of Utah Press, 2003).

The Unlimited Freedom to Come

By way of stories about a perfect future, American civil religion generated an expectation for unprecedented freedom to come. The founding fathers envisioned a country dedicated to the persistent pursuit of liberty, a goal never quite fulfilled, yet coming.[14] Generations later, the Civil War and Reconstruction brought a conception of a more perfect freedom still to be achieved, the result of concern for emancipation of slaves.[15] During the twentieth century, great efforts to preserve democracy in two world wars produced a vision for expansion of liberties worldwide. Soon thereafter, Martin Luther King, Jr. helped revitalize national devotion to ever more liberty, inspiring faith in a mythic "land of freedom," not yet reached.[16]

Baseball illustrates the American mythology of unlimited freedom to come. Players easily transcend the boundaries set for them, expressing the anticipation of unrestricted movements in the future. Frequently, fielders run across the foul lines to record an out, free of concern. The catcher remains completely out of bounds, liberated from need to stay in fair territory.[17] At the end of each half inning, teams freely pass over the two foul lines without a change in active status. After reaching the dugout, they become hitters to launch the ball well beyond the home-run boundary, portraying an aspiration for futuristic accomplishments that will far exceed established limits. Sluggers like Babe Ruth, Mickey Mantle, and Albert Pujols hit home

---

[14] Martti J. Rudanko, *James Madison and Freedom of Speech: Major Debates in the Early Republic* (Dallas: University Press of America, 2004); Ronald A. Wells, ed., *Liberty and Law: Reflections on the Constitution in American Life and Thought* (Grand Rapids MI: Eerdman's Publishing Company, 1987).

[15] Michael S. Green, *Freedom, Union, and Power: Lincoln and His Party during the Civil War* (New York: Fordham University Press, 2004); Eric Foner, *Slavery and Freedom in Nineteenth Century America* (New York: Oxford University Press, 1994).

[16] King, *Speeches of Martin Luther King, Jr.*

[17] Perhaps because of this transcendent view of the field, catchers frequently become managers (e.g., Yogi Berra, Bob Brenly, Joe Torre), benefiting from the unique perspective.

runs hundreds of feet further than the designated fence. Sometimes, they provide a glimpse of coming freedom from every recognizable boundary by hitting the ball "completely out of the park." Barry Bonds often belts a home run into "McCovey's Cove" beyond the limits of the stadium and even the North American continent.[18] Displayed on a diamond of play, ease of movement across boundaries portrays faith in future freedom from longstanding limitations.

The American expectation of unprecedented liberty pervades baseball. Players have opportunity to hit, run the bases, catch, throw, and pitch free of interference. They even possess liberty to steal or take a base, depicting a coming level of freedom similar only to actions today thought unethical. In game action, a player is free to benefit from personal strengths and is able to fully concentrate on use of strong hand to throw, catch, and hit. Pitchers exhibit great independence in the ability to pick the type of pitch, location, speed, and arm angle. Free of interference, they focus on mechanics, details of personal performance. The pitcher receives signs from a catcher about the next pitch, yet he "holds the ball" and the freedom to decide. Fielders exhibit much freedom in determination to throw quickly or with deliberate pace and the "fielder's choice" of where to throw. Hitters exercise free will to "pick the right pitch" from several in an at-bat. They freely choose to pull the ball, go with the pitch, or hit the ball up the middle. Freedom to make personal decisions in the game conveys the mythic vision in the United States for great liberty of opportunity to come.

Baseball portrays the American myth of a futuristic freedom even from the limits of time. Theoretically, a game could last forever since it recognizes no clock and teams can tie into infinity. The Brewers and White Sox nearly did in 1984 playing for twenty-five innings and just short of nine hours.[19] Players remain free from time

---

[18] Chicago Cubs fans await a long ball over the outfield stands, onto Waveland Avenue, and out of sight.

[19]*The Guinnes Book of World Records* (New York: Encyclopedia Americana, 2004) 399.

constraints during every moment of a contest, at liberty to take what seems like an eternity to hit or pitch. Pitchers hold the ball and take their time, liberated from time, while base runners circle the bases in counterclockwise fashion, depicting freedom from the clocked movement of the present. Immersed in the timeless flow of a game, fans sing "I don't care if I ever get back" to the timed conditions of everyday life. Games occur day after day in a season of many months, enhancing the never-ending quality of the play.[20]

Beyond the timelessness of a game and season, baseball expresses the aspiration in the United States for long-lasting liberty from time. Stars play on for decades, quite prominent even at age forty and beyond. Longevity of players creates memorable situations of fathers and sons as teammates, most recently involving the Griffeys and Clemens. Though not much older than football and basketball, baseball seems far more timeless in the national consciousness, known as "the grand old game." Legendary individuals, immortals of the game, live on in a way unmatched by the other sports. Almost ancient players like Babe Ruth, Ty Cobb, and Satchel Paige remain present in the country's imagination, almost on par with Washington, Jefferson, and Lincoln, while living legends (e.g., Henry Aaron, Willie Mays, Ernie Banks) frequent games today, much more than the once-famous retirees of football (e.g., Gale Sayers, Joe Namath). The timeless character of the game conveys the American expectation of unlimited freedom to come from the clock dominated life of the present.

The mythic freedom of baseball gives great power to the players, illustrating the futuristic story of unprecedented ability by humanity to revolutionize conditions. Game action pivots on the crack of the bat and the pop of the catcher's glove, unmistakable acts of consequence by the human beings who play. Players possess

---

[20] Former manager of the Baltimore Orioles, Earl Weaver preached the virtue of daily character to baseball: "This ain't football, we play this everyday." Quotations by Earl Weaver, BrainyQuote, http://www.brainyquote.com/quotes/authors/e/earl_weaver. html.

uncompromised freedom to determine the conclusion of a game, contrasted to the supreme power of the clock in current life. On offense, a hitter is free to bring a contest to an end with the game-winning hit, ideally in a "walk-off home run." Luis Gonzales has a place in the national imagination, especially in Arizona, for one bloop hit to halt the 2001 World Series, while the country still remembers the "shot [homer] heard around the world" by Bobby Thompson to finish the 1951 National League Championship. Pitchers hold similar freedom to influence, having the ability to end a game or season dramatically through recording the final out. The game-ending capability of players discloses the aspiration in the United States for unparalleled freedom to shape circumstances, depicting a belief in a coming time when remarkable accomplishments will produce dramatic results.

According to baseball, the great liberty to come promises to bring freedom from the fate to commit many mistakes. A team rarely commits more than one or two errors in a game, conveying hope for liberation from the mistake-ridden present. Beyond highly visible errors, miscues are subtle in the game.[21] The pitcher throws a pitch in somewhat too predictable a manner or delivers the ball a few inches too high, inaccuracies detectable only to the well-trained eye. Hitters fail by recognizing the spin on the ball a split-second too late and through slight raise of the front shoulder during a swing. Fielders mess up by failing to take one more step forward to field a batted ball in time for a successful throw. Rarity of errors and fine failures express anticipation of freedom from the gross mistakes of life now.

Most dramatically, baseball portrays the American imagination for liberated human beings of the future, free to achieve the remarkable. Players propel a small ball that swerves and dips at ninety-five miles an hour far into the distance. Pitchers make the ball

---

[21] The mistakes of football and basketball are much more grievous errors, often the cause of dramatic "turnovers."

curve, drop, sink, tail away, bore in, and rise.[22] Fielders race to snag an apparent base hit and dive across the field with their full body extended, portraying the vision of nearly unbelievable accomplishments to come. Compared to other sports, baseball features the most revered achievements. Even casual fans know exact numbers of statistical records, expressing intimate association of the game with national aspiration for mythic accomplishments to come. Like the legendary meaning of 1776 and 1944, record numbers of 714, 755, 60, and 61 carry abundant significance as symbols of remarkable feats still to be achieved. Remarkable accomplishments in baseball illustrate the expectation of future freedom to produce the incredible.

The Harmonious Future

Alongside the vision of unlimited freedom to come, American civil religion promotes the anticipation of harmonious relations between human beings. The nation early envisioned a more unified country to move beyond the loose affiliation of thirteen commonwealths.[23] In defiance of the divisiveness brought by the Civil War, Abraham Lincoln upheld faith in "the mystic chords of unity," generating devotion to a futuristic story about a more perfect union of states.[24] During the twentieth century, Martin Luther King, Jr. inspired aspiration for greater social harmony. He nurtured a belief in an "inescapable web of mutuality," expecting much closer relations for the future of the country and world.[25] Historically, diverse movements emerged in expression of expectation in the United States for the grand togetherness of people, groups with idealistic

---

[22] Because of baseball's association with ultimate achievements, American culture promotes use of the term "hardball," a nickname for baseball, to describe especially difficult activities throughout society.

[23] Richard Bernstein, *Are We to Become a Nation? The Making of the Constitution* (Cambridge MA: Harvard University Press, 1987).

[24] Kenneth R. Johnston, ed., *The Rhetoric of Conflict* (Indianapolis: Bobbs-Merrill Publishers, 1969); Melinda Lawson, *Patriot Fires: Forging a New American Nationalism in the Civil War* (Lawrence: University of Kansas Press, 2002).

[25] King, *Speeches of Martin Luther King, Jr.*

goals for community like the Amana commune of the nineteenth century or the hippies of more current times.

Baseball portrays the American story of coming unprecedented harmony in human relations. It is a nonviolent competition, an illustration of hope for a peace someday that will supersede enmity. With an exception or two, physical aggression represents illegal interference, depicting national imagination for a struggle of skill rather than of brute force.[26] Like the idyllic laws of the future, rules demand peace-loving acceptance of advancement by the opponent through a team's defended territory, unheard of in football and contentious life of today. Baseball produces a peaceful and even helpful interaction with the opposition on each play of a contest, requiring an offering of fair opportunity to the opposing batter by way of a pitch within the reachable strike zone. Beyond the required activities, players show heartfelt camaraderie with opponents through friendly conversations at home plate and on the base paths. They practice kindly courtesies toward the enemy, returning a dropped mask to the opposing catcher or a flung bat to the rival hitter. Peaceful exchanges and much cordiality in the game express imagination in the United States for a more unified and even welcoming society of the future.

The American mythology of a harmonious life to come generates the expectation of a remarkable acceptance and forgiveness between people. Gradually, the country embraced the expectancy of immigrants who arrived in hope for incredible hospitality. Recently, leaders like Martin Luther King, Jr. sharpened the national aspiration for a gracious future with the prophetic story of a time when citizens "will not judge based on the color of skin but on the content of one's character."[27] Baseball portrays a civil vision for a much more forgiving life. It encourages a gracious overlook of failure 70 percent

---

[26] One dramatic exception, a base runner can physically blast into the catcher who blocks access to home plate, like Darin Erstad running over Johnny Estrada of the Atlanta Braves in 2005.

[27] King, *The Speeches of Martin Luther King, Jr.*

of the time by a hitter, deeming a .300 batting average a great success.[28] Coaches and fans forgive a hitter for inability to hit safely in kind recognition that the mere "tip" or "flick" of the ball foul uses up precious energy by the opposing pitcher and reveals information about future pitches. Perhaps most dramatically, the game mercifully allows a player to fail indefinitely by hitting an infinite number of foul balls, disclosing anticipation of abundant grace.

Every position player benefits from the mythic forgiveness of baseball. Fans and teammates abundantly forgive pitchers who cause great difficulty by giving up runs to the opponent, extending much love for keeping the game close. Even the most judgmental of managers, Earl Weaver forgave often: "I gave Mike Cuellar more chances than my first wife."[29] Frequently, pitchers fail several times in a row, allowing hitters to reach base, yet still they gain great favor when they yield just one or two runs from the ominous situation. Execution of a double or triple play brings the remarkable grace of wiping away several mistakes by the pitcher in one dramatic moment. Players of other positions often find forgiveness for an error on defense through one run-producing hit on offense. Conversely, he who fails on offense receives mercy because of ability to "save runs" defensively. The long-lasting season of games prompts fans and team officials to forgive poor play whether early or late, while the extensive length of many careers produces toleration of much failure by a player in gracious recognition of future promise or past achievement.[30] Displayed on a diamond of play, this prolific forgiveness expresses the American foresight for incredible care and concern among human beings.

In the United States, the mythic expectation for great harmony extends into relations with nature. Soon after the Revolution, the

---

[28] Ty Cobb achieved the highest lifetime average among long-term players, failing sixty-three percent of the time.

[29] Michael Hill, "When Oriole Way Meant Class," *The Baltimore Sun*, 7 July 2004, .

[30] "Slumps" of poor performance are an accepted "part of the game."

nation envisioned a future of wondrous benefit from close relations with the seemingly boundless land to the west.[31] Legendary explorations by Meriwether Lewis and William Clark enhanced the national anticipation of great promise from nature's provisions.[32] Near turn of the twentieth century, Theodore Roosevelt revived imagination for a wondrous connection to nature through the establishment of spectacular national parks. More recently, space exploration and the environmental movement help maintain the expectancy of amazing things to result from intimacy with the natural world.

Baseball portrays the American mythology of coming harmony between people and nature. Inclement weather delays or cancels games, encouraging the expectation of ideal conditions from nature's climate. Routinely, the game takes place in short-sleeve comfort in a near-perfect setting of inspiration for fans to arrive early and stay late in enjoyment of naturalistic ambiance.[33] Most importantly, game action exalts the earth. It depicts the natural land as a great helping agent, providing abundant ability to produce the all-important runs. Fast players like Lou Brock and Ichiro Suzuki hit the ball on the ground to benefit from much potential for reaching base. A line-drive hitter propels the ball hard on a line not far from the turf but over the infielders to maximize chances of the hit falling safely to earth, while sluggers smack the baseball to a distant and especially joyous landing beyond the home-run fence. As base runners, players slide on the ground for a safe journey around the bases.[34] According to the description, the land acts as a helping agent to propel the player into

---

[31] Ellen Hovde and Muffie Meyer, dirs., *Liberty: The American Revolution*, video (PBS Video, 2004).

[32] Kris Fresonke and Mark Spence, eds., *Lewis and Clark: Legacies, Memories, and New Perspectives* (Berkeley: University of California, 2004); Harry W. Fritz, *The Lewis and Clark Expedition* (Westport CT: Greenwood Press, 2004).

[33] Typically, baseball parks have picnic and barbeque areas, furthering the sense of ideal conditions.

[34] The sliding in baseball contrasts sharply with the slamming and throw-down action of football.

the safety of a base. On defense, outfielders skip the ball off the ground in a one-hop fashion to nail a base runner. Infielders benefit from the world underneath when teammates scoop throws deflected up by the dirt. Abundant aid from nature below illustrates the imagination for future harmony with the earth.

In complement to the vision for the help of nature's land, baseball presents the airborne hopes of the United States. Each play of a game begins with sophisticated movement through the air in the form of a pitch, while a perfect game would involve eighty-one strikes delivered by the pitcher without the ball ever leaving the air, not even on return throws from the catcher. Hitters "lift the ball" in "moon shots" of great promise, threatening to "bring rain" like the productivity of some futuristic device for weather. Even a bunter pushes the ball for a few crucial moments of air travel to reach intended destination on the grass.[35] Fielders make such frequent use of the air that throws for "assists" bring little recognition or fanfare, only the label "routine." Frequently, they create a rapid succession of high-speed flights in the spectacle of a double play. The prolific benefit from the air and ground in the game conveys the American expectation of wondrous relations with the earth and natural world above.

In its story of futuristic harmony, baseball illustrates remarkable use of technology to come. The main piece of equipment, the bat, is a tool of much empowerment. It enables players to launch the ball with fantastic speed and distance in production of the pivotal runs, disclosing the aspiration for amazing accomplishments by way of inventions. The "heavy lumber" wielded by a hitter symbolizes faith in the nation's capacity to transform natural resources into incredibly productive tools. Consequently, hard-hit balls resemble "shots" or "smoked" objects, propelled in like manner to bullets fired by a finely crafted gun. Similar to the telephone and television, the baseball bat

---

[35] The legendary Rod Carew could tap the ball airborne for a perfect flight of twenty to thirty feet, producing a base hit. See Rod Carew, *Rod Carew's Art and Science of Hitting* (New York: Viking Press, 1986).

represents the American trust in unlimited potential of human beings through technological innovations, especially in a more peaceful future, free of present hostilities.

The mythic empowerment by inventions emanates from many features of baseball. On the bases, players benefit from a path cleared and leveled like a grand highway of the future, liberated from today's traffic and road rage. Fine leather gloves aid fielders in the difficult effort to catch the speeding ball, softening the impact in cushioning action. Of much help to the pitcher, the carefully landscaped mound provides a heightened perspective and acceleration as a result of downhill motion. Warning tracks signal potential trouble near the outfield fence, expressing a vision for improved ability to prevent collisions of the present. Teams spend much time in dugouts, shelters that illustrate imagination for a future time of closeness to the natural world just beyond the open front porch and of even greater intimacy with human beings like those nearby on the bench.

The Much Anticipated Circle of Life

Movements in baseball are cyclical, portraying a coming cycle of life to end the frantic search for fulfillment. From the beginning, the United States promoted the "pursuit of happiness," a settled lifestyle not yet achieved. With the late nineteenth century, industrialization produced a heightened expectation for a much more convenient way of life, bringing an aspiration for freedom from strenuous labor someday.[36] In the twentieth century, the invention of ever better technology persistently regenerated national vision for a much easier future. Today, the country pursues a more relaxed living by way of lofty expectations for coming weekend days and retirement still to be reached.

Baseball portrays story of a much anticipated circle of life, which is envisioned to come after the end to the current striving. Consistently, players follow a pattern of cyclical return to a point of

---

[36] Thomas F. Tierney, *The Value of Convenience: A Genealogy of Technical Culture* (Albany: State University of New York Press, 1993).

origin, ever back to an established and well-known location. Hitters circle the bases in a journey of return home, a very familiar place. Great pitchers come back inning after inning and game after game to take the mound in glorious repetition. Similarly, fielders circle back to predetermined positions in preparation for each play, making circular designs on the infield dirt and outfield grass. After each pitch, the pitcher checks to ensure that every fielder has returned to their position of origin. Even the umpires circle back to established locations in sharp distinction from nomadic referees of football. Cyclical movements of the game express expectation in the United States for a future life cycle that will perpetually return society to already ideal conditions, abolishing the need for movement to a distant place or time.

Circular baseball presents the American hope for more settled patterns of social interaction. Infielders take up positions around the pitcher, forming a circle of defense within comfortable talking distance of each other. On offense, players follow teammates on their journey around the bases to illustrate the exemplary life to come. In attempts to score, base runners circle next to, rather than away from, the opponent, portraying an anticipation of future achievements that will not create distance between competitors. The ultimate accomplishment, a home run, does not cause a departure from the other team, as the opposition stays in previously held positions while the catcher returns to greet the next batter. Because of close proximity to opponents, games produce remarkable moments when a player celebrates the record-breaking feat of someone on the opposing team. In 1998, Sammy Sosa of the Chicago Cubs nearly circled the bases with rival Mark McGuire when McGuire broke the longstanding record for home runs in one season. Cyclical actions near others convey a vision for a coming time when relations between rivals will consistently follow a friendly pattern.

The mythic circle of baseball upholds the American faith in a coming way of life, expected to maintain current conditions in attentiveness to the now and end the hurried pursuit of a better future. Routinely, players take their time in dedication to present circumstances. Frequently, the pitcher stands motionless to await signs from the catcher. Fielders avoid hurrying throws. When in trouble, he receives visits with message to settle down and reject a rushed manner. Awaiting the next pitch, the catcher sits in focused attention to the moment. Hitters remain silent and relatively still for extended time in meditation on the incoming pitch, requesting a time-out when feeling hurried. Base runners walk off leads in deliberate steps from a base with eyes fixed to study the current motions of the pitcher. Teams are not even in a hurry to leave town when on the road and far away from home. They stay for days, taking time to rest and take in the present surroundings. Concentration on the now in baseball expresses the aspiration for a future end to the rushed life of today, portraying the anticipation of amazing accomplishments to come through focus on present conditions.

Baseball generates simple patterns of action, an illustration of the American imagination for coming freedom from the frantic search for a better way to accomplishments. The game does not demand the leadership of geniuses or brilliant tacticians. Teams have "skippers" or "captains" who lead by facilitation of good interpersonal relations without the need of novel inventions. Baseball managers do not stay up late or arise early to discover groundbreaking strategies. They encourage players to get plenty of rest and stay out of trouble, focusing on ways to motivate in a manner like managers of old. Today, players are bigger, stronger, and faster, but they pitch, score, and record outs in simple sequence of activities started long ago. Like in 1906, the pitcher in 2006 initiates play with a pitch to the batter who swings in hope of hitting the ball safely to the ground, while fielders attempt to catch the batted ball or throw out a base runner. Currently, pitchers use new and refined pitches compared to years past, yet they throw in much the same overhand motion and with longstanding strategy of changing speeds, type of movement, and location. Hitters hit in old approach of a level swing with eyes on the ball, front shoulder pointed down, and feet planted softly in a spread fashion on the ground. Like in decades past, fielders field grounders with a glove on the turf and a fly ball with two hands in front of the eyes. Displayed on a diamond of play, long established methods of performance convey the aspiration for a grand simplicity to life and an expectation for a future pattern of living that will produce remarkable refinement of efforts.

Finally, the mythic cycle of baseball portrays the American story of a synergistic circle to connect every element of the world. Prolific travels of the ball in the air are for the purpose of productive contact with the earth, highlighting the connection of things above and below. Pitchers focus on successful use of airspace to minimize the time their team spends on defense, away from opportunity to produce runs by way of the land. Fielders throw the ball through the air to record an out and generate a chance for a link to the earth on offense. The player who completes the third out of a half inning expectantly drops the ball to rest on the fertile grass or dirt, symbolizing anticipation of great things to come through interaction with the realm underneath as a hitter. Ritualistically, groundskeepers spray the field with water to soften and improve conditions, a portrayal of the ocean's importance for the coming creation of an ideal environment. Similarly, players provide watering through incessant spitting, mixing water with the ground, ball, hands, and bat in hope of aid for their efforts. Baseball expresses the vision in the United States for a future circle of life, expected to produce remarkable interplay between air, land, and sea. Through the story of a game, it presents the national perception of a much better world to come.

Chapter Five

Basketball:
American Story of
Irreversible Progress

The third element to the mythology of the United States, stories portray a belief in unstoppable progress to a much better future. They give great importance to the beginnings of the country, representing the origins of an unstoppable momentum toward an ideal life. Shortly after the Revolution, founding fathers encouraged thinking of the new nation as a "great experiment" of vital significance to "millions yet unborn."[1] Amid the despair of the Civil War, Abraham Lincoln inspired hope through a story of "four score and seven years ago," generating renewed confidence that the country's beginning had set in motion powerful forces determined to produce greater freedom and equality.[2] During similar circumstances of war in the twentieth century, Franklin Roosevelt fostered trust in a "rendezvous with destiny," believed the result of historical commitment by the nation to democracy.[3] Subsequently, Martin Luther King, Jr. helped revitalize national faith in unalterable powers

---

[1] Ellen Hovde and Muffie Meyer, dirs., *Liberty: The American Revolution*, video (PBS Video, 2004).

[2] Abraham Lincoln, *The Gettysburg Address* (Boston: Houghton Mifflin, 1995).

[3] Franklin D. Roosevelt, *Rendezvous with Destiny* (, repr., New York: Kraus, 1969).

initiated by "the architects of the Constitution," then pushing for increased equity in race relations.

Basketball portrays the American story of irreversible progress to an ideal life. Fans watch the score build rapidly from zero to a lofty number, bringing the perception of dramatic advancement by the human beings who play the game. NBA games produce final scores of 110 to 108, 101 to 100, and sometimes 130 to 128. Beyond the elevated numbers of point production, players succeed a high percentage of the time. Good shooters score in more than 50 percent of attempts from the field and at a much higher rate from the free throw line. They rack up astronomical digits of accomplishment during a career, indicating highly advanced conditions like the gaudy figures of the gross national product or stock market. Jerry West tallied 25,192 points, and Oscar Robertson 26, 710. Prolific scoring expresses the understanding of much progress achieved in the United States for people with goals under the influence of the flag above the court.

Basketball conveys the American confidence in dramatic improvement of society by way of the ability to score in rapid bursts of success. Frequently, players become hot or on fire with the capacity to score fast and often. The legendary Wilt Chamberlain scored 101 points in one game, while even mediocre players are unstoppable at times, scoring thirty or more points in a short period before returning to more unspectacular performance.[4] In both the NBA and college competition, teams often explode in runs of twelve or more points in a row, quickly changing the complexion of a game. Displayed on a court of hardwood, explosive capabilities of players and teams express the faith in forces of social advancement that make possible quick and remarkable achievements by individuals or groups.

The ease of accomplishments in basketball further illustrates the American belief in the progression of human abilities. The smooth and sweet moves in a game resemble the convenient flow of efforts

---

[4] *The Official NBA Encyclopedia* (New York: Doubleday, 2004) 137.

associated with the microwave and drive-through restaurant, national symbols of progressive movement to an easier life. Players almost effortlessly lay the ball in over the field goal rim or gently kiss the basketball off the backboard for a lay up. In the tradition of Wilt Chamberlain and George "Iceman" Gervin, others finger roll the ball with one arm outstretched in a delicate flick into the hoop. Shooters often benefit from open shots and free throws, presenting the perception of a well-developed quality to life with many open-ended opportunities for individuals.

Finesse and sophistication of motion pervade basketball, portraying the American trust in growing refinement of human beings. Routinely, players use "touch" to shoot the ball in soft descent through the hoop or skillfully backspin a pass with style indicative of refined abilities. Perpetually, they dribble the ball, showing accomplished use of the prized object compared to simple carrying action of football. Often, a player employs both hands in remarkable ambidexterity. Dazzling manipulations of the basketball behind the back and between the legs, resemble the super fast and complicated maneuvering of phenomenon like the human voice by ever improving technology. Fine skills of the game illustrate complex movements associated with social advancement in the United States.

Representative of progress toward a more perfect life, basketball generates an association with perfection, though without concept of a "perfect game." On the individual level, however, a player can achieve a kind of perfection. He or she accomplishes a perfect game of shooting by making every field goal attempt, a feat that grows in significance with the number of attempts. Others reach the perfection of sinking every free throw in a contest or through shutting out an opponent in perfect defense. Frequently, shooters "hit nothing but the bottom of the net," a near perfect moment similar to an event of social change that provides temporary glimpse of the ideal society to come.[5] Perception of the perfect in the game communicates the American mindset of ideals perceived but not yet fulfilled.

The basketball is a perfect circle, symbolizing the pursuit of perfection. Perfectly round, it bounces in a true way to enable the use of anticipatory powers. The game features great anticipators who steal the ball by quickly moving to the expected spot of the next dribble. Others are prolific rebounders (e.g., Bill Russell, Ben Wallace) as a result of the capacity to foresee the bounce of the basketball from the rim. The benefit from the abilities of anticipation conveys the understanding in the United States of well-developed people who follow strong intuition to accomplishments in search of perfection.

Though symbolic of perfectionist goals, the basketball provides a far-from-ideal object. Its significant size and slippery surface produce difficulty in handling, especially compared to the small and easy to grip baseball.[6] Because of the frantic pace to a game, profuse sweating makes control of the ball even more perilous, illustrating the hardships in life regardless of advancements achieved. Teams suffer through long periods of scoring drought, bringing realization that the basketball is only slightly smaller than the field goal hoop. Difficulties in use of the big "roundball" express the American faith in efforts to achieve the perfect, a pursuit still far from fulfillment.

The basketball appears orange, distinct from the earthy brown football and white baseball. It resembles the sun, encouraging an association with prime settings for betterment of living conditions like sunny California or the sunshine state of Florida.[7] In the United States, orange also draws a connection to the fireball of a NASA rocket or the combustion of an automobile engine, national icons of

---

[5] For example, the victory of civil rights activists in 1955 against bus segregation brought a momentary sense of great liberty but did not establish anything close to perfect freedom. See Sanford Wexford, *The Civil Rights Movement: An Eyewitness Account* (New York: Facts on File, 1993).

[6] The big ball often causes dislocated or broken fingers.

[7] The Phoenix Suns make much use of the resemblance between the basketball and the orange sun.

well-propelled advances in society. Across the country, orangish signs signify places of construction, disclosing devotion to building and development. The orange ball symbolizes the dedication to push for rapid advancements, especially by way of explosive movements.

Along with the ball, a basketball court offers a setting for the depiction of the American story about fast movement from ordinary circumstances to the ideal. It is a rectangle, giving an everyday look to the context for a game. The half court line divides the playing surface into two areas of rectangular shape, while free throw lanes at each end define another pair of prominent rectangles. Attached to the two field goals, backboards convey further rectangular appearance, especially by way of inner boxes to guide eyes of the shooter. Though presenting many rectangles, the court also features circles, highlighting pursuit of something more perfect.[8] One circle identifies center court, which is often in eye of the fan, while the free throw lanes lead to two circles at top of the key, prime spots for shooting to the hoop. Nearby are other lines of circular shape, marking a space of opportunity for the optimal score of three points. Most importantly, the field goals display two circular hoops, ever the purpose of game action. Displayed on a court of hardwood, a blend of rectangles and circles reveal the national commitment to fast-paced advancement from common conditions of today to ideal and seemingly perfect goals to come.

In basketball, each contest starts with a toss of the ball into the air in a "jump ball," illustrating the perception in the United States of progressive forces in motion but yet to be controlled. The opening jump requires players to secure control of the loose ball, which represents the potential for great productivity in need of further human direction.[9] Similarly, missed attempts at field goals or free

---

[8] See Barbara Rose, *Ellsworth Kelley: Curves/Rectangles* (New York: Blum Helmun, 1989); Dorling Kindersely, *My First Look at Shapes* (New York: Random House, 1999).

[9] The start to a basketball game contrasts with the secured and gripped baseball at the start of play with a pitch.

throws create loose ball situations, demanding effort to first gain control of the basketball before proceeding to more sophisticated acts in search of a score. Even after a field goal or successful free throw, play begins by gaining use of the bouncing ball, still in motion from the previous shot. Efforts to possess the ever-moving ball express the American faith in an already generated momentum for greater development of society, a promise for increased progress that requires more controlled action.

The March to Freedom

Basketball features strict boundaries and restrictive conditions, depicting a highly limited humanity. The ball is out of play on or beyond the end lines, while players cannot cross the half-court line after entering the frontcourt on offense.[10] Scoring occurs only by way of shooting the basketball through a quite limited location, a field goal with diameter of just eighteen inches.[11] Teams restrict ball handling mostly to specialists (i.e., point guards) who pass to teammates in search of the best shot. They limit touches of the ball for most teammates to feed one or two stars. The intensity of play restricts participation of each player, demanding significant periods of rest on the bench. Even the greatest players (e.g., Michael Jordan, Shaquille O'Neal) show much finitude with time out of action. The legendary Wilt Chamberlain could play each of forty-eight minutes in a game, but he eventually succumbed to a more restricted role after age thirty. Strict limitations in the game portray recognition in the United States of restrictive circumstances in life.

First and foremost, time restricts basketball players, illustrating the American perception of severe limits on human beings with the timed conditions of history. Frequently, the clock compels ball handlers into poor decisions and shots of desperation, prayers without much chance of success. Games occur at restricted moments

---

[10] Infringement of this rule is a "back-court violation."

[11] Therefore, television provides excellent coverage of the action with cameras perched above the game's permanent goals.

of the week, the result of limited capability to play the game. Time exercises power in a playing career, as players retire on average well before age thirty. Basketball stars older than forty, like Roger Clemens or Barry Bonds of baseball, are absent, while quickly aging greats (e.g., Magic Johnson, Shaquille O'Neal) display a quite limited span of productive years. Limitations of time in basketball disclose restricted abilities of even the greatest individuals.

Alongside the acknowledgement of restrictions on humanity, civil religion of the United States generates confidence in increasing freedom for human beings. According to national mythology, origins of the country produced belief that "all ranks are marching to freedom," inspiring faith in the initiation of long-term movement toward ever more liberty.[12] A century later, the Civil War produced a rededication to the pursuit of a freer society as the result of emancipation for slaves.[13] During the twentieth century, success in two world wars brought a sense of expanding liberties abroad.[14] At home, legendary activists for civil rights led in liberation from restrictive conditions of racial segregation. They enacted a mythic "march to freedom," continuing in the struggles of the nation to overcome current and future barriers to human liberty.[15]

Basketball portrays the American story of progress toward great freedom. Players show remarkable ability to use both hands in handling the ball, free of restriction to one hand and arm of strength. They score from much distance to the field goal, showing freedom from need to be physically near the hoop. Great shooters like Jerry

---

[12] Benjamin Rush, *The Selected Writings of Benjamin Rush* (New York: Philosophical Library, 1947).

[13] Eric Foner, *Nothing But Freedom: Emancipation and its Legacy* (Baton Rouge: Louisiana State University Press, 1983); James E. Byrd, *Walk to Freedom: Reconstruction and the Ratification of the Fourteenth Amendment* (Westport CT: Praeger, 1997).

[14] Peter Eisner, *The Freedom Line: The Brave Men and Women who rescued Allied Airmen during World War II* (New York: Morrow Press, 2004).

[15] James M. Fendrich, *Ideal Citizens: The Legacy of the Civil Rights Movement* (Albany: State University of New York Press, 1993).

West and Larry Bird are "deadly from anywhere on the court," free from longstanding limitations of space like the nation's use of wireless technology. Teams freely pass to each teammate in search for an open shot. Ideally, everyone touches the ball, expressing a national faith in liberty of opportunity for every individual as the best means to group advancement. Displayed on courts of hardwood, freedom from restrictions illustrates a belief in an increasingly free humanity.

The mythic freedom of basketball extends into liberty from limits of time. During the shooting of free throws, players become free from timed constraint in relaxed moments, depicting the American anticipation of liberation to come from the pressures of time. As a game nears its conclusion, teams offset the power of the clock through ability to commit fouls and call time-outs. They possess freedom from time by way of overtimes, sometimes delaying the outcome for three or more extra periods. Theoretically, a contest could last forever if the two teams remain tied, conveying an expectancy of liberty someday from authority of the clock. Basketball communicates hope in the United States for progress to freedom from the restrictions of timed conditions, an aspiration for advancement to the end of history.

Most dramatically, the prolific success of African Americans on courts of hardwood accentuates the American perception of development to ever greater freedom. More than any other area of professional life, basketball depicts remarkable progress for people of African descent, expressing the improvement from harsh discrimination of the past. Today, African Americans represent 90 percent of players in the NBA and more than 60 percent of college team members. Black individuals dominate the game, disclosing a significant advancement from strict exclusion not so long ago.

Beyond representation in quantity of players, African Americans further the idea of progressive movement toward great liberty through much influence on the quality of play in basketball. Largely by way of innovations from blacks, games follow fast-paced, explosive, and high-flying style, representing liberation past bigotry against the leadership of African Americans. Before racial integration, play plodded along in a slow, deliberate, and close-to-the-floor fashion. Today, players flash to the basket in creative and quite personal moves, exercising freedom of expression that once drew ridicule.[16] Individuals suddenly take flight to soar high above the rim in displays of free will to achieve the remarkable, especially compared to more grounded efforts of the pre-integration player. Currently, basketball provides fast-break action, punctuated by explosive moments of dramatic change, liberated from the restrictive style of earlier times. Free to use the call-and-response ritual of African-American tradition, players pursue inspirational interaction between teammates or challenging jive with opponents to produce enhanced performance. The greats like Michael Jordan and "Magic" Johnson lift teammates to advanced levels of play, revealing much power to make others better.[17] Presented on hardwood courts, freedom of expression, liberating events of spectacular success, and free interaction with others offer strong indication of national advancement to legendary freedom to come.

Irreversible Progress to the Harmonious Future

American civil religion upholds stories of unstoppable advancement to unprecedented unity between human beings. According to national mythology, the country progressed from loose affiliation of thirteen commonwealths to become the United States, much more closely linked. Decades later, the nation pushed beyond the sharp

---

[16] The current style of the game is quite similar to distinctively African-American forms of religion, highlighted by freedom of expression, community interaction, and dramatic moments of achieved aspirations. See Timothy E. Fulop and Albert J. Raboteau, eds., *African-American Religion: Interpretive Essays in History and Culture* (New York: Routledge, 1997).

[17] The motivating abilities of players resemble acts of "lifting the preacher," inspirational interaction between church participants and ministers in African-American Christianity. See Clifton H. Johnson, ed., *God Struck Me Dead: Voices of Ex-Slaves* (Cleveland: Pilgrim's Press, 1993).

differences of the Civil War to achieve a stronger union.[18] In the twentieth century, industrialization and mass communications produced an ever more connected culture from coast to coast.[19] Difficult years of World War and Cold War strengthened the faith in growing unity of purpose across the states, motivating concern to hunt down sources of disunity.[20] Recently, the globalization of society generates perception of movement toward greater harmony worldwide.[21]

Basketball expresses an American story of dramatic advancement in human relations. It demands nonviolent and highly disciplined interaction with opponents, portraying progress to a state of competition free of crude aggression. On offense, players drive aggressively to the basket but refrain from running into the opposition. Good defenders establish position on the floor, impeding the opponent without violent force. Illustrating advanced conditions of respect for individual rights of opportunity, each player possesses an equal right to occupy every space on the floor, free of physical attack from others.

The accomplished thieves of the game steal the ball but do not commit act of violence, while a shot-blocker swats away scoring attempts yet avoids physical contact. Beyond the nonviolence of the game, the shooting of free throws brings friendly conversation between competitors, depicting the expectation of a much more intimate relation to come at the end of history's time.

Upholding the belief in movement toward social harmony, basketball conveys the conviction in the United States that human

---

[18] Melinda Lawson, *Patriot Fires: Forging a New American Nationalism in the Civil War North* (Lawrence: University of Kansas Press, 2002); Allen Johnson, ed., *Readings in American Constitutional History, 1776–1876* (Boston: Houghton Mifflin Company, 1912).

[19] International Association for Mass Communication Research, *Mass Media and National Culture* (Warsaw:, 1978).

[20] Jim Tuck, *McCarthyism and New York's Hearst Press: A Study of Roles in the Witch Hunt* (Lanham MD: University Press of America, 1995).

[21] Michael Leigh, *Unity in Diversity: Globalization, Democracy, and Cultural Vitality* (Sarawak, Malaysia: Institute of East Asian Studies, 1998).

relations remain adversarial at present. Players confront "in your face" opposition, a contentious situation in the effort to succeed. On offense, they encounter towering giants, fierce defenders like Bill Russell and Ben Wallace who generate fear and intimidation from their ability to reject shots. Others cause trepidation through capacity to steal, similar to belligerent members of society ready to take the most prized of possessions. A player runs into traps with double and triple teams of pressure, a gang of forceful opposition, forced to make sharp and quick moves to create a shot. On defense, teams confront the attack of the opponent and "crash the boards" with overwhelming force. At the home of the opposition, they face hostile crowds nearby, seemingly hovering over game action. Displayed on courts of hardwood, the contentious action of a game portrays the American sense of adversarial relations despite the social progress achieved.

The mythic progress of basketball expresses the perception of remarkable improvement in relations with nature. Games begin in early November when the weather turns difficult for most of the country but concludes with the transformed and comfortable setting of spring. Even in the middle of January, a game takes place in advanced conditions of an arena, consistently providing seventy-degree temperature. Like the revered air conditioners of the nation, the basketball arena symbolizes faith in dramatic advancement through ability to offset nature's hardships.[22] It offers sanctuary from the often harsh environment just beyond the perimeter walls. Similarly, the floor gives superior footing and a level surface in contrast to less ideal ground of nature.[23] The arena and court

---

[22] According to national mythology, the pioneers initiated remarkable advancement in interactions with nature through the building homes in the otherwise harsh "wilderness." In the twentieth century, the country moved forward in ability to control the climate, especially by way of air conditioning, bringing capability to live in areas previously considered too hot (e.g., Arizona, Florida, California, Texas). See Clifford Strock, ed., *Air Conditioning Engineer's Atlas* (New York: Industrial Press, 1939).

[23] An arena is quite similar to a church or synagogue, providing concrete foundation and walls that separate from the natural world.

represent American confidence in an ever developing capability to overcome natural adversities.

The abundant use of the air in basketball expresses a belief in the unstoppable progress associated with prolific air industry of the United States. Oftentimes, players take flight to snatch a rebound, shoot, or slam dunk, rising above for achievements.[24] They have much bounce like astronauts beyond the atmosphere. On offense, individuals benefit from airspace to float past an opponent, while defenders soar to snuff out a scoring attempt. Passes and shots of the ball through air space occur frequently in a game, portraying the development of conditions to a context where the airborne is almost commonplace. Like productive signals of satellites, alley-oop passes float upward to a high-flying receiver for "throw down" to earth in scoring fashion.[25] Frequent and sophisticated air travel communicates the national conception of the advancing capabilities of human beings.

Though presenting the progress in connection with the air, basketball conveys the recognition of limited developments to date. Air movements are restricted to an elevation of just over 10 feet and for only a few seconds of time, disclosing much still to be accomplished in the world above. Airborne actions happen at a sporadic pace in a game, outnumbered by the incessant dribbling and running on the floor, reminiscent of grounded action in everyday life. Beyond the strong limitations in relation with air space, games take place within a rather unremarkable setting of all-encompassing concrete and man-made materials, distant to more majestic features of nature.[26] Uninspired by the surroundings, fans rarely show up

---

[24] Recent TNT broadcasts highlight the airborne element of basketball, featuring "the flight of the game," sponsored by Southwest Airlines. NBA Playoffs, TNT Television, 28 May 2006).

[25] Andrew F. Inglis, *Satellite Technology: An Introduction* (Boston: Focal Press, 1997); P. L. Bargellini, ed., *Communications Satellite Technology* (Cambridge MA: MIT Press, 1974).

[26] The setting for basketball contrasts sharply with the striking natural beauty of a baseball park.

early or stay late, while players lack the benefit of the much fresher atmosphere outdoors. Within the sports trinity, they "suck the most air" but breathe the worst oxygen, playing in stale and enclosed circumstances. Not so long ago, contests occurred in a smoke-filled room, today in non-smoking but still far from ideal conditions. Teams compete on fine hardwood, nevertheless the cause of many bumps, bruises, burns, and broken bones. Restricted use of the air, indoor environment, and hard materials of the game display the incompleteness of social advancements, stopping well short of the synergy with the larger and softer world of nature.

Limited in scope, the mythic progress of basketball illustrates fast-paced development to a more accomplished life through the use of technology. The backboard and rim for the field goal provide great benefit in a game, expressing trust in tools to aid achievements. Backboards produce the capability to soften and guide the flight of the ball during a scoring attempt. Players toss the ball to the board for a gentle fall through the hoop in a lay up or bank a shot off the inner square for deadly accuracy, allowing the glass to improve the potential for success. Periodically, the backboard gives almost miraculous help when an errant shot hits the board to carom into the basket. If help of the board is not enough, the rim can give a shooter's bounce, a softened deflection of an imperfect shot to roll into the hole. At other times, it offers protection from a menacing opponent for a reverse lay up or to create an opportunistic rebound for the unsuccessful shooter who follows a shot.

Beyond the aid of backboards and rims, basketball takes place on the finest hardwood, furthering the perception of remarkable advancement by way of inventive effort. Famous courts like the Boston Gardens display a decorative design similar to the distinctive flooring in buildings of national significance. Bright paint marks the lane to the field goal, expressing the conception of an already established pathway to much productivity. The greats of the game (e.g., Wilt Chamberlain, Shaquille O'Neal) score through an exceptional ability to benefit from optimal positioning "in the paint."

The floor for hoops action communicates the belief in carefully crafted and paved avenues to accomplishment, considered the result of societal development.

Though representative of faith in the aid of technology, basketball lacks tools for direct handling, portraying the American conviction that technological empowerment remains unfulfilled, not to be achieved until the more distant future. Players use bare hands in offensive and defensive pursuits. They score through completely self-generated means, depicting the benefit of technology as beyond reach. Related to its poverty of equipment, the game maintains great popularity with inner city youth who lack in material resources yet have large numbers ready to play. Near the streets of cities across the nation, individuals gain fame through legendary feats, using only a ball, hoop, and harsh playing surface.[27] Basketball happens on shiny wood and under the bright lights of NBA arenas but also on the unspectacular blacktop of an urban playground, presenting the perception of dramatic progress accomplished in the United States and of much still to achieve.

Sacred Departures for the Circle of Life

Like heroes of American mythology, basketball players move directly away from the present location in search for success elsewhere. They drive to the basket in sharp departure, similar to the direct flights of planes across the country. Teams go coast to coast in end to end action like the pioneer push west. Offensive-minded individuals blow past opponents en route to a field goal, creating even greater departure in the score. Others shoot the ball in straight line to the hoop from great distance, able to depart situation with a menacing opponent nearby. A team builds points in a linear fashion far from the starting point of zero to cause ever more distance from the rival in a blow out. Defenders strive to strip the ball from the other team in a fast break departure to the opposite end. Departing actions of a

---

[27] In recent years, ESPN featured a program about the "street ball" of urban America.

game illustrate dedication in the United States to movement decidedly away from present situations to pursue advancement somewhere else.

Basketball expresses American devotion, especially to the departure up and away from the ground. Game action portrays the nation's expansion across the continent and globe before moving upward through air travel. Teams "push the ball" from end to end in pursuit of elevated activity for score of a field goal. Players take flight like the legendary air force of the country, depicting a strong faith in leaving earth for success above. Individuals who play close to the floor are at a huge disadvantage, rarely making an impact in major college or professional competition. The greats like Michael "Air" Jordan possess the ability to defy nature's pull down. Kareem Abdul Jabbar excelled through the sky hook, moving the ball high above the ground to deadly scoring position. Basketball conveys a commitment to the high-flying culture of the United States and the search for social progress by way of dramatic movement to depart the world below.

As the purpose of departures on a court of hardwood, the circular field goal represents American pursuit of a more settled life to come. Players move the ball to a future rest inside the net, conceptualizing the goal as a basket or bucket, something with the capacity to end the movement of objects. Originally, field goals were peach baskets to bring the ball's motion to a complete stop.[28] Today, restful imagery remains in the form of a net under the hoop, there to soften and slow momentum of successful shots. Aspiration for the circular rim presents civil trust in fast-paced and elevated activity to push life toward a very relaxed future, a public display of hope by the nation's commuters who rush to fly in pursuit of a more restful someday in the coming weekend and beyond.

---

[28] Larry Fox, *Illustrated History of Basketball* (New York: Grosset and Dunlap, 1974).

The celebrated hoop of basketball expresses the expectation in the United States for a coming cycle of great productivity. Frequently, individual players become automatic in ability to use the circular basket successfully, "unconscious" with ability to put points on the scoreboard. "In the zone" shooters seem led by a cyclical force to return the ball into the hoop repeatedly. He "plays out of his mind," conveying the national anticipation of future power to repeat a pattern of remarkable accomplishment. When unsuccessful, a player works to put the ball back in the basket, led by mindset of circular movement back to a pre-established place. The repetitious nature of scoring portrays the American imagination for a more accomplished future, a vision for the establishment of a set way to prolific achievements and an end to the frantic search for a better method.

Like the repetitions to produce points, teams follow a mythic pattern of up-and-down movement. After taking flight for a moment, they inevitably come down, revealing the perpetual support of the world underneath. Similarly, the ball enters the hoop for a score high in the air but persistently falls back to the earth. Players ascend high above by way of repeated contact with the ground in a display of increasing productivity through leveraging of a longstanding reality. The rhythmic bounce of the ball from the underworld inspires the fast pace of a game, giving the action a rapid heartbeat that produces explosive moments in a dunk or blocked shot. Basketball illustrates the American aspiration for the cycle of life to connect people, the earth, and air in remarkable productivity. Games of hoops convey civil devotion to sharp departures of football in forward and upward progress to pursue the mythic synergy of forces, portrayed by baseball.

Chapter Six

Doctrines of the Sports Trinity

In their mythic portrayals of life, football, baseball, and basketball convey the doctrines of the United States, core beliefs about the nature of truth. First, they express convictions on matters of theology, thinking in regard to the source of truths.[1] In theological concerns, the sports trinity upholds common tenets of American faith, trust in one supreme being of three-fold expression. Second, the three games communicate more diversified concepts in cosmology, beliefs about where to find knowledge of ultimate truths. Third, each sport presents a distinctive element of doctrine in soteriology, directives for how to solve problems.

Beyond a unified message about theology, the trinity of sports illustrates a three-part perspective in the United States on issues of cosmology and soteriology. In cosmology, football depicts the national conception of supreme truth as transcendent to common conditions of life, highlighting an extraordinary means of revelation.[2] Conversely, baseball portrays the imagination for a future of immanent knowledge, an ideal time when every understanding will

---

[1] For discussion of theology within religion in general, see Wilfred C. Smith, *Towards a World Theology: Faith and the Comparative History of Religion* (Philadelphia: Westminster Press, 1981); Leonard J. Swindler, *Toward a Universal Theology of Religion* (Maryknoll NY: Orbis Books, 1987).

[2] On element of the transcendent, consider Alan M. Olson and Leroy S. Rouner, *Transcendence and the Sacred* (Notre Dame IN: Notre Dame University Press, 1981); John Hick, *An Interpretation of Religion: Human Responses to the Transcendent* (New Haven: Yale University Press, 1989).

result from the study of ordinary circumstances. The final piece to the cosmological equation, basketball presents the belief that guidance is increasingly available from the everyday, faith in progressive realization of absolute truth. Concerning soteriology, football asserts the devotion of the nation to self-help by human beings, forceful resolution to solutions of exceptional adversity (e.g., war).[3] Baseball expresses a futuristic expectation for an unprecedented level of help from forces greater than humanity, while basketball communicates a mode of reasoning for most current circumstances, upholding a dedication to a balance of self-help and reception of aid from someone or something greater. Football, baseball, and basketball convey the American trinity of doctrines about how to discern the greatest truths and problems.

Theology

Civil religion of the United States promotes theistic faith, belief in a divine person as the source of truth.[4] Guided by pledge of allegiance to the flag, citizens aspire to be "one nation under God," a theological tenet challenged unsuccessfully by atheists.[5] Founders of the country directed attention to the "Creator," a supreme being of endowing power.[6] In the Civil War, President Lincoln prescribed trust in a sovereign God more directly at work in human affairs than the deity of Washington and Jefferson.[7] For each decade of the twentieth century, presidents encouraged faith in personified origin of national truths, while social reformers (e.g., Martin Luther King,

---

[3] Also see Hick, *An Interpretation of Religion*, for soteriology in the world's religions.

[4] Mark A. Noll, *America's God: from Jonathan Edwards to Abraham Lincoln* (New York: Oxford University Press, 2002).

[5] Richard Ellis, *To the Flag* (Lawrence: University Press of Kansas, 1994).

[6] *The Politician's Pocket Companion: The Declaration of Independence, the Constitution of the United States, with Amendments* (Morristown NJ: Henry P. Russell, 1804).

[7] Noll, *America's God*; John W. Hill, *Abraham Lincoln: Man of God* (New York: G. P. Putnam and Sons, 1920); Gordon Leidner, *Lincoln on God and Country* (Shippensburg PA: White Mane Books, 2000).

Jr.) inspired by way of devotion to an Almighty character of justice.[8] Most recently, President George W. Bush speaks often of God, especially in the most formal of addresses.[9]

Football, baseball, and basketball express the American faith in the personal nature of the ultimate reality. Beyond abundant references to "the Lord," players first think of a special person for guidance in how to play, conveying the national belief in the search for knowledge from a personified source.[10] They gain understanding through the study of a great player who presents truths for success in form of a personality. Barry Bonds thinks of Willie Mays, and Tom Brady reflects on Joe Montana, while Kobe Bryant remains mindful of Michael Jordan, concentrating on personal sources of knowledge. Especially when faced with much adversity, a player conceives of an exemplary individual in a similar dilemma to a find sense of direction like the national reverence for heroic individuals of history (e.g., Lincoln, King). Exalted personalities of sports portray devotion in the United States to personal foundation of truth.

Post-game activities further reveal the American association of supreme person with the most inspirational thoughts. Players often speak of gratitude to a particular loved one, disclosing a personal source of motivation. Frequently, they move quite smoothly to praise for God in talk of inspiration from the ultimate person. Not simply believers in personality, players strive to be recipients of the public trust, hoping to benefit from civil dedication to personal objects of faith. Ultimately, they aspire to be inducted in a Hall of Fame and

---

[8] See James M. Washington, *I Have a Dream: Writings and Speeches that Changed the World* (San Francisco: Harper and Row, 1992); Martin Luther King, Jr. *The Speeches of Martin Luther King*, video (Corlan Park: MPI Video, 1990).

[9] Paul Kengor, *God and George W. Bush* (New York: Regan Books, 2004); Tom Freiling, *George W. Bush on God and Country* (Fairfax VA: Allegiance Press, 2002).

[10] The personal mindset of American players differs from the more impersonal thinking in other societies. For example, Japanese baseball upholds concern for following a formula of action rather than a person, more of a scientific, step by step learning pattern in contrast to the imitation of people in the United States. See Robert Whiting, *You Gotta Have Wa* (New York: Macmillan Press, 1989).

immortalized as a personality of significance for generations unborn. Similar to national monuments, each Hall of Fame houses shrines of reverence, sites for veneration of persons given extraordinary value. Hundreds of thousands visit every year, displaying strong faith in personified truths. Like Washington and Jefferson, "immortal" persons of football, baseball, and basketball illustrate the abundant meaning of exemplary individuals in the United States, deemed representatives of a greater and supreme being.

Expressing the American trust in a personal origin of truth, the sports trinity gives ultimate importance to select personalities in the conduct of a game. The arbiters on the field or court make many errors in judgment, publicly revealed by replay technology, yet they retain sovereign power, portraying a belief in a person with final authority. The decision-making ability of referees and umpires conveys national faith in an animate being. They rule in a quick, direct, and decisive fashion and are believed more responsive to dynamic circumstances of life than something impersonal. Inanimate forms of information, instant replay, and computer programming grow in use but with minimal impact on game action.[11] Teams and fans expect an umpire or referee to employ every capacity of personhood in service of the truth, showing a close connection between personal qualities and the greatest truths. Like the personified source of truth in civil religion of the United States, an extraordinary person makes authoritative rulings in contests of football, baseball, and basketball.

Beyond the game action, fans show dedication to a supreme personality of guidance. They give great significance to one favorite player on a team, often displaying the beloved name of the individual in distinction from every other name on a jersey or some other object

---

[11] The more personal game of baseball contrasts with football where computer programs have much influence on determining the champion of major college football. Baseball best illustrates the ideal of a personal source of truth, while football represents the nation's compromise of ideals for difficult realities (e.g., more impersonal or collective effort).

of devotion. Frequently, a fan aspires to know every intimate detail about the exalted person in search for ever more personal knowledge. Like the supreme being conceived of by the nation, good teams look to a leader, a personality who exemplifies the winning mindset for the group. Teams feature mascots that add more personification to the meaning of a game. The "Philly Fanatic," the "Gorilla" of the Phoenix Suns, and the "Minnesota Viking" provide a personalized image for franchises of professionals, while the "Trojan" of the University of Southern California, the "Chief Seminole" of Florida State University, and the "Nittany Lion" of Penn State symbolize personality-like conception of college organizations. Special concern for a particular personality conveys the American devotion to one person of truth.

Like players, fans often believe in some higher force of justice at work in the games, indicating faith in a personal and sovereign power who can even things out between two teams and deliver on the promise of a player who is due. Many expect quite personalized answers to requests of "please help," "let him get a hit," or "allow us to score this time." In moments of dire circumstances, the die-hard fan offers up prayerful plea of "why?" Frequently, he or she senses that a game or season follows a highly organized and predestined design for success or failure, disclosing a sensibility for some greater person of influence, able to predetermine events on the field or court. During game action, the thoughts of fans express the American trust in a supreme personality, a supreme someone of determining power.

More than a purveyor of simple belief in personal source of truth, the civil religion of the United States upholds the three-and-one character of ultimate reality.[12] Three constitutional documents present one set of truths for the country, while three forms of federal

---

[12] Undoubtedly, the Christian doctrine of the trinity had much influence on the nation's thinking. For the trinitarian concept of Christianity, see Jaroslav J. Pelikan, *The Emergence of the Catholic Tradition, 100–600* (Chicago: University of Chicago Press, 1975).

government guide national search for oneness of political effort.[13] One verdict of court justice results from a three-way interaction between judge, jury, and lawyers. Three branches of the military represent one force of comprehensive defense. From the beginning, citizens looked especially to three founding fathers (i.e., Washington, Jefferson, Franklin) for knowledge to become one nation. As a result of exceptional leadership in the Civil War, Abraham Lincoln became one in a trinity of exemplary presidents (i.e., Lincoln, Washington, Jefferson), ever-present for posterity. [14] One hundred years later, Martin Luther King, Jr. inspired a rededication to one set of ideals, producing much support from Protestants, Catholics, and Jews, the three major religions in the country.[15] American civil religion generates faith in the three-and-one nature of the greatest truths.[16]

Football, baseball, and basketball express strong devotion in the United States to a three-and-one truth, leading the nation through one year with three-sport action. Each game produces one grand conclusion (i.e., the final score) by way of a three-fold exchange involving a home team, visitors, and referees or umpires. Teams strive for oneness of thinking, chemistry between three primary groups (i.e., players, coaches, and management officials or administrators). Among the players, three parties work to accomplish one collective victory. A football team features offensive, defensive, and special units, while infielders, outfielders, and batteries (i.e., pitchers and catchers) complete one team for baseball. In basketball, guards, forwards, and centers work for oneness of identity, win or lose. For each sport, players perform in a three-part manner on

---

[13] American Political Science Association, *The Constitution: Our Enduring Legacy* (Washington DC: Congressional Quarterly, 1986); Syl Sobel and Pam Tanzey, *How the U.S. Government Works* (Hauppauge NY: Barron's, 1999).

[14] The national monument at Mount Rushmore honors the three along with Theodore Roosevelt, commissioner of the site.

[15] Miskit Airth, *Dr. Martin Luther King, Jr.: An Amazing Grace*, video (Del Mar CA: McGraw Hill, 1985).

[16] These two types of expectation convey competing Republican and Democratic versions of the civil faith.

offense, defense, and in vocal or moral support of teammates, actions of devotion to one group.[17] Post-game, individuals frequently speak of inspiration from family, teammates, and coaches, a unified set of triune guidance like the three sets of federal figures and documents of directive influence for the country. In prolific ways, the sports trinity portrays American trust in one-and-three quality of the most foundational elements in life.

Similar to the teams, fans show dedication to oneness of truth with three expressions. They expect a coach or manager to establish one set of rules for unification of the three factions on a team, intolerant of disunity among tripartite groups of teammates. Shaped by the worldview of the United States, a fan sees double standards in the treatment of players as highly problematic, and they are concerned about the violation of the oneness expected on a field or court of play. Most fans maintain devotion to three teams that make up one source of nonstop inspiration, triune sets of athletes associated with one city, region, or state. Near a large city, professional franchises of the sports trinity draw the attention of one fan, while three teams of a college or university generate similar commitment in areas of more statewide identity.[18] Routinely, one fan has three favorite players (e.g., Allen Iverson, Bobby Abreu, and Donovan McNabb for Philadelphians) in a trinity of characters who most represent one metropolitan place or state. Even when allegiances shift after moves across the country, many fans replace one set of triune teams with a new group of three, maintaining a trinitarian devotion rather than adopt a special concern for a more diverse cast of exalted figures. Most often, they preserve the oneness of faith in the three teams of personal affiliation from early in life, frequently despite moving thousands of miles to other side of the

---

[17] With highly specialized roles, the offensive and defensive personnel of football perform in regards to running and passing the ball plus the cheering for teammates in three way effort for one success.

[18] For example, the University of Nebraska is the source of ultimate concern across Nebraska and the University of Oklahoma in "Sooner" territory.

continent. Dedication to three teams of one place illustrates American belief in three and one truth.

Cosmology

Though unified in portrayal of theology, the sports trinity presents divergent views on cosmology, beliefs about where to look in the surrounding world for knowledge of ultimate reality. Historically, civil religion of the United States encourages faith in the transcendence of truth, trust in looking well beyond common realities of life to extraordinary locations for directives.[19] It directed attention to constitutional documents for understanding of supreme truths, highly specialized sources of information.[20] Through the guidance of these exceptional texts, Abraham Lincoln inspired national rededication to transcendent precepts of "freedom and equality," concepts that represent "the task undone," ideals far from realization in everyday life during the Civil War.[21] A century later, Martin Luther King, Jr. regenerated a special concern for the disparity between constitutional values and unjust realities of ordinary living in the country.[22] He helped revive a nationwide commitment to ideas (e.g., justice, freedom) deemed transcendent to existing laws and practices, especially those of racial segregation. The nation's worldview has generated devotion to convictions that sharply transcend the commonplace.

Football expresses the American trust in the transcendence of truth. Players find guidance in specialized places, looking well

---

[19] Hick, *An Interpretation of Religion*; Benson Saler, *Conceptualizing Religion: Immanent Anthropologists, Transcendent Natives, and Unbounded Categories* (New York: Oxford University Press, 2000).

[20] William Dudley, *The Creation of the Constitution: Opposing Viewpoints* (San Diego: Greenhaven Press, 1995); Ronald Wells and Thomas A. Askew, *Liberty and Law: Reflections on the Constitution in American Life and Thought* (Grand Rapids MI: Eerdmans Publishing Company, 1987).

[21] Abraham Lincoln, *The Speeches and Addresses of Abraham Lincoln* (New York: Little Leather Library Company, 1911).

[22] King, *Speeches of Martin Luther King, Jr.*

beyond ordinary conditions inside themselves and on the field to something or someone transcendent. For a sense of direction, they think of the end zone, typically far from familiar circumstances along the nearby line of scrimmage. The goal line remains at remote end of the playing field, generating thoughts of transcending everything close at hand just as national beliefs point to yet-to-be-reached truths. Besides the end zone, a player looks to the distant sidelines for understanding, consistently thinking of someone or something not close. Resembling the country's faith in special officials of federal government, he trusts in the ideas of a few extraordinary persons (i.e., the head coach and an elite group of assistant coaches) rather than easier-to-access internal thoughts. Similarly, the individuals on a team receive directives from one exceptional book (i.e., the playbook of strategy), believed to transcend other information like constitutional writings. The mindset of players illustrates faith in the transcendence of ultimate truths, concepts perceived as distant and extraordinary, disassociated from the ordinary conditions of life.

Belief in a transcendent truth emanates from many aspects of football. Common situations of nature are not the focus of concern during a game, often deemed the cause of adversity to be rejected. Players renounce ordinary thoughts of weather to concentrate focus on more transcendent precepts of the game plan, extremely specialized and human-centered concepts for how to proceed. Teams give exclusive attention to ideas of transcendence to natural provisions, illustrated by the absence of birds, flowers, plants, or any other inspiring thing from nature. Team names declare the supreme significance of human beings, believed on a level of existence far superior to nature's circumstances. "Steelers," "Packers," and "Cowboys" highlight extraordinary abilities of humans, while teams of naturalistic association communicate mindset of distance to the much more important people on the field. "Eagles," "Hawks," and "Falcons" fly remote to human affairs, similar to "Bears," "Lions," and "Dolphins" that roam well removed from society, never within sight of play on the gridiron. Thoughts of a distant nature express dedication in the United States to transcendence of the commonplace.[23]

Football exemplifies transcendent truth by way of a strong trust in modern medicine. Players often ingest chemical prescriptions or supplements, formerly properties of nature now rearranged in an exercise of human ability to conceive the transcendent. Frequently, they inject medication in rejection of natural pain from an injury, a dramatic display of a mindset for transcendence.[24] Frequent use of surgery by teams communicates belief in the capability of human beings to comprehend mysteries of healing quite distinct from the more gradual process of nature. Generating much commitment to modern medicine, football upholds the American doctrine of transcendent truths, existent remote to conditions of the natural.

Through a source for devotion to transcendent thinking, civil religion of the United States nurtures expectation for immanent truth in a future when prolific knowledge will be available through the study of the everyday.[25] From the beginning, the nation envisioned ideal conditions to come, anticipating an end to the search beyond the here and now for sense of direction. In the early nineteenth century, many communities emerged across the country with an aspiration for utopian goals within daily living (e.g., Oneida, Brook Farm).[26] Decades later, reconstruction from the devastation of the Civil War and the subsequent era of progressive reform rekindled a vision for a coming time of truth as common sense, especially expectant of remarkable truths associated with emerging technology.

---

[23] Mary E. Jones, *The American Frontier: Opposing Viewpoints* (San Diego: Greenhaven Press, 1994).

[24] See Paul W. Sharkey, *A Philosophical Examination of the History and Values of Western Medicine* (Lewiston NY: E. Mellen Press, 1992).

[25] For a classic description of belief in divine immanence, see William Temple, *Nature Man, and God* (London: Macmillan, 1964).

[26] Mark Holloway, *Heavens on Earth: Utopian Communities in America, 1680–1880* (New York: Dover Publications, 1966); Dolores Hayden, *Seven American Utopias: The Architecture of Communitarian Socialism, 1790–1975* (Cambridge MA: MIT Press, 1976).

In the twentieth century, worldwide wars produced a more pessimistic mindset, pushing national hope for realization of grand knowledge into the futuristic distance. Nevertheless, Franklin Roosevelt helped inspire renewed faith in "destiny" to realize idealistic concepts, while Martin Luther King, Jr. spoke persuasively of a "someday" when everyone in the nation will possess great "truth," a full comprehension of constitutional ideals without much effort.[27] Historically, the national worldview has produced imagination for a future of easily known truths, knowledge to be gained through focus on common circumstances.

Baseball expresses the American expectation of immanent truth to come, ideal time of finding abundant understanding from within the commonplace. Players receive guidance through concentration on the familiar and nearby, mostly by way of an internal search for readily available thoughts. Hitters follow easy-to-find intuition, sitting on or guessing about the next pitch while pitchers use quick working "feel" to select a pitch, exercising inner foresight for how to deliver the ball. Fielders benefit from anticipation of the soon-to-be-hit baseball. Portraying the aspiration for a time of commonly known truths, players rarely look beyond themselves for directives, only infrequently receiving directions from the third base coach or manager on the bench. Frequent gazes to the dugout for help draw much chastisement, highlighting trust in already possessed information. Good players "have an idea," while the greats possess "feel for the game," keen instincts for how to play independent of external influence. Similarly, managers pursue "gut instinct," inner sensibility for the next move in a contest rather than strict adherence to prescribed rules. At times, they consult a book of strategy, internalized guidelines for how to proceed, ever able to "throw the book away." Displayed on a diamond of play, trust of inner capabilities conveys vision in the United States for immanent truths in a future when each individual will possess great knowledge.

---

[27] King, *Speeches of Martin Luther King, Jr.*

Hope for readily available truth radiates from baseball, especially through thoughts about the natural environment. Players find inspiration in the commonplace provisions of nature, discerning much purpose within the familiar. Warm weather prompts exuberant thoughts of "let's play two [games]" and "today is a perfect day for baseball," while strong winds generate visions of belting home runs.[28] Bright sunshine excites a hitter, bringing perception of an increased capability to see the incoming pitch, and enlivens pitchers by way of confidence in their enhanced ability to grip the ball for spinning difficult to hit curves. When faced with a situation of two outs and no runs scored, teams seek "two out lightning" in imitation of explosive power from nature with loud cracks of run-producing hits. If trailing in the score by seemingly insurmountable margin, a team prays for rain in plea for miraculous work of nature to halt the ill-fated contest. Names of teams in Major League Baseball further indicate aspiration for guidance from the natural. "Orioles," "Cardinals," "Blue Jays," and "Phillies" represent life forms of nature that live close to human beings, providing inspirational sound and look.[29] Concepts of inspiration from nature express the American expectation of easily discernible truths to come, a time when natural provisions will reveal a prolific sense of purpose.

According to baseball, the earth provides much guiding influence, illustrating a vision in the United States for coming realization of truths by way of a thoughtful focus on nature below. Near home plate, players dig into the soil to bring a greater awareness of the soon-to-be-delivered pitch, expecting productive contact with the land by hitting the ball safely to the ground. Pitchers

---

[28] Hall of famer and "Mr. [Chicago] Cub," Ernie Banks is infamous for articulation of such thoughts.

[29] Symbolic of more ominous creatures, "Tigers" and "Diamondbacks" are the exception. Seemingly, they represent the inclusion of big cats and reptiles in an ideal world to come, befitting baseball's portrayal of futuristic perfection. Former Oakland A's owner, Charles Finley provided diverse animals for the setting of a game in expression of the idyllic vision.

"toe the rubber," touching the mound of earth for enhanced concentration on delivery of pitches. With perception of directive impact from the land, the game generates much concern with the feet and legs, body parts near the earth to guide more elevated efforts of hands and eyes. Star hurlers possess great legs for benefit from strong contact with the ground, sometimes using dramatic leg kicks to maximize leverage from below.[30] Faced with many grounded balls, fielders focus on deep-bending knee action to gain prime position close to the turf. Hitters become ready through thoughts of legs and feet in an open, closed, or balanced stance, mindful of the stabilizing support from earth. As base runners, they frequently leap forward feet first, visualizing safe passage around the bases by way of sliding low into the dirt. Displayed on a diamond of play, belief in the land as a directing force conveys the American imagination for an easy-to-find sense of direction, a futuristic expectation of productive knowledge from study of nearby conditions just below the feet.

Beyond perceptions of nature, thoughts about health and healing in baseball express an aspiration for immanent truths someday, anticipating the discovery of solutions from inside the commonplace. Most of the time, teams prescribe rest as the remedy for an injury in search for resolution to a health problem within easy-going activities of familiar life at home. Frequently, they place players on the "fifteen day disabled list," an excused absence from game action to pursue healing within the flow of ordinary living. For guidance, a player follows the lead of pain, easily accessible and internally provided information, reducing or ceasing sport activities until the end to the hurtful messages.[31] If the problem persists, methods of more transcendent thinking (e.g., chemical intake, surgery) become possibilities but only after much effort to find a solution inside common actions, sometimes giving years to nature's process for

---

[30] For illustration, see delivery of Dontrelle Willis today or Vida Blue from decades past.

[31] Such concern with pain often contrasts with the more transcendent philosophy of football.

healing.[32] Recent controversy about use in baseball communicates special association of the game with natural methods.[33] In response to health difficulties, dedication to familiar ways of remedy presents a belief in a time to come when every piece of knowledge will be readily available, even the mysteries of medicine.

The complement to football and baseball, basketball portrays the American faith in the progressive realization of ultimate truth, disclosing trust in a historical movement ever closer to a future when transcendent truths of history will become immanent in the everyday.[34] Routinely, teams receive guidance from sources that transcend nearby and familiar circumstances. They concentrate on set plays that are revealed by the coach, not easy to find information. In preparation for a game, players look well outside themselves to gain knowledge from a unique book (i.e., the playbook), writing about highly extraordinary concepts like the ideals in constitutional documents. A player puts aside inner thoughts and feelings to focus on transcendent ideas of prescribed plays. When having exceptional difficulty in a contest, he or she glances to the bench for help with perspective, seeking an external point of view. Ideally, teams remain mindful of scoring through lifting of the ball up and away to the field goal rim, resembling the country's pursuit of goals transcendent to things close at hand. Located at end of the court and elevated high above, the hoop symbolizes the transcendence of highly pursued truths that are found in the remote and higher thoughts of human beings rather than in the ordinary.

Devotion to transcendent truth echoes from many elements of basketball, disclosing a mindset in the United States of much still to be realized. The setting for a college or professional game, an arena

---

[32] In search for healing through rest, a team may place an individual on the "sixty day disabled list."

[33] Though generating steroids intake, football does not draw similar outrage from the public.

[34] Basketball expresses belief in progressive revelation like the modernistic and optimistic thinking of Reform Judaism and liberal Protestants.

houses thoughts of strict concern with specialized efforts of human beings, quite distant to common conditions of nature outside. Arenas feature impenetrable slabs of concrete under the floor like every building of importance in the nation, symbolizing hard faith in transcendence of the natural world below. Birds, grass, flowers, wind, sunshine, rain, and everything else from nature stay invisible to the game, out of sight and mind. In the NBA, team names further the mindset of human progress at a distance to nature. "Hawks" fly far above humanity, while "Bulls" require seclusion from society.[35] "Suns" and "Lakers" bring to mind people who live under sunny skies in Arizona and near the water in California, not first and foremost the natural conditions. Players conceive of achievement by way of transcending nature's pull to the earth. Frequently, they reject common thoughts of existence near the ground to embrace transcendent ideas of flight like the extraordinary concepts associated with the lift off of NASA rockets and satellite technology. In arenas from coast to coast, the perception of distance from nature displays a belief in the transcendence of supreme truths and dedication to knowledge discerned from study focused beyond the common provisions of life.

Alongside a philosophy of transcendence, basketball expresses the American confidence in truth becoming increasingly immanent inside the familiar, progressive realization of ideals previously considered distant. After following specialized directives from the coach and playbook, players concentrate on internal information, a readily available understanding of how to play. On offense, they exercise imagination to create a shot, drawing on an inner vision for guidance. When in doubt, a player trusts in internalized precepts such as "pass the ball," "go to the basket," or "follow your shot." Similarly, he or she focuses on ideas that naturally come to mind as a defender (e.g., "stay on your feet," "box out"). The greats possess

---

[35] The "Heat" of Miami communicates sense of something natural to keep at a distance outside the air-conditioned arena.

court awareness, easy to access intuition for how to proceed. Like the close-at-hand sense of direction possessed by stars of the game, the targeted field goal is often near to the players. Though at a distance to start most plays, teams quickly move within shooting range of the hoop, making their objective quite accessible. A good team frequents the space near the basket, which is representative of national belief in historical movements closer to once remote goals. Displayed on courts of hardwood, concentration on internal thoughts of much familiarity and prolific moves near to the hoop portray the conception in the United States of progress toward the immanence of every truth, approaching a coming time of remarkable understanding to result from awareness of nearby conditions.

Depicting the American faith in a growing comprehension of ultimate truths, basketball communicates the recognition of highly productive guidance received from the most common features of nature. Players find guiding influence from nature's solid world below, support of the earth under the constructed floor. They think of great leverage by way of a massive foundation underneath to explode above for the spectacle of a dunk or long distance jump shot. Showing aspiration for gaining a sense of direction from the nearby ground, the game gives special significance to the feet and legs, parts of the body close to nature below. Oftentimes, a player upholds a special concern for shoes in exalted thinking about foot action, while fans spend billions to buy footwear of stars, inspired by strong conviction that "it's the shoes."[36] In like-minded focus, teams strive to "find [their] legs" in search for supremacy in a contest. They envision "spring in the legs," imagination for beneficial contact with an immovable source of power below. Belief in the directive influence from the very familiar ground conveys a sense of historical progress to immanent truths, national confidence in movement toward a future when conditions of nature below will provide a remarkable

---

[36] Walter E. Meanwell, *The Care of the Feet in Basketball* (Rock Island IL: Servus Rubber Company, 1994); Roslyn Jordan and Kadir Nelson, *Salt in his Shoes: Michael Jordan in Pursuit of a Dream* (New York: Aladdin Paperworks, 2004).

sense of direction, ending human dependence on concepts of distant meaning.

Soteriology

Beyond cosmology, the sports trinity expresses doctrines of soteriology in the United States, beliefs about how to solve problems and achieve ultimate truths. The national worldview encourages devotion to self-help efforts by human beings rather than simple reliance on the aid of someone or something greater. Constitutional documents uphold the supreme importance for voluntary actions by individuals, asserting faith in the free will of the people.[37] Harsh conditions on the frontier produced increased commitment to self-determination, strong belief in "pulling yourself up by your own bootstraps." During the Civil War, Abraham Lincoln periodically lost the sense of God's help, yet he preserved dedication to moral action in anticipation of improving conditions. In the twentieth century, World War I and II brought heightened resolve to forceful works against evil powers, while the civil rights movement inspired the nation "to keep moving" in democratic pursuit even when support seems unavailable. The belief system of the country pivots on trust in the capability of human beings to resolve great difficulties, a tenet of faith most relevant during times of crisis, moments seemingly devoid of aid from some higher power.

Football expresses the American doctrine of self-help. In a game, success comes only after long-lasting and intense struggle, portraying the national devotion to strenuous efforts by individuals to improve conditions. Ball carriers earn every inch of progress on the field, acting as workhorses who rarely release the ball in deferment to another. Great quarterbacks "will" teams to victory through self-determined action, while offensive linemen "put teammates on their back" in exceptional personal output that clears the way for "skilled"

---

[37] Thomas E. Patterson, *We the People: A Concise Introduction to American Politics* (Boston: McGraw Hill, 2004); Jon Pahl, *Paradox Lost: Free Will and Political Liberty in American Culture, 1630–1760* (Baltimore: John Hopkins Press, 1992).

colleagues. Defenders disrupt progress of the opponent through willful acts of aggression. Linebackers and defensive backs "jump" plays to stop the opposition by way of highly self-initiated activity. Frequently, players continue in a contest after being injured, sometimes severely, providing an inspirational example of courageous effort. Winning teams "bring their lunch pales" in exemplary labor to do whatever it takes. Illustrated on a gridiron of play, aggressive acts of self-determination convey strong dedication to works by human beings, believed capable of overcoming the severest adversity.

American belief in self-help emanates from every corner of football. Players remain relatively free of superstitions, without much time for ritualistic routine to seek the aid of greater forces. The timed conditions of a game also discourage expectations for miraculous change in the score and seemingly help by some higher power.[38] At some point in a contest, the losing team has no chance for turn of fate, powerless before the clock. They have no hope for intervention of natural forces since play continues regardless of the weather, leaving the humans on the field solely responsible for results.[39] Similar to the scant possibility of a team for dramatic turnabouts, little support is available to the individual player during games. Routinely blocked from clear view of plays, referees provide infrequent help, furthering the "do it yourself" mindset. Most of the time, a player responds to illegal tactics by the opponent in self-determined manner by "settling the score" with personal act of retribution inside flow of game action. Football depicts the devotion in the United States to efforts of self-determination, especially for times of extraordinary difficulty, moments when the possibility of intervention by someone or something greater seems absent.

Alongside trust in human works, American civil religion generates the expectation for aid from a higher power, particularly in

---

[38] Lack of hope for miracle turnarounds is especially evident in comparison to baseball.

[39] A strong earthquake would end the game action, but with such trauma as not to be beneficial.

an ideal future. Early, the nation envisioned incredible benefits to come from boundless resources, anticipating abundant blessings of divinity.[40] With the victory of the Union in the Civil War, Abraham Lincoln helped revive national hope in the intervening powers of God.[41] Fueled by grandiose success in World War I and II, the country enhanced its faith in supernatural "destiny," apparently the source of its exalted position worldwide.[42] Within the states, Martin Luther King, Jr. inspired increased awareness of "spiritual and moral forces" at work to move the nation ever closer to constitutional ideals.[43] Recently, George W. Bush led a resurgence of trust in the direct aid from God, perceiving a divine push for increased democracy, peace, and justice across the globe. Throughout its history, the belief system of the United States upheld the doctrine of other help from a higher power, encouraging the anticipation of strong support from divinity.

Baseball expresses the American aspiration for a future of manifold benefit from divine forces. Routinely, players perform dramatic feats with an ease that seems miraculous, illustrating the national imagination for divinely empowered events to come. Without breaking a sweat, hitters swing in level and easy motions, yet they propel the ball many hundreds of feet, often at speeds of over 100 miles per hour, seemingly aided by some invisible force. At times, they nudge the pitch softly between two infielders in a "seeing eye base hit" as though directed by a higher power. Frequently, players benefit from highly provided for opportunities, "bases loaded" situations of providence. They become incredibly hot, hitting safely several times in a game, game after game, as if propelled by energy from beyond. The greats rack up gaudy numbers of

---

[40] Benjamin Rush, *The Writings of Benjamin Rush* (New York: Philosophical Library, 1947).

[41] Lincoln, *Speeches of Abraham Lincoln.*

[42] Roosevelt, *Rendezvous with Destiny.*

[43] King, *Speeches of Martin Luther King, Jr.*

prolific achievement, which are the causes of wonderment about their nearly unbelievable level of success.[44]

Like hitters, pitchers perform amazing acts with a grace that is difficult to explain, throwing in smooth motion yet slinging the ball at speeds almost too fast to see. A major league pitcher exhibits many types of pitches, able to doctor the baseball with magic-like movements. Oftentimes, he mystifies the hitter with the ability to "pull the string" in dramatic "change up" of speed. In particular, knuckle-balls generate a sense of help from outside forces. These pitches "dance and dart" in wild unpredictability. Straighter, fastballs often move upward in remarkable defiance of nature's pull down as though pushed by transcendent power. Curve balls loop and drop in a sharp fashion like an object forcefully turned by divine will. Infielders also offer an indication of benefits from some higher force. They are routinely the recipients of easy-to-field "gifts" of a hop by the batted ball. At times, they charge a bunt at full-speed intensity for a bare-handed catch and an off-balanced throw in a nearly unexplainable sequence of events. Outfielders sprint and leap in full extension to rob the opponent of an apparent base hit, enacting an almost miraculous turn of fate. Displayed on a diamond of play, remarkable actions and the ease of effort convey a vision for a coming time when greater forces will empower human activity.

Unpredictability pervades baseball, portraying the American faith in unprecedented events to come by way of divine intervention. The timelessness of a game makes amazing comebacks possible since no deficit is too great to overcome. Fantastic turnarounds in the score, especially during the ninth inning, bring sense of higher powers at work. Unbelievable, magical, and miracle come-from-

---

[44] ESPN broadcaster, Jon Miller speaks of long-standing records by old-timers like Babe Ruth and Lou Gerig as "Old testament" stories of miraculous events since "things like that don't seem to happen anymore." *Sunday Night Baseball*, ESPN Television, 10 April 2005).

behind wins highlight the season of a successful team.[45] Similarly teams and their supporters experience a reception of unmerited favor when inclement weather arrives to cancel a game and wipe away a pending loss. Recognizing the influence of someone or something greater, players believe that "it's better to be lucky than good," while fans expect a player to lead off the next at bat on offense after making an exceptional play on defense. The long-lasting season of play allows teams to lose many games in a row yet still gain a sudden and sharp rise in the standings. Incredible revolution in the standing of a team generates a belief in the work of destiny, some transcendent energy of determining power. Dramatic changes in a game and season express the aspiration in the United States for a future of powerful benefit from forces of divinity, which is expected to cause miraculous turns for the better.

In baseball, abundant aid is available to players, expressing the American expectation for other help. Pitchers gain nonstop support from teammates who "talk it up" to provide encouragement. When in trouble, the pitcher receives visits and helpful words of comfort or guidance from a teammate, coach, or manager. If the adversity persists, he benefits from team members pledged to his "relief," others dedicated to rescue work like super prepared emergency professionals of the future. Resembling mythic fireman, the best relievers intervene to hold or save a win, producing images of a saving action of a more grandiose fashion to come. Unable to drive base runners home, hitters find a teammate soon present at the plate to "pick him up" with a run scoring hit. After failure against a particular pitcher, they benefit from teammates ready to "pinch hit" and lift the burden of responsibility. On defense, players "back each other up," conveying a futuristic expectation for prolific support when difficulty arrives. In response to a threatening hit deep into the outfield, they move into the formation of a human chain for a

---

[45] As an Orioles fan, I vividly remember the "Orioles magic" of 1979 and the miraculous turns of fate delivered by Eddie Murray, Ken Singleton, Doug DeCinces, or some other Oriole near end to a game.

supportive relay of throws to the proper base. Subsequent to extremely troublesome moments, a fielder may hand-deliver the ball in act of aid to the pitcher, helping to restore order and some calm. Readily available help in a game illustrates the anticipation of a future with boundless forces of support.

Portraying the American hope for the helping influence of divinity, baseball generates rampant superstition, ritual acts of trust in aid from someone or something greater. During hitting streaks, players will not shave or change underwear, hoping not to offend whoever or whatever may be ultimately responsible for their success. Hall of famer, Wade Boggs ate chicken before every game, expecting grand results.[46] In game action, teams strictly avoid touching the foul lines when walking on or off the field and refrain from talking about a teammate who has not allowed a hit in a contest, fearing alienation from some higher power. If behind in the score, they turn team headgear inside out in a display of "rally caps," which are believed to be capable of drawing support from an invisible force for dramatic change in the outcome.[47] Like the players, fans exhibit superstition, upholding detailed practices for watching or listening to facilitate help to a beloved team. Many speak incantations like "he's due" or "we only need a hit" while sitting or standing in a purpose-filled manner to prompt the intervention of divinity into a game situation. Widespread superstitions in baseball communicate the aspiration for an ideal life to come with overwhelming influence from divine powers of good.

The perfect complement to football and baseball, basketball expresses the American devotion to a balance of convictions for how to solve most problems, encouraging both belief in self-help and the aid of greater forces. First, the game conveys a dedication to works by human beings. Players often work hard just to produce one field goal

---

[46] Wade Boggs, *My Favorite Chicken Recipes* (Wakefield RI: Narraganset Graphics, 1984).

[47] Recently, the "Rally Monkey" practice at Anaheim Stadium revived the old rally cap ritual in new form.

attempt with some chance of success. Frequently, they run end to end in a display of exceptional effort to reach elevated achievements. On defense, teams "gut it up," producing desire from within to "out hustle" the opponent. The greats feature a strong will to win, confident in a self-generated power to determine the results of competition. Even coaches exert themselves greatly, giving emotional, intellectual, and physical effort to influence play on the court. Fans too offer fervent works of support to help produce the winning equation. Presented on courts of hardwood, commitment to strenuous actions portrays faith in acts of self-determination.

Depicting the civil doctrine of self-help, basketball players routinely lack support, leaving each individual to quite personal resources. As defenders, teammates are often too engaged in a "man to man" struggle with an opponent to aid each other. To rebound of a missed shot, they exercise a sense of self-responsibility in a "box out" effort, unable to perform the required work for other members of the team. On offense, players dribble in solitary action, left alone to succeed or fail against menacing opposition, striving to minimize moments of lost control after the release of the ball to bounce from the floor below. Periodically, teams encounter long times of inability to score, "ice cold" streaks when no help seems available to end the string of failures. Then, they appear unable to "throw the ball in the ocean," as though abandoned by invisible forces of support previously unrecognized. Coaches provide aid but are oftentimes in a position on the sidelines where they are difficult to see and hear. Help is hard to find during the intense action of a game, illustrating the devotion in civil religion of the United States to helping oneself.

Diverse features of basketball communicate the American dedication to self-help. Similar to the scarcity of aid from teammates, referees give quite limited support. They make many inaccurate calls or miss violations of rules altogether as a result of the frantic pace of activity. Consequently, players settle most injustices on the court in self-initiated acts, often unseen by the officials. Generating reliance on oneself, the tempo of play is too quick for much use of superstition, encouraging personal spontaneity rather than ritualistic acts to seek help from a higher power. Because of the time limitation, the losing team has no chance for a change of fate at some point in a contest, discouraged from hope for miraculous intervention by someone or something greater. [48] Seclusion indoors precludes aid from forces of nature to halt a pending defeat, giving full attention to influence of the individuals who play. Win or lose, the weighty importance of works by the players in a game portray strong belief in human responsibility for the outcome of history.

Though illustrative of human self-help, basketball also expresses the American faith in aid from other forces, communicating trust in the increasing support from a higher power of great good. Frequently, players exhibit an ease of accomplishment that hints of outside help, indicating gifting associated with much gracefulness. "Pure" shooters (e.g., Jamaal Wilkes, Dirk Nowitzki) flick the ball softly up and through the distant hoop in silky smooth motion, while others pass in "no look" fashion, as though aided by visionary force. Even mediocre performers become incredibly hot, able to score in an unstoppable manner like "a man possessed" by someone supernatural. The greats excel with remarkable effortlessness over hundreds of games, believed born to star in the game, somehow predetermined by something greater. Over the course of a game, prolific scoring brings about seemingly impossible comebacks by teams and encourages hope for miraculous turnabouts of fate. If losing by a small margin near the end of a contest, a team will "throw up a prayer" in petition for higher aid, and once in awhile they are answered in an unbelievable finish. Displayed on the hardwood, the ease of accomplishment and remarkable changes convey the perception in the United States of growing help from divine forces.

Often difficult to find, help is frequently available to the player in basketball, depicting the American belief in the partially realized

---

[48] This moment typically arrives later in a basketball game than in football where the more limited time and greater difficulty in scoring destroy hope much earlier.

advancement to a future of abundant support. On defense, teammates talk and switch responsibilities to aid each other, initiated by loud appeals for help. Periodically, a "beaten" defender benefits from the saving intervention by a teammate to block a shot attempt of the driving opponent. Offensively, players find deliverance from the situation of a stalled dribble through rescue efforts by another team member who arrives to pick up possession of the ball. At times, they receive easy opportunities to score, "set up" by team members in well-provided-for circumstances. A player gains much support through another's "pick" of a pesky opponent, opening personal access to the hoop. Though sometimes out of sight and sound, coaches deliver helpful guidance, especially during extended time-outs and other stoppages of play. Referees miss many infringements of rules, but they call many violations, bringing a sense of intervening justice. Consistent reception of aid in hoop action presents the civil faith in the historical movement to a time of prolific benefits from agents of divinity.

Expectation of other help echoes from many aspects of basketball. Routinely, players release the precious ball in a dribble, pass, or shot, turning some measure of control over to outside forces. Once in awhile, they receive a miraculous gift when a seemingly errant field goal attempt falls through the hoop. Game action generates hundreds of chances for redemption from failure through the opportunity to rebound or steal the ball. Referees intervene to grant free throws like instruments of divine justice, giving an uncontested shot to score. At times, they rule with special favor to a star performer in disclosure of exceptional grace available for extraordinary accomplishments.[49] Similarly, the point guard distributes the basketball for team members, indicating the influence of rewarding force. He or she offers opportunities to those who have earned supreme status and passes to "role players" in a less frequent,

---

[49] This reality sparks controversy among fans and analysts. Nevertheless, it expresses belief in the giving of other help.

yet rewarding, response to great effort. A coach gives extra minutes of playing time to individuals with exceptional work yet also bestows unmerited chances to inexperienced players in hope for future potential, showing faith in acts of graciousness. Displayed on a court of end to end action, the prolific reception of rewards and undeserved support portrays trust in increasing help from forces of divine grace. Basketball illustrates the American dedication both to strenuous efforts by human beings and the expectation of aid from someone greater, blending the self-help doctrine of football with baseball's anticipation of other help. Presenting a unified message in theology about the source of truth, the sports trinity provides for matters of cosmology and soteriology, beliefs about how to gain knowledge of truths and resolve problems.

Chapter Seven

The Ethical Dimension of Football, Baseball, and Basketball

Alongside the more abstract themes of doctrine, the sports trinity portrays ethical values of American civil religion, beliefs that define standards of conduct.[1] Football conveys moral thinking for times of crisis (e.g., war), while baseball depicts the ethical ideals of the nation, illustrating how people will live in a perfect someday. Basketball expresses the country's pragmatic reasoning about most current situations. It presents a commitment to a balance of principles, an adjustment to the realities of life and the striving for heights of moral virtue. Together, the three games represent national guidelines for ethical response to diverse situations, offering directives for the worst of circumstances, ideal conditions, and more commonplace scenarios. Beyond their presentation of the three modes for moral decision-making, football, baseball, and basketball provide guidance on the use of violence, relations of the individual with society, and use of wealth.

Moral Decision-Making

Though a strong source of democratic beliefs, the civil religion of the United States generates a dedication to strict obedience of orders

---

[1] For a description of the ethical dimension in religion, see Ninian Smart, *Worldviews: Cross-cultural Explorations of Human Beliefs* (Englewood Cliffs NJ: Prentice Hall Publishers, 2000) 104–17.

from authorities.[2] During situations of national crisis, it demands submission from each individual to directions from the appropriate authority, calling for temporary suspension of right to self-determined actions. At such times, the federal government has power to enlist citizens into the military, dictate daily work of the nation, and even control the use of privately-owned resources.[3] It possesses eminent domain over property and the public broadcasting of information.[4] In periods of national emergency, the president exercises sovereign authority to command the activities of the nation, acting as commander in chief.[5]

Football portrays the American belief in strict obedience to orders during times of crisis. Coaches dictate every play of a game under the command of the head coach, resembling federal officials who direct the nation by way of presidential power. Players strictly follow orders, scripted plays conceived of in a team's "war room" like military commands. With great self-restraint, they do a job and perform the demanded actions regardless of personal thoughts and attitudes. The prescribed act is of supreme importance, expressing trust in submission to detailed directives from the proper authorities. Displayed on a gridiron of play, obedient efforts by players convey the morality of sacrificing individual wants and goals for the national good in times of emergency.

---

[2] Undoubtedly, the deontological or obedience morality of Protestant Christianity had much influence on this aspect of the national culture. For an overview of Protestant ethics, see James Gustafson, *Catholic and Protestant Ethics* (Chicago: University of Chicago, 1978).

[3] For the Constitutional power of federal institutions, see Nancie G. Mazulla, *Property Rights: Understanding Government Takings and Environmental Regulation* (Rockville MD: Government Institutes, 1997); David A. Schultz, *Property, Power, and American Democracy* (New Brunswick NJ: Transaction Publishers, 1992).

[4] Bruce Ackerman, *Private Property and the Constitution* (New Haven: Yale University Press, 1977).

[5] See Geoffrey Perret, *Lincoln's War: The Untold Story of America's Greatest President as Commander in Chief* (New York: Random House, 2004); Joan Biskupic, *The Supreme Court and the Powers of the American Government* (Washington DC: Congressional Quarterly, 1997).

The obedience ethic of football illustrates devotion in the United States to a command approach for wartime. Coaches scream clear-cut directions, expecting absolute conformity. They order players to "get over here now," "move left," "explode into the hole," and a litany of other direct demands. The head coach will abruptly yank players out of game action like the dictatorial removal of officers by a general or the president. At times, he grabs a player by the face mask to command attention of the disobedient individual in chastisement to fall in line.[6] Among players, the quarterback barks out directives to start each play, acting as a field general similar to commanders on the battlefield. Frequently, teammates shout at each other in demanding statements to produce better performance.[7] On defense, the signal caller (e.g., the middle linebacker) points and commands others into position, sometimes pushing the player to a spot without verbal request. The commanding character of the game generates prolific cursing by players in direct condemnation of others, harsh words with directions that would send the opponent to grave states of degradation if taken literally. Fans too take on the crude mode of interaction, making the attendance of a game not a family atmosphere. Football expresses national dedication to the use of commands, detailed and direct orders of prescribed actions, believed necessary to meet the demands of crisis situations.

In complement to situational belief in obeying commands, American civil religion upholds a commitment to the ideal of self-determined action. National stories exalt voluntary efforts, acts inspired by motives and convictions within the individual. According to the mythology, founding fathers led in creation of the new nation as a result of personal commitments to ideals of freedom and democracy. Decades later, legendary pioneers pursued a strong inner

---

[6] Former coach of Notre Dame and South Carolina, Lou Holtz frequently exercised such commanding authority.

[7] Recent events showed Terrel Owens try to motivate fellow star Donovan McNabb with repetitious commands to "relax" while Ray Lewis demands excellence from teammates on the Baltimore's Ravens.

hope to create a better life and transformed the frontier, while reformers followed privately held values to fight the liquor and slave trades.[8] In the early twentieth century, women organized through self-generated efforts to enact suffrage for nearly half of the adult population.[9] More recently, civil rights activists inspired millions to rededicate themselves to the ideals of freedom and equality, widespread voluntary decisions that dramatically changed the United States.[10]

Baseball illustrates the American devotion to the ideal of self-motivated action. Routinely, the manager of a team sits passively in the dugout, giving players on the field the power to make most decisions. A manager dictates few plays, only rarely commanding a player to "sacrifice" in a bunt or "hit and run." He creates a "game-plan," but in general he gives guidelines rather than clear-cut directives. The vast majority of the time, players choose how to execute the envisioned plan in self-determination of how to hit, run, field, and pitch. Expressing the voluntary character of the game, coaches encourage team members to develop a mindset rather than prescribe actions. They advise hitters to be prepared and focused for the next pitch, and then they counsel pitchers to relax and concentrate on the catcher's glove. Fielders remain mindful of potential situations to exercise good choices about how to handle the ball, benefiting from practice of every possible circumstance in a game to develop the ability to make autonomous decisions. Presented on a diamond of play, the decision-making by each player depicts the civil aspiration for a coming time when every person will self-determine activities.

---

[8] See Timothy L. Smith, *Revivalism and Social Reform: American Protestantism on the Eve of the Civil War* (Gloucester MA: Peter Smith, 1976).

[9] This reform was not relevant to the majority of African-American women who lived in the South and who were disenfranchised by Jim Crow laws.

[10] For the persuasive and voluntary element of the movement, see Martin Luther King, Jr. *The Speeches of Martin Luther King*, video (MPI Video, 1990); Donald H. Smith, *Martin Luther King, Jr.: Rhetorician of Revolt* (University of Wisconsin, 1964).

The self-determination of baseball generates abundant discussion during a game in an effort to facilitate good decisions by each member of the team. Oftentimes, a manager visits the pitcher to offer suggestions in a conversation rather than lecture on what to do. Similarly, catchers suggest possible pitches, but pitchers frequently veto or "shake off" the idea in exercise of personal will. Periodically, fielders gather for the friendly sharing of strategy, typically without pointing and yelling directions at each other. As hitters, players share information about the opposing pitcher, offering knowledge to inform the self-directed swings by each individual at the plate. Fans and teammates root for others in support of independent thinking by the player at the center of action, especially the hitter in the batter's box or the pitcher on the mound. They "talk it up" to build personal confidence in team members for the making of good decisions, promoting command of the ball in controlled throws and hard hits, not the commanding of human beings. Baseball inspires prolific encouragement of independent choices by others. It illustrates the expectation in the United States for an ideal life where individuals will receive abundant guidance and support to inform highly voluntary decisions.

Like football, the game of basketball expresses the American belief in obedience to commands for response to adversity. The head coach dictates set plays and defenses for a team, depicting the national faith in following the orders of appropriate authorities. Players put aside personal feelings and thoughts in acts of conformity to the prescribed actions. Exaltation of the obedience ethic in a game generates the commanding of others. Frequently, coaches yell and gesture orders, sometimes calling time-out to castigate teams for lack of compliance. "The General," Bobby Knight moves within an inch of a disobedient player in a red-faced demand of more submission. Similarly, teammates "get in the face" of each other to deliver direct demands for better play. Routinely, the point guard shouts detailed directions to initiate the next play, often pointing players into position. The great ones like Magic Johnson or Steve Nash possess the masterful ability to direct an offense in a demanding fashion. Displayed on courts of hardwood, the dedication to commands portrays the national faith in obedience to orders in restraint of self-determination, believed necessary to meet the difficult conditions of life.

Though generating an obedience ethic, basketball also communicates the devotion in the United States to historical progress toward more self-determined decisions. Initially, players follow prescribed orders from the coach but inevitably move to improvisation, disclosing the limited and soon-to-be-outdated value of commands.[11] Only able to dictate the start to plays, the head coach offers encouragement to develop the right mindset in a player to make good choices when clear-cut directions no longer apply. Coaches admonish players to "use your head," "think clearly," and "play smart" in stress on personal decisions. Inevitably, the set play "breaks down," causing the need for a self-determined pass, cut to the basket, or "creation of a shot" by players. Fast breaks bring decision-making by the individuals on the court in a burst of energy and choices for a quick score, while defenders make equally fast and individual determination to contest the offensive push. Resulting from the fast-paced action, the self-initiated acts of basketball express the American recognition of the decided limits to the value of obeying commands, conveying the belief in the swift advancement of history to more voluntary actions by each individual.

Use of Violence

Beyond the portrayal of ethical decision-making, the sports trinity depicts convictions about the use of violence. National stories exalt warrior figures who symbolize disciplined aggression to protect life, upholding the justice of violent acts for welfare of the country. The founding fathers led the nation in an original "just war" against

---

[11] For improvisation in basketball, see John E. Wideman, *Hoop Roots* (Boston: Houghton Mufflin, 2001); Dan Palladino, "The Basketball/Jazz Connection," Riddleworks, http://www.riddleworks.com/.

English tyranny.[12] Four score and seven years later, Abraham Lincoln commanded aggressive military ventures in the Civil War, dedicated to higher purpose of "unity with liberty" across the states.[13] Throughout the twentieth century, the United States engaged violent opponents, exhibiting devotion to employment of overwhelming force in two world wars, the Cold War, and today's War on Terror. Representatives of a civil commitment to just warfare, great leaders of fighting forces often become icons of public veneration, especially Generals Grant, McArthur, Eisenhower, and Powell.[14] Fictional characters of popular culture like Superman, Batman, or those played by John Wayne and Arnold Schwarzenegger present warriors that utilize violence to oppose evil enemies of "peace, justice, and the American way."[15] Football expresses the just war ethic of the United States. Games are battles and wars against an opponent dedicated to violent attack. Similar to heroes of national mythology, players represent warriors who act with physical aggression for greater good of the group. Running backs "fight for every inch of territory" to advance the team, leading a "pounding" of the opposition by way of "smash mouth action." To supplement this "ground attack," the quarterback conducts an "air assault" with throws of the football, launching "bombs" through the sky, much like the Air Force of the nation that leads in strikes to pacify a belligerent enemy. Good quarterbacks resemble gunslingers who shoot down threatening opponents with propelled objects like heroic sheriffs of the old West. They lead a "march down the field" in offensive use of force to

---

[12] The United States Continental Congress, "The Just War into Which the United States has been Forced" (repr., Hartford: Eben, Watson, 1776); Colony of Massachusetts Bay, "The War, Resistance, and Opposition" (Watertown MA: Benjamin Edes, 1776).

[13] Philip B. Kundardt, *Lincoln: The Pivotal Year*, video, dir. Peter W. Kunhardt (PBS Video, 1992).

[14] See Edward T. Linenthal, *Changing Images of the War Hero in America: A History of Popular Symbolism* (New York: E. Mellen Press, 1982).

[15] John K. Muir, *The Encyclopedia of Superheroes* (Jefferson NC: McFarland and Company, 2004).

weaken a menacing foe, disclosing a belief in a periodic need to invade enemies. Defensive units "blitz" and "attack the quarterback" to counter offensives by the opposition. They "storm" the ball carrier in a "jail break" of overwhelming force to "blow up a play." Displayed in action on the gridiron, "bone-jarring" violence depicts national dedication to violent action when faced with a hostile enemy and in service of the common good.

Football portrays the American commitment to the disciplined use of violence, conveying the morality of selective aggression. Players act with violent force, but they are restricted by many rules, representative of faith in ethical limits to aggressions even if employed for moral ends. Helmet-to-helmet collisions, "spearing" the opponent with the helmet, tripping or kicking with the feet, blows to the head, and the "horse collar tackle" are taboo, expressing a sense of fairness for the most bitter of wars.[16] Regulation of "unsportsman-like" behavior communicates the national belief in the unethical character of unrestrained and absolute violence. Football presents dedication to ethical guidelines for acts of violence, standards believed necessary to maintain the morality of the fighting.

Though supportive of war for "just" causes, American civil religion upholds great expectations for nonviolence and peacemaking. After combat against native tribes to expand the country westward in the nineteenth century, the federal government promoted the assimilation of conquered peoples, fostering a vision for peaceful coexistence.[17] After the fierce fighting of the Civil War, the belief system of the nation generated hope for peace, bringing cooperative relations between North and South.[18] Following World

---

[16] The rules represent laws for military behavior.

[17] Then, the goal was not equality or self-determination for Native Americans but nevertheless represented a sense of peaceful inclusion. For the inequities in the government's policy, see Vine Deloria, *God Is Red: A Native View of Religion* (Golden CO: Fulcrum Publishers, 2003).

[18] This was a peace, however, that overturned gains made by African-Americans during Reconstruction, setting the stage for civil rights movement of the mid-

War I, President Woodrow Wilson cultivated the national aspiration for the nonviolent resolution of international conflicts to establish the League of Nations.[19] Reoccurrence of violence during World War II produced an increased devotion to peacemaking actions worldwide, prompting support for the newly formed United Nations.[20] Through courageous leadership in the nonviolent movement for civil rights, Martin Luther King, Jr. inspired a stronger faith nationwide in the supreme importance of efforts for peace.[21] Subsequently, a "peace movement" emerged in protest against the Vietnam War, establishing an ongoing concern for peaceful interactions. Today this concern is focused on the war in Iraq.[22]

Baseball expresses the American aspiration for peace in relations between human beings. It is a nonviolent competition, portraying a vision for an ideal life of competitiveness without physical aggression. The use of bodily force represents illegal interference, while the game generates the peaceful acceptance of the opposition's passage through a team's defended territory. Occasionally, pitchers hit a batter intentionally with a "purpose pitch" and fights or "brawls" erupt, but these rare moments normally end without any physical contact. Almost all the time, opponents interact in nonviolent and even in ways helpful to the rival. On each play of a game, the pitcher

---

twentieth century. See C. Vann Woodward, *The Strange Career of Jim Crow* (New York: Oxford University Press, 1958).

[19] Thomas J. Knock, *To End All Wars: Woodrow Wilson and the Quest for a New World Order* (New York: Oxford University Press, 1992); Nordholdt J. W. Schulte, *Woodrow Wilson: A Life for World Peace* (Berkeley CA: University of California Press, 1991).

[20] Patrick J. Hearden, *Architects of Globalism: Building a New World Order during World War II* (Fayetteville: University of Arkansas Press, 2002).

[21] Della Rowland, *Martin Luther King, Jr.: The Dream of Peaceful Revolution* (Englewood Cliffs NJ: Silver Burdett Press, 1990); Ed Clayton, *Martin Luther King, Jr.: The Peaceful Warrior* (Englewood Cliffs NJ: Prentice-Hall, 1964).

[22] Charles F. Howlett, *The American Peace Movement* (Boston MA: G. K. Hall, 1991); John Lofland, *Polite Protesters: The American Peace Movement of the 1980's* (Syracuse NY: Syracuse University Press, 1993).

pitches an "offering" of fair opportunity to the opposition by throwing the ball within the strike zone, which makes the ball quite available to the opposing batter. Fielders record outs free of physical contact with nearby base runners from the other team. Hitters forcefully hit the ball, not the opponents, putting the ball "in play" for use by the opposition. The nonviolence of game action illustrates the anticipation in the United States for perfect situation with competition of skill rather than of brute force.

In portrayal of a harmonious future, baseball presents the American expectation for abundant peacemaking in human relations. To begin a contest, the managers of competing teams conduct warm exchange of information at home plate to set a friendly tone. During play, they courteously notify each other of changes in personnel, conveying an aspiration for a coming time when knowledge will be freely shared. Players practice "courtesies" to establish good will with opponents. They pick up the dropped mask of an opposing catcher, return a flung bat to the rival hitter, and sometimes even helpfully flip an uncaught pitch to the opponent behind the plate. Frequently, the catcher greets the hitter from the other team upon arrival in the batter's box, while base runners engage in friendly conversation with the opposition on the journey around the bases, exemplifying the hope for a friendliness to come that will transcend the present standards of tolerance for others.[23] Baseball portrays national ideals of peacemaking and friendship, even with the most intense of rivals, depicting the imagination of a nonviolent and even welcoming society someday.

Ever the complement to baseball and football, basketball expresses the American commitment to the use of highly restrained force in most current situations, aggressive actions that stop short of violence. Forceful physical contact is a "foul" with penalty of "free throws" for the victim and the reestablishment of expectation for

---

[23] For the limitations of modern tolerance, see Herbert Marcuse, *A Critique of Pure Tolerance* (Boston: Beacon Press, 1969).

nonviolent interactions with opponents. The frequent use of excessive force brings disqualification from a contest. Direct acts of violence draw the charge of "flagrant fouls," possible ejection from the game, and a fine or suspension from future participation.[24] The aspiration for nonviolence on the court communicates the national faith in advancement beyond the more violent relations of past societies. Alongside the ideal of nonviolence, game action portrays the dedication to engage in the contentious competition of daily life, producing assertive actions in pursuit of personal and team goals. Players "fight" for the ball and to achieve position on the floor. They "pound the boards" in shows of great force, while using "aggression" to drive toward the hoop. The intense competitiveness of a game resembles the nonviolent tensions that drive pivotal institutions of the country. Opposing lawyers wage a forceful struggle of words and ideas to produce legal decisions, while the federal government has three competing branches for a balance of power, often involved in sharp conflict.[25] Fierce competition on courts of hardwood illustrates the national faith in the capacity to compete at present and not to resort to violence yet without achievement of the more peaceful life to come.

Though revealing that the present is far from friendly, basketball portrays the American belief in historical progress to a time of peace-making between human beings. Opposing teams greet each other at the opening moment of a game to set a cordial tone for the competition to come. Routinely, players conduct respectful and even intimate talks with the referees, expressing hope for less adversarial disagreements, even when decisions have negative consequences. During timeless moments of free throws, opponents converse in a relaxed and often warm manner, representative of expectation for

---

[24] The National Basketball Association, "Official Rules of the National Basketball Association," http://www.nba.com/analysis/rules_index.html.

[25] Philip B. Kunhardt, dir., *The American President*, video (PBS Video, 2000); James A. Thurber, ed., *Rivals for Power: Presidential-Congressional Relations* (Washington DC: CQ Press, 1996).

friendlier exchanges between rivals at the end to timed conditions of history. Nonviolent and cordial interactions of basketball express anticipation in the United States for more peaceful human relations, disclosing faith that the present ethic of tolerance will someday give way to more ideal friendship.

The Individual and Society

Presenting the ethical beliefs of American civil religion, the sports trinity communicates convictions about the relationship of the individual to the nation. Symbolic of national values, it upholds freedom for the individual but with the limitation of dedication to the national welfare and the rights of others.[26] In times of crisis, the belief system of the nation demands temporary suspension of devotion to individual freedom for collective action as a nation. [27] During the Civil War, the Union and Confederacy expected rejection of personal pursuits—over half a million in the ultimate sacrifice of death—to act as a powerful unit for the greater good.[28] President Lincoln enacted the draft and censured the press to wage a unified fight against disloyalty to the country. In the twentieth century, two world wars and the Cold War produced situations for restraint of individuality in mass action against totalitarian forces. Recently, George W. Bush led the institution of the Patriot Act to scale back freedoms of the individual to conduct the War on Terror.[29]

Football expresses the American dedication to sacrifice of individual freedom for collective effort during periods of crisis. It

---

[26] "Welfare" of the nation provided motivation for both sides.

[27] The pledge of allegiance to the flag is the most direct expression of this civil devotion.

[28] See Ellis Katz and G. Alan Tarr, eds., *Federalism and Rights* (Lanham MD: Rowman and Littlefield, 1996); Robert A. Goodwin and William A. Schambra, eds., *How Does the Constitution Secure Rights?* (Washington DC: American Enterprise Institute for Public Policy Research, 1985).

[29] Stuart A. Baker, ed., *Patriot Debates* (Chicago IL: American Bar Association, 2005); Jennifer Van Bergen, *The Twilight of Democracy: The Bush Plan for America* (Monroe ME: Common Courage Press, 2005).

generates cooperative actions in denial of individuality, "the ultimate team sport" in the United States.[30] The running back follows collective blocking by teammates, while offensive linemen work together to also protect a quarterback, allowing other members of the team to throw or catch the ball for the group benefit. Defenders cooperate to "team tackle" the ball carrier and to tip a threatening pass for someone else to intercept. On special teams, players almost link arms in creation of a human wall to keep opponents away from the kicker or kick returner who carries the ball for good of the team. The individual player "sacrifices his body" by way of blocks or through stopping the charge of opposing linemen to free up a teammate to "make a play." Displayed on a gridiron of play, cooperative and self-sacrificial actions portray devotion to the restraint of individual freedom for collective effort as a nation.

The collectivist ethic of football pervades every corner of the game. Players are members of a mass group numbered one to ninety-nine. Helmeted faces and heavily padded bodies further the mostly selfless identity. Many teams prohibit personal names on the uniforms with the number of a player as the only distinctive feature.[31] Defensive and offensive units of a team run onto or off the field as a group unannounced and without distinction of the individual for the audience. After each play, teammates huddle together in expression of great uniformity. Even fans exhibit the collectivism of the sport, frequently screaming in unison to create a deafening roar. Cooperative efforts of a fan start with the sharing of food, drink, and conversation in "tailgating" long before game time. With the ball in play, actions en mass by spectators intensify with chants and gestures

---

[30] For one among many commentators on this theme, see Mike Golich, ESPN Radio broadcast, 29 May 2005.

[31] Teams vary on the printing of names and other forms of individual recognition. NFL teams often present individual names on uniforms, illustrating the greater fame of individuals in the NFL than college. Nevertheless, even the more recognized players of professional football play in relative selflessness due to the collectivist nature of the game.

of group devotion. Devotees of the Pittsburgh Steelers wave "terrible towels" in a unified show of force, while members of "Eagle's Nation" join together for an earth-shaking mantra of "let's go Eagles" or some derision of the opponent. The players, coaches, and fans of football express the American faith in special times of self-sacrifice for collective action, disclosing prescribed morality for national emergencies.

Though demanding the denial of individual freedom in unusual circumstances, civil religion in the United States upholds the ideal of individuality, an aspiration for individual freedom with the limitation of respect for the freedoms of others.[32] Dedication to individuality originated with constitutional documents, early established in sacred print to inspire many reforms of the nation to come. During the nineteenth century, a renewed commitment to the freedom of the individual brought the expansion of voting rights to every "white man," ending privilege for property owners.[33] Decades later, the rededication of the country to individual rights produced the emancipation of slaves, while a similar rediscovery of individuality led to women's suffrage in the early twentieth century.[34] More recently, the civil rights movement inspired fresh devotion to freedom for every individual, producing federal enforcement of constitutional rights for African Americans.[35] Today, national faith in individual liberty has many expressions, the basis for advocacy of gay and

---

[32] The ethic of individuality is distinct from individualism, which gives absolute power to the individual.

[33] Gyndon G. Van Deusen, *The Rise and Decline of Jacksonian Democracy* (Huntington NY: R. E. Krieger Publishing Company, 1979); Faye Rattner, *Reform in America: Jacksonian Democracy, Progressivism, and the New Deal* (Chicago: Scott, Foresman, 1964).

[34] Ann Bausum, *With Courage and Cloth: Winning the Fight for the Women's Right to Vote* (Washington DC: National Geographic, 2004); Jill Liddington, *One Hand Tied behind Us: The Rise of the Women's Suffrage Movement* (London: Rivers Oram Press, 2000).

[35] King, *The Speeches of Martin Luther King, Jr.*

lesbian causes at one end of the spectrum and for the "right to life" coalition in support of an unborn fetus on the other.

Baseball illustrates the American devotion to the ideal of individuality, individual freedom with responsibility for the freedoms of others. Occasionally, a manager compels players to sacrifice for the good of the team, just as the constitution demands allegiance to the nation in restriction of individual rights. Primarily, however, game action generates independent efforts by an individual to represent the team, not the uniform actions of a mass group or collective. The hitter walks to home plate alone, very much in an individualistic effort with the personal introduction of names and the playing of favorite music, while the scoreboard adds many other details about a player's hometown and hobbies. One batter at a time faces one person on top of the mound. Through offensive and defensive performances, players produce a unique set of statistics, a long list of distinctive numbers that highlight the individuality of each team member.[36] Because of the highly personalized accomplishments, the game features enduring stars, great individuals like Ruth, Aaron, and Mays who never seem to lose personal presence. Individualistic actions on a diamond of play express the national belief in the supreme good of individuality, portraying aspiration for much liberty to come.

The individuality of baseball extends into every element of the game. Teams wear uniforms of group identity, but each player exhibits a distinctive way to shape the cap and wear prominent game socks in self-expression.[37] Individual faces of players are at center of attention, the focus for zoom-in cameras of television coverage, while substitution of one player for another brings announcement over the public address system. Game action stops to allow an individual

---

[36] The collectivist ethic of football limits statistical documentation only for "skill players," leaving out masses of offensive linemen.

[37] Belief in the American ethic of individuality causes problems for players in Japan where traditional morality prescribes strict uniformity. See Whiting, *You Gotta Have Wa*.

player, coach, or manager to express personal opinions about the ruling of an umpire.[38] The authority figures on the field, umpires give the opportunity for discussion and argument about their decisions, portraying national devotion to the right of every individual to free speech. Fans declare thoughts and feelings with individual voices that are remarkably audible during a game, recognizable in radio or television broadcasts and even from a crowd of many thousands. Especially devout spectators keep score in a deeply personal study of the performance by individual players in a contest. Furthering the individuality of the game, well-known personalities announce games, presenting the action with the unmistakable voice of a special person. Highly individualized sounds of Vin Scully, Jon Miller, Curt Gowdy, and Ernie Harwell bring immediate association with other individuals who play with a bat and ball. Baseball illustrates the American ideal of individuality, generating the expectation of a future when unprecedented freedom for the individual will motivate ever greater accomplishments.

The third part to the moral equation, basketball expresses the dedication in the United States to a balance of principles in most current situations, combining commitment to collective efforts with aspiration for future independence of individuals. On the one hand, it gives significance to self-sacrifice for cooperation with others. Game action encourages almost constant interaction with teammates, especially by way of passing in collective effort, illustrating a belief in the unified actions of service to the nation. Great teams keep the ball moving in a show of exceptional togetherness, and then they play "team defense" to extend the group effort. Back on offense, players "dish the ball off" and "feed" teammates in unselfish manner or give up the effort to score to "pick" for someone else to shoot. As defenders, they take responsibility for struggling members of the team, stepping out to impede the charge of a threatening opponent.

---

[38] Baseball upholds a rich heritage of individual freedom to argue with the authority figures: umpires. As a Baltimore Orioles fan, I grew up watching a legendary exemplar of this tradition: Earl Weaver.

In "loose ball" situations, a player will dive on the floor in sacrifice of personal comfort to secure the basketball for the team to advance up court. Displayed on courts of hardwood, acts of self-sacrifice and cooperation communicate devotion to the collective action for the national good.

On the other hand, basketball portrays the American pursuit of individuality, representing faith in the historical push for ever greater importance to the individual. Individuals can dominate a game well beyond what is possible in football or baseball.[39] Greats like Michael Jordan or Shaquille O'Neal dramatically influence the success of a team like great individuals that highlight American mythology (e.g., Abraham Lincoln, Martin Luther King, Jr.), showing the great power of efforts by an individual. Game action generates one-on-one activity, engaging players in a personal struggle with an opponent. Long lists of statistics underscore individual accomplishments by each team member, while the slight uniforms reveal much self-expression by way of prolific tattoos, piercings, and hairstyles. Fans recognize individuals like Allen Iverson or Ben Wallace from distant locations as a result of their distinctive appearances. Television coverage broadcasts the unique faces of individual players, particularly during close-up moments of "free throws." Strong focus on individuals in basketball conveys a belief in the fast-paced movements of history toward unprecedented value for the individual in future societies.

Use of Wealth

Addressing the ethical issues foundational to the American way of life, the sports trinity presents beliefs about the use of wealth. National stories depict the virtue of early settlers who took possession of land and resources in the New World, seeking to produce prosperity. According to the mythology, prospectors of the

---

[39] This is largely the result of limitation to five participants in a game, making possible a greater level of influence by an individual compared to football or baseball.

nineteenth century pursued the moral goal of acquiring abundant wealth in "rushes" to find gold.[40] Decades later, legendary industrialists amassed huge fortunes to finance the remarkable economic expansion of the country, while immigrants arrived in pursuit of a mythic pot of gold. The Great Depression and costly world wars of the twentieth century made financial security even more pivotal to the nation's belief system. Martin Luther King, Jr. inspired faith in a national "ocean of prosperity," trust in the country's ability to generate almost unlimited resources of potential for African Americans and other minorities.[41] Today, the promise of the stock market and other get-rich ventures like gambling disclose a passionate devotion to acquisition of wealth, maintaining an expectation in the United States for the quick amassing of prosperity.[42]

Football expresses the American ethic of acquisitiveness, a dedication to the accumulation of great wealth. Players aspire to "possess" the ball, the prized item of the game that provides the ability to produce points. Sharing the football with the other team or even with "unskilled" teammates is taboo like the shared property ideologies of communism and socialism, upholding national faith in private ownership of resources.[43] An individual player takes control of the ball for benefit of the team, a portrayal of the civil commitment to personal acquisition of property as the means to best serve the national good. Illustrated on a gridiron, heightened concern for possession of the ball presents the nation's trust in the accumulation of economic power by individuals, even if by a select few.

---

[40] See Fred Rosen, *Gold!: The Story of the 1848 Gold Rush and How It shaped the Nation* (New York: Thunder's Mouth, 2005); Kenneth N. Ownes, ed., *Riches for All: The California Gold Rush and the World* (Lincoln: University of Nebraska Press, 2002).

[41] King, *Speeches of Martin Luther King, Jr.*

[42] Based on this aspiration for personal turn of financial fate, the city of Las Vegas holds tremendous appeal for individuals across the nation.

[43] On Anti-Communism in the United States, see John E. Haynes, *Communism and Anti-Communism in the United States* (New York: Garland Publishing, 1987).

Beyond control of the pigskin, the acquisitiveness of football promotes devotion to the possession of land and time. Teams strive to "possess territory," expressing the dedication to gain as much land as possible. They move end to end in effort to "dominate" every yard of space, like the country's historical push for ownership of the continent and beyond. Players work to "take control" over a particular area of responsibility on the field similar to the laboring of citizens to earn title for a piece of real estate. Ball carriers "eat up territory," while quarterbacks "use the whole field" similar to wealthy individuals who acquire vast amounts of property. In pursuit of ever more territory, a team seeks possession of time, conveying the national commitment to acquire of power over the time in a day, year, and lifetime. Control over territory and the prized ball brings the capability to determine the use of remaining game time, just as the nation pursues wealth for power over time remaining in a person's life. Offensive units act promptly in highly planned efforts to maximize the benefit of ticks of the clock, resembling busy members of the country who divide up each day into strictly scheduled moments for heightened efficiency. Football illustrates the American belief in the morality of acquiring ownership of more land and time.

Alongside the commitment to accumulation of property, civil religion of the United States generates aspiration for generosity, especially in an ideal future of sharing from great prosperity. Soon after the Revolution, the nation embraced a vision to become a society of generous givers, initiating an era of voluntary effort to help the poor, uneducated, and abused.[44] Decades later, emancipation brought anticipation of giving to the freedmen, as the country considered the possibility of granting "forty acres and a mule" to supplement federal aid for education and enforcement of civil

---

[44] Timothy L. Smith, *Revivalism and Social Reform: On the Eve of the Civil War* (New York: Harper and Row, 1965).

rights.[45] As a result of industrialization, increased prosperity produced enhanced imagination for more charitable distribution of wealth during the late nineteenth century, motivating financial gifts to fund social service organizations like the Hull Settlement House.[46] In the twentieth century, Franklin Roosevelt's "New Deal" and the popularity of figures such as Huey Long and Charles Coughlin expressed growing "share the wealth" expectations.[47] Not long ago, Martin Luther King, Jr. sparked national hope for a more generous society to end poverty, public anticipation still evident in the concern for social welfare programs and prolific forms of charitable giving.

Baseball portrays the American hope for generosity, particularly in a future of unprecedented prosperity. Each player roams large areas of territory without interference from anyone else, illustrating the national vision for abundant land ownership by every individual someday. Teams wear fancy-looking uniforms with hats and decorated socks, like the dressy clothing of wealthy individuals to come. Players display many possessions, depicting trust in the permanence of private property and the coming prosperity for every individual. Frequently, they wear jewelry, gold chains, and benefit from abundant items like fine leather gloves, sunglasses, rosin bags, pine tar rags, jackets, and metal files. Even umpires use many prized items. Beyond the protective equipment, they possess a brush to clean the plate, a counter for tracking game situations, and a pen with paper to monitor the lineups of teams. The field features prolific signs of affluence, traditionally full of commercial advertisements, expressing the hope for ever more prosperous living. Ball parks provide picnic areas, food courts, playgrounds for children, and even

---

[45] The country did not enact "forty acres and a mule," but the policy received much consideration. See Claude F. Oubre, *Forty Acres and a Mule: The Freedmen's Bureau and Black Land Ownership* (Baton Rouge: Louisiana State University, 1978).

[46] Deborah Kent, *Jane Addams and Hull House* (Chicago; Children's Press, 1992).

[47] See Alan Brinkely, *Voices of Protest: Huey Hate Radio Long, Father Coughlin, and the Great Depression* (New York: Vintage Books, 1983); Donald Warren, *The Radio Priest: Father of Hate Radio* (New York: Free Press, 1996).

swimming pools, amenities associated with pursuit of luxury. Expectancy of great wealth radiates from the nearly endless supply of baseballs for a game of Major League Baseball, expressing a vision of the nation for unlimited reservoir to come for the most precious resources.

In portrayal of a much more prosperous time to come, baseball illustrates the American aspiration for the remarkably generous use of possessions. It generates charitable sharing of the ball with the opposition on each play of a game, conveying a futuristic expectation for shared use of the most valuable things. The pitcher "releases" possession of the ball in a pitch to the opponent, sometimes "serving up fat pitches" of extreme generosity. Hitters also send the ball away through contact with the bat, turning access over to the other team, sometimes in a gift-wrapped and easy-to-field "can of corn." Fielders employ a rapid throwing action and move the ball rapidly out of personal possession to record an out or stop the advancement of opponents on the bases, quickly leading to the next pitch and chance for the opposition to make contact with the baseball. Similarly, game action produces generous distribution of many balls to the fans, providing dozens of "souvenirs" each game. The prolific sharing of the ball presents the national vision for a future of incredible giving.

Along with the ball, land is the focus of much sharing in baseball, depicting the anticipation in the United States for overflowing charity in future use of territory. On defense, players possess a special relationship to a particular territory, yet their coverage areas overlap, illustrative of the shared benefit from real estate to come. Fielders back up each other, communicating the imagination for a coming time when society will be ready to offer generous support to individuals in caring for property. The pitcher and opposing batter "share the plate" and the use of the pivotal strike zone. They have equal access to the same prime space for the production of success. Perhaps most dramatic, the game gives opportunity for "safe" movement through an opponent's territory by way of route around the bases. Displayed on a diamond of play, shared access to key places portrays the American hope for the mutual benefit from the land even between rivals in an ideal life of the future.

The generosity ethic of baseball extends into use of time. The pitcher allows fielders many moments to prepare for the next pitch. He offers more generous opportunity for the opponent to settle into the batter's box before delivery of the ball, while the batter reciprocates by granting much time to the pitcher in making the next offering. Hitters will "take a pitch" or two in giving a period of benefit to teammates for the purpose of stealing a base or studying an opposing pitcher. Sometimes, they walk slowly to the plate or back to the dugout in generosity to a teammate who needs some rest before taking the mound to pitch. Managers frequently call a time-out to stroll leisurely onto the field and offer extended time for a struggling pitcher to regain composure. Umpires generously grant stoppages of action to players who feel hurried by the opponent. Fans and coaches give a player many days and even weeks to overcome a slump in performance. They allow young prospects periods of five years or more to develop before expecting a major league level of play. Baseball expresses the aspiration in the United States for abundant generosity with time, illustrating the expectation of a future era when charitable giving of opportunity to others will supersede the importance of pre-established schedules.

A complement to American ethic for emergencies and an ideal future, basketball portrays the dedication to a combination of acquisitiveness and generosity in most situations. First, it upholds the national devotion to acquisition of many possessions, though the slight clothing and poverty of personal equipment discloses a sense that present conditions remain distant to coming affluence. Game action generates the pursuit of possession over the ball, territory on the court, and time. Players possess the basketball to score and avoid "turnovers" in the giving up of points to the other team. They control the ball for power to succeed in the game through scoring, while defenders work to "swipe" or "steal" possession of the ball. When two opposing players share a hold on the basketball, referees stop play and restart with a "jump ball" to determine personal power over the ball, showing the national commitment to the individual rather than shared ownership of property.

Beyond the use of the ball, basketball players take control of strategic areas on the court like powerful individuals who own vital places within the country. The greats "own" space "in the paint" near the hoop similar to highly influential people who dominate pivotal locations on Wall Street and in Washington DC. Ownership of key areas on the floor and of the ball produces an anticipated ability to dictate the use of time in a game. Then, teams can employ a deliberate pace of play to make the clock work in their favor. Otherwise, a team acts in a crisp and quick fashion to gain maximum benefit from the time remaining, conveying a concern for heightened efficiency to meet timed restrictions. Presented on a court of hardwood, the frenzied pursuit of possessions discloses the civil devotion to the accumulation of prime spaces, items, and time, the ownership of abundant property to best advance personal and societal conditions.

In balance to its ethic of acquisitiveness, basketball portrays the American commitment to generosity, upholding the belief in historical progress to a time for the sharing of resources. As ball handlers, players repeatedly "release" possession of the ball in a dribble that offers the opposition opportunity to "steal." Frequently, they give up ball control in a shot for the opponent to rebound or in passes to teammates. The sharing includes space on the floor, illustrating the aspiration someday to achieve the charitable use of real estate. On offense, a player will use a personal location to set a "pick" in generous provision of more open spaces for a teammate to utilize. On defense, he or she gives help to a team member by moving in front of a driving opponent in shared responsibility for prime spots on the court. The use of physical force to move someone from an established place is taboo, representing the civil dedication to the equal right of every individual to land ownership. Commitment to sharing extends into the use of time. Oftentimes, teams allow the opponent many ticks of the clock to bring the ball up the court before applying pressure as defenders. On offense, they routinely give the opposing unit time to settle into formation. Coaches call many time-outs to give players extended moments for reestablishment of proper perspective. The sharing of the ball, space on the court, and time in basketball reveals the expectation in the United States for growing generosity, at present practiced in limited fashion as a result of the need to acquire possessions, someday to be perfected in an ideal life to come.

Chapter Eight

Social Tenets of the Sports Trinity

Multidimensional in significance, football, baseball, and basketball portray the dedication in the United States to certain social arrangements, addressing relations with people both outside and inside the nation. Football expresses devotion to strict separation from outsiders and a hierarchy of authority in domestic affairs, prescribed modes of interaction for times of national crisis. Baseball illustrates futuristic ideals of integration with other nations and equality between individuals inside the nation. Basketball presents the commitment of the country to a balance of convictions about societal exchanges in most situations. It depicts a belief in the periodic need for distance from foreigners and a commitment to a domestic hierarchy, while pursuing long-term goals of integration with outsiders and equity within the nation. Together, the sports trinity provides an illustration of American beliefs for relationships with outsiders and insiders, giving directives for times of emergency, ideal conditions, and commonplace circumstances.

Relations with Outsiders

American civil religion upholds a belief in the situational demand for actions of separation from other countries. The founding fathers inspired devotion to the early independence of effort, especially from "parent" England in events surrounding the Revolution.[1] Over eighty

---

[1] For example, Daniel Webster admonished the nation to stop acting like children and become independent beings, a "new Adam" of humanity. See Daniel

years later, the Civil War revealed an intense focus on domestic life and a lack of concern with affairs outside the country, disclosing an isolationism most evident in widespread prejudice against the Roman Catholic Church.[2] World War I revitalized the isolationist tendencies of the nation and the desire to remain separate from troubling events in Europe.[3] Eventually, World War II brought a more active form of national separatism as the country "closed ranks" to fight threatening outsiders abroad and to round up groups with suspicious foreign ties at home.[4] More recently, the War on Terror revived the longstanding commitment in the United States to separate action from the rest of the world, independent efforts deemed necessary by extraordinary difficulties.

Football expresses the American dedication to separation from people outside the nation during times of crisis. The line of scrimmage strictly divides "us" from "them," identifying outsiders as enemies to push away and keep distant. Players act in strict separation from opponents. On offense, a team works to keep the ball far away from the opposition, ever seeking greater distance from the other team. Similarly, defenders strive to separate the football from opposing receivers or ball carriers, recover a fumble, and take the ball away into the scoring distance. Displayed on a gridiron of play, acts

Webster, *The Diplomatic and Official Papers of Daniel Webster* (New York: Harper and Brothers, 1848) and *The Life, Eulogy, and Great Orations of Daniel Webster* (New York: Mckee Publishers, 1855).

[2] Jenny Franchot, *Roads to Rome: The Antebellum Protestant Encounter with Catholicism* (Berkeley: University of California Press, 1994); George E. Pozzetta, ed., *Nativism, Discrimination, and Images of Immigrants* (New York: Garland, 1991).

[3] John M. Cooper, *The Vanity of Power: American Isolationism and the First World War* (Westport CT: Greenwood Publishing Corporation, 1969); Ronald E. Powaski, *Toward an Entangling Alliance: American Isolationism, Internationalism, and Europe, 1910–1950* (New York: Greenwood Press, 1991).

[4] The federal government imprisoned Japanese and German Americans in internment camps. See Diane Yancy, *Life in a Japanese American Internment Camp* (San Diego CA: Lucent Books, 1998); Mary M. Gruenewald, *Looking Like the Enemy: My Story of Imprisonment in Japanese American Internment* Camps (Troutdale OR: New Sage Press, 2005).

of separation portray a belief in isolation from menacing foreigners during national periods of emergency.

The separatism of football pervades many elements of the game. After each play, teams huddle together in a secluded distance from the other team. Showing the separateness of purpose, they line up facing the opponent to move in the opposite direction. Teams occupy separate sides of the field, further divided by the wide playing surface and mass of participants in a contest. During game action, players refrain from helping the opposition up from the ground, following a "no fraternization with the enemy" policy to preserve distant feel.[5] Like neutral observers of a crisis for the country, the referees stay separate as well, rarely engaging in conversation. Residing near their beloved teams, most fans sit in separate parts of the stadium from supporters of the other team, divided by great gulf of the field and nearly 200 players. Even greater separation between fans results from facing an opponent once each year, making the opposition seem extremely foreign. Football illustrates a devotion to sharp separation from people outside the nation during exceptionally harsh circumstances. Not coincidentally, it remains almost completely an American game, separate from the rest of the world.[6]

Alongside advocacy of timely separation, the civil religion of the United States generates an aspiration for a highly integrated life with people outside the country, producing a vision of close relations to come with other nations. The founding fathers envisioned a long-term alliance with France and others in Europe to broaden the scope of democracy into the future.[7] In the nineteenth century, the nation nurtured anticipation of multinational support for leadership by the

---

[5] Much more than in baseball and basketball, NFL players gather to pray with opponents after a contest, perhaps because of the intense opposition during play.

[6] The Canadian Football League generates significant support to the north but with players almost exclusively from the United States. Similarly, NFL Europe presents American players, attracting a relatively small following.

[7] For the promise of France for American founding fathers, see Paul M. Spurlin, *The French Enlightenment in America: Essays on the times of the Founding Fathers* (Athens: University of Georgia Press, 1984).

United States to civilize the Western Hemisphere, while millions of immigrants inspired the national imagination for becoming the guardian of those yearning to be free everywhere.[8] The result of world wars in the twentieth century, superpower status produced expectancy of increasing cooperation across the globe, encouraged by postwar efforts to rebuild Germany and Japan. [9] Today, hope for closer relations with other countries motives "nation-building" in Afghanistan and Iraq, led by George W. Bush.[10]

Baseball illustrates the American aspiration for integration with people outside the nation, depicting an ideal life of friendly relations to come. The game generates opportunity-giving interaction with the opponent. Pitchers work with opposing hitters by offering use of the ball inside the strike zone, within prime area of the batter's swinging ability. He "delivers" the baseball to the opposition, portraying national vision for a coming cooperation among human beings, even between strong rivals. On defense, players throw the ball close to the opponent on the base path in a "bang-bang" exchange that provides a chance for the rival runner to knock the baseball free from a "tag" or to show evidence of "beating" the putout attempt. As hitters, they strive to hit the ball safely away from the opposition, yet they almost always create a situation of opportunity for the other team to make a play and record an out. As base runners, most players engage in

---

[8] In the nineteenth century, the "Monroe Doctrine" guided national policy, gaining intensity with the leadership of President Theodore Roosevelt at beginning of the twentieth century. See Ernest R. May, *The Making of the Monroe Doctrine* (Cambridge MA: Harvard University Press, 1992); Richard H. Collin, *Theodore Roosevelt, Culture, Diplomacy, and Expansion: a New View of American Imperialism* (Baton Rouge: Louisiana State University Press, 1985).

[9] Sung-jo Park, *U.S. Labor Policy in Postwar Japan* (Berlin: Express Edition, 1985); Constantine C. Menges, ed., *The Marshall Plan from Those Who Made It Succeed* (Lanham: University Press of America, 1999); John B. Bonds, *Bipartisan Strategy: Selling the Marshall Plan* (Westport CT: Praeger Press, 2002).

[10] Consider Stanley Hoffman, *Gulliver Unbound: American Imperial Temptation and the War in Iraq* (Lanham: Rowman and Littlefield Publishers, 2004); Anthony H. Cordesman, *The War after the War: Strategic Lessons of Iraq and Afghanistan* (Washington DC: Center for Strategic and International Studies Press, 2004).

friendly conversations with members of the other team, conveying the anticipation of a future time when accomplishments by one nation will not threaten close relations with others. Presented on a diamond of play, helpful and friendly interactions between opponents reveal the expectation in the United States for a much more integrated society to come.

The integration of baseball reaches into every corner of the game. Teams occupy two distinct and somewhat secluded dugouts, but they are relatively near each other. They face the same direction to open-ended field of play, expressing an imagination for shared purpose between nations in focus away from domestic details that could foster hostile divisions. Players communicate in open space, within clear view of the opponent, only rarely huddling together in more separate conversation. The third base coach signals team members in front of everyone present, exhibiting vision for a coming time when countries will pursue self-determined plans within an international community of open relations. Fans of opposing teams often sit close to each other rather than in separate sections, integrated throughout the ball park. Oftentimes, they engage in friendly wagers, verbal jousting, and simultaneous cheers, depicting hope for a friendlier future of national loyalties without much friction.[11] In professional baseball, games occur in series and several times a year. Consequently, opponents are more like a competitive neighbor than a distant enemy and are quite familiar by season's end. Frequent player movement from team to team further lessens the sense of separation from the other team since an opposing player today can quickly become member of the beloved team tomorrow or next year. In prolific ways, baseball expresses the aspiration in the United States for achievement of closer relations with people from other countries. Within the sports trinity, it has the most participants not from the fifty states.

---

[11] This is less true in certain places like Boston, Philadelphia, and New York, more hostile and football like.

Ever the third element to the national equation, basketball portrays the American commitment to separate action from outsiders in moments of great adversity, while pursuing the futuristic goal of integration with the larger world. Routinely, players act in separation from the opponent. They work to keep the ball distant to the other team, dribbling and passing in an isolationist effort. Defenders block "the passing lane" and box out to "steal" or "swipe" the basketball in a keep-away action from the opposition. Teams move in diametrically opposed directions, expressing a separate purpose from each other. During time-outs, a team huddles together in seclusion from outsiders. The separateness is evident in the on-court demeanor of players, as opponents rarely help each other and often "talk trash" in verbal division from the rival. Most of the time, teams face an opponent once or twice a year, keeping the opposition separated and unfamiliar. Acts of separation on the hardwood convey devotion to isolation from people outside the United States in a domestic push to overcome situations of great difficulty.

In supplement to the periodic need for separate action, basketball illustrates the American faith in historical progress to a much more integrated future when rival countries will work with each other. Game action generates opportunity-giving interaction with the opponent. A ball handler dribbles in an opening to the opposition, continually moving the ball from the air to the floor with potential for a steal. He or she throws a pass into open airspace in a gift of chance to the other team, depicting the recognition of current advancement to conditions where rivals provide opportunities to each other but not yet directly in work together. Teams sit on separate benches, yet they face the same direction, representative of shared purpose to come between competitors. Most of the time, players communicate plans in clear view of the other team, expressing a hope for movement to more open relations among nations. During timeless moments of free throws, opponents stand next to each other in striking contrast to the face-to-face separation of direction when time is a factor, relaxed moments that portray the national anticipation of working alongside individuals from other countries in a future beyond time. The interactive and sometimes close relations of basketball communicate faith in the fast-paced flow of history toward a more integrated society still to be reached.

Domestic Relations

Though a source of strong democratic beliefs, American civil religion gives value to a hierarchy for relations within the country, especially during times of emergency. The federal government possesses eminent domain, supreme power to direct citizens and to use resources for the national defense or welfare. The president is "commander in chief," the executive authority empowered to dictate orders for the country in times of crisis. During the Civil War, Abraham Lincoln instituted the draft, rapidly fired generals, and censured the press in an exercise of presidential position. In World War II, Franklin Roosevelt drafted hundreds of thousands into combat, while commanding masses of citizens at home in civil service projects.[12] The belief in the sovereignty of federal institutions worked to enforce civil rights for African Americans during nation-changing events of the 1950s and 1960s.[13] More recently, George W. Bush used executive privilege to invade Afghanistan and Iraq in the War on Terror.[14]

Football expresses the American dedication to a hierarchy of domestic relations, particularly in situations of emergency. The head

---

[12] See Matthew J. Dickinson, *Bitter Harvest: FDR, Presidential Power, and the Growth of the Presidential Branch* (New York: Cambridge University Press, 1997); Martin S. Sheffer, *Presidential Power: Case Studies in the Use of the Opinions of the Attorney General* (Lanham MD: University Press of America, 1991).

[13] For a detailed case studies of federal authority in the civil rights struggle, see Peter Wallenstein, *Blue Laws and Black Codes: Conflict, Courts, and Change in Twentieth Century Virginia* (Charlottesville: University of Virginia Press, 2004); Kenneth T. Andrews, *Freedom is a Constant Struggle: The Mississippi Civil Rights Struggle and its Legacy* (Chicago: University of Chicago Press, 2004).

[14] Louis Fisher, *Presidential War Power* (Lawrence: University of Kansas Press, 2004).

coach has supreme and nearly absolute authority, acting as commander in chief like the president in response to extraordinarily harsh circumstances. Head coaches empower assistants to dictate every play, set apart in dress and authoritative behavior from the players. Each team upholds a chain of command like the nation for times of great difficulty. On offense, the quarterback is a "general on the field," commanding movements of the group. Offensive linemen represent "front-line solders," set apart from more acclaimed and trusted "skilled" players. Defensively, one "captain," normally the middle linebacker, directs the others. Often close to the ball by way of an interception or tackle of the ball carrier, defensive backs and linebackers garner most of the praise from fans or commentators, gaining an unequal amount of attention compared to players on the line of scrimmage. Defensive linemen are the "grunts" of the team, laboring "in the trenches" without much statistical or media coverage. Even the referees exhibit hierarchical authority in exchanges with players and coaches. They rule with nearly unquestioned power, rarely engaging in discussion about a call.[15] Inequities in relations on the gridiron portray the commitment in the United States to a hierarchy of power during times of national crisis, illustrating a faith in temporary suspension of search for social equality.

The dedication to hierarchy emanates from many interactions in football. Owners and players have a decidedly unequal relationship, as the players union remains quite weak. Team officials possess the authority to limit the amount of guaranteed money to a free agent, release a player, and "franchise" or stop the departure of the best players. Compared to members of society, however, players represent an elite group, set apart from common citizens by huge physical stature and abilities like the military vanguard of the nation. Teams often develop hierarchical relations with each other. Until recently, a

---

[15] Recent use of instant replay in the NFL and college competition allows for a few moments of contested rulings in a game.

few "dynasty" franchises in the NFL and "elite" college programs dominated the game, while other hapless teams stayed at the bottom of the game's food chain.[16] Consequently, the quantity and quality of fan groups are decidedly unequal. The Dallas Cowboys and Michigan Wolverines command hordes of followers, whereas the Arizona Cardinals or Rice Owls generate far fewer and more timid supporters. Perhaps the most dramatic inequity of the game, a ruling elite of voters and computer programmers determines the champions of Division I college football, not the players on the field. Football depicts the American devotion to hierarchical authority in periods of exceptional difficulty, delaying push for egalitarian ideals.

Alongside situational advocacy of hierarchy, the civil faith of the United States inspires an aspiration for equality in social relations. Constitutional documents uphold supreme dedication to "equal rights" between individuals, establishing a high standard of inspiration for later reforms.[17] "Jacksonian democracy" brought increased equality during the early nineteenth century, specifically for "the common man," "white" men without land ownership.[18] The Civil War and Reconstruction produced a rededication to greater equity within the nation by way of an effort to emancipate slaves.[19] Enacted in 1920, women's suffrage represented an ongoing struggle for further equality. The devotion to egalitarianism in society

---

[16] The Cardinals and Saints remained at the bottom of the NFL hierarchy for decades. University of Southern California, Miami, Oklahoma remain perennially in the top ten of college football, while Rice, Temple, and Vanderbilt stay consistently at the bottom of collegiate rankings.

[17] Bernard Schwartz, *The Great Rights of Mankind: a History of the American Bill of Rights* (Madison WI: Madison House Press, 1992); *The French Declaration of the Rights of Man and the American Bill of Rights* (Washington DC: United States Senate, Congress, 1989).

[18] William MacDonald, *Jacksonian Democracy: 1829–1837* (New York: Harper and Brothers, 1906); Walter E. Hugins, *Jacksonian Democracy and the Working Class: a Case Study of the New York Workingmen's Movement, 1829–1837* (Stanford: Stanford University Press, 1960).

[19] Herman Belz, *Abraham Lincoln, Constitutionalism, and Equal Rights in the Civil War Era* (New York: Fordham University Press, 1998).

motivated a fight against belligerent monarchies during World War I and against the even more aggressive totalitarianism in World War II.[20] Later, the civil rights movement, the "right to life" coalition, women's rights advocates, and gay activists conveyed persistent concern across the states with pursuit of social equity.

Baseball expresses the American aspiration for an ideal state of equality within the nation. Managers of teams rarely command the actions of players. They determine the line-up of participants for a game, and then they defer authority in "letting the players play." A manager sits or stands passively in the dugout to empower individuals on the field, conveying the expectation of a time when leaders will confer great power to others in the creation of remarkable equality. Managers wear uniforms like everyone else in expression of egalitarianism. Within a team, certain positions (i.e., the pitcher, catcher, short-stop) handle the ball more than others in a hierarchy of importance. However, the game requires every player—except for the pitcher in many leagues—to perform both offensively and defensively, equalizing the value of teammates. Typically, the best performers on defense are not the best hitters and vice-versa. On offense, the batting order seems to represent inequity by way of ranking, yet it guarantees virtually an equal amount of chances in a game for each player, varying at most by one plate appearance. Even the greatest hitter gives equality of opportunity to eight less able individuals before entering the batter's box again. Interactions on a diamond of play illustrate egalitarianism in the United States, the expectation of unprecedented equity to come between human beings.

The civil dedication to equality extends into many relationships within a baseball team. Among pitchers, teams feature a "number one starter" of exalted status but within a "rotation" that gives equal opportunities to each member. The very best pitchers sit inactive in

---

[20] Kenneth P. O'Brien and Lynn H. Parsons, eds., *The Home-Front War: World War II and American Society* (Westport CT: Greenwood Press, 1995); William L. O'Neill, *A Democracy at War: America's Fight at Home and Abroad in World War II* (New York: Free Press, 1993).

the dugout for four out of every five days in deference to the others on the staff. Teams also give relievers rankings, yet in fluid roles, changing frequently in the course of a season. Similarly, abundant movements of players from the minor leagues generate a sense of equal chance to progress through rewarded performance. Prolific changes in roles and personnel communicate the American trust in the equality of opportunity but not of results.

The egalitarianism of baseball reaches well beyond the relations on a team. Within the sports trinity, the game offers the most equal chance for the average-sized person in society to succeed through hard work and intelligence, nicknamed "the common man's sport."[21] Major League players are remarkably equal with owners in power to negotiate salaries, as they command many millions of guaranteed dollars in multi-year contracts.[22] Moreover, many players possess rights of arbitration to win disputes with ownership even before signing a long-term deal. Among teams, a relatively small group of franchises wins consistently over the decades, however, eighteen different teams have won the World Series in the past twenty-five years, a testimony to the game's equalizing power.[23] The elite teams lose sixty or more times each year, while the worst organizations win sixty to seventy games and often one in a three-game series, producing many days of more or less equal status. On any one day, a team has a nearly equitable chance to win, while the score of most games is quite close, frequently a difference of only one or two runs in expression of equality between the rivals. In diverse ways, baseball

---

[21] In the early twentieth century, the average sized player was about 5'10" and 170 pounds. Today's players are considerably bigger but so are common citizens. Many professional players today stand close to or less than 6 feet tall, while scores of others are overweight like people across the nation.

[22] For example, Alex Rodriguez signed his current contract for $252 million over ten years. The power of the player's union gives much importance to another group of people—agents for the players like Scott Boras and Jeff Moorad, the latter who is part owner of the Arizona Diamondbacks.

[23] "The World Series," Wikipedia, http://www.wikipedia.org/wiki/World_Series/html/.

portrays the American devotion to achievement of an egalitarian society.

Like football, basketball conveys the commitment in the United States to a strong measure of hierarchy during circumstances of adversity. The head coach exercises lots of power, often dictating actions of players from domineering stance on court's edge. The "General," Bobby Knight demands absolute submission, while "Zen Master" Phil Jackson directs teams from posture of great teaching authority. Powerful coaches wear formal suits, authoritative looking in contrast to the scant uniforms of individuals who follow their directives. Similarly, unequal relations exist between players, expressing the civil faith in inequity of power today to best overcome difficulties on court or in society. The point guard and one or two stars handle the ball majority of the time compared to "role" players of more limited importance. Within a team, the star possesses far superior status, generating expectations to "carry" or "lift" a team to championships like the great Michael Jordan.[24] A hierarchy also characterizes exchanges between players and owners in the NBA, as the players union commands limited authority. The salary cap restricts capabilities of a free-agent player, making huge long-term deals infrequent. Among teams, inferior squads rarely upset the very best, while frequent point differentials of large margin in a game indicate inequity between the two opponents. Inequality of relations in the game reveals national dedication to hierarchical authority for meeting the demands of difficult conditions.

In complement to the promotion of unequal power, basketball portrays the American pursuit of equality between human beings, illustrating faith in a historical drive for future equity in society. Often authoritative, the head coach gives power to players for making many decisions in a game. Frequently, he or she remains quiet on the bench in trust of the individuals on court, sitting next to team

---

[24] This inequity of importance given to players causes the evaluation of non-winning and otherwise exception individuals as "not great."

members in equitable fashion. Today in the NBA, players have nearly equal, if not superior, power to that of the coaches, often commanding a higher salary and input into decisions by team officials. Stars "run the show" with ability to "fire" a coach, revolutionizing authority relations. Performance equalizes the value of players. Prolific scorers like Jerry West and Reggie Miller often look inept and overmatched when playing defense. On offense, individuals routinely pass the ball, giving authority to others. The great teams keep the basketball moving in egalitarian action. Among teams, sixteen franchises make the NBA playoffs each year in expression of equal opportunity. The "March Madness" of NCAA basketball empowers sixty-five teams with chance to win, including many small colleges and undistinguished state universities. Each year, schools like Bethune Cookman, Valparaiso, St. Joseph's, Southwest Missouri State, and Montana University receive the opportunity to become champions of college competition, showing an egalitarian concern for far-reaching inclusion. Displayed on courts of hardwood, the pursuit of equal relations depicts the national dedication to push for ever more social equality, an idealistic effort balanced by the practical need for hierarchy.

Great Individuals of Public Veneration

Civil religion of the United States exalts a select group of individuals, people who capture the national imagination. After the Revolution, a small consort of "founding fathers" (i.e., Washington, Jefferson, Franklin) drew devotion from across the thirteen states, while legendary personalities of frontier life (e.g., Daniel Boone, Davy Crockett, Wyatt Earp) dominated popular culture of the next century.[25] Abraham Lincoln ascended to a place of veneration through exceptional leadership during the Civil War, pushing the individual holder of the presidential office into a position of supreme

---

[25]Adrien Stoutenberg, *American Tall Tales* (New York: Viking Press, 1966); Mark Derr, *The Frontiersman: The Real Life and Many Legends of Davy Crockett* (New York: W. Morrow Press, 1993).

public concern, especially compared to the more impersonal workings of Congress and the Supreme Court. In the twentieth century,
heroic individuals of fighting action received great reverence from
society, some real (e.g., Alvin York, Douglass McArthur, Dwight
Eisenhower) and others of fiction like the characters played by John
Wayne and Arnold Schwarzenegger.[26] Currently, Republicans and
Democrats have contrasting sets of venerable persons who symbolize
each party's version of the national faith.[27]

Football, baseball, and basketball provide individual stars of
nearly equal status to the exalted figures of American politics, the
military, and movies. Great players become idols, objects of civil
praise and devotion.[28] Fans show an intense dedication to the study of
their game actions and personal affairs, bestowing authority to the
stars of sports. A fan cherishes knowledge about a beloved player,
always in search of more information. As a result, certain players have
a great deal of influence on charitable giving, the sale of commercial
products, and even on social issues, commanding imitative behavior
from a particular segment of society. Highly revered, they receive
millions of dollars and a diverse array of gifts or perks from the
public. The fans decorate the special people of sport with money and
lavish living to declare lofty status. The quantity and quality of
attention given to sports stars express the American trust in a very
select group of individuals who most represent the national way of
life.

---

[26] Edward T. Linenthal, *Changing Images of the War Hero in America: a History of
Popular Symbolism* (New York: E. Mellen Press, 1982); Ronald L. Davis, *Duke: The
Life and Image of John Wayne* (Norman: University of Oklahoma Press, 1998).

[27] The Republican list begins with Ronald Reagan and Rush Limbaugh, while
Democrats give concentrated importance to John F. Kennedy, Bill Clinton, and
others.

[28] David L. Andrews and Steven J. Jackson, eds., *Sports Stars: the Cultural Politics of
Sporting Celebrity* (London: Routledge Press, 2001).

The greats of the sports trinity are icons of the United States, personified symbols of pivotal convictions for the nation.[29] Symbolic of the civil faith, Michael Jordan, Hank Aaron, and Joe Montana possess informal power in contrast to institutionalized authorities of politics and the military. They lead by example, modeling directives for the country by way of dramatic accomplishments on the court or field.[30] Intimately associated with national beliefs, a sports star generates a sense of societal crisis when charged with questionable or immoral behavior. The recent steroids controversy in baseball provoked questions regarding the integrity of several stars (i.e., Bonds, McGuire, Sosa), prompting the intervention of Congress on behalf of the public trust in the indicted individuals. Loss of credibility for great players of the national pastime resembles the trauma caused by the disclosure of corruption in the White House or Senate.[31] Personalities from the sports trinity receive a remarkable amount of condemnation when they detract from the lofty meaning of the games. Like the extraordinary love directed to sporting stars, the depths of bitterness and anger toward a fallen star reveal the immense significance given to the three sports played by people who may quickly rise and fall.[32]

Sports fans convey the American belief in great individuals through the exalted importance of physical objects associated with a star player. The most mundane item takes on incredible meaning and

---

[29] For an overview of American icons, see Marshall Fishwick and Ray B. Browne, eds., *Icons of Popular Culture* (Bowling Green: Bowling Green University Press, 1970); Roger Horrocks, *Male Myths and Icons: Masculinity in Popular Culture* (Houndsmills NH: Macmillan Press, 1995).

[30] In basketball, Charles Barkley vehemently opposes belief in athletes as "role models" because society gives such high status to the stars of sports. Exemplified by greats of the games, the dimensions of civil belief are the topic of this entire manuscript.

[31] For example, the Watergate and Clinton-gate scandals shook millions of people and rocked public faith in core beliefs of the nation.

[32] Conversely, recent problems in hockey and boxing have drawn little outrage, not close to the fervor about stoppages or corruption of play in the big three games.

worth when used by a popular athlete. Chewed gum by Luis Gonzales of the Arizona Diamondbacks sold for $ 10,000 on Ebay, while one trading card of Honus Wagner cost $640,500.[33] The multi-billion-dollar industry of collectibles pivots on the passionate and personal devotion to a very select group of individuals in society, including the special personalities of sports.[34] Fans believe in the weighty significance of seemingly commonplace things, having great reverence for barely legible marks of a pen made by beloved players on a napkin or five-dollar baseball. Major corporations recognize the intense veneration for great individuals of sport by paying millions of dollars to the stars who endorse their products. Apparently, the mere association of a famous player with a commodity brings an increase in value, no matter how orchestrated the connection.[35] The lofty expense and popularity of material things connected to star athletes express the strong devotion in the United States to a small group of persons inseparable from the national belief system.

Beyond the giving of immense monies, corporate advertising underscores the legendary status of sports stars. Many decades ago, Babe Ruth became "the Sultan of Swat," a royalty-like figure who directed fans to drink Coca-Cola and drive a Ford. In the sixties and seventies, the prince of football's airspace and New York's night-life, "Broadway Joe" Namath, revealed the great value of pantyhose. More recently, "everyone want[ed] to be like Mike" in a devoted imitation of "his highness," Michael Jordan, running and jumping with Nike sneakers and Hanes underwear.[36] Currently, NBA star Kevin Garnett "has the whole world in his hands" and is associated with messianic

---

[33] Bob Ley, "Outside the Lines," ESPN Television, 22 July 2005.

[34] Ibid. Reportedly, a jar of air breathed by Angelina Jolie and Brad Pitt sold for $530.

[35] Not coincidentally, telecast of the Super Bowl has the most expensive and innovative commercials each year, making it the holiest time for advertisers.

[36] Steven J. Jackson and David L. Andrews, eds., *Sport, Culture, and Advertising: Identities, Commodities, and the Politics of Representation* (London: Routledge Press, 2005); Robert Goldman, *Nike Culture: The Sign of the Swoosh* (London: Sage Publication, 1998).

predictions through his use of Nikes. Inspiring a mass of "witnesses," LeBron James is "the One" person of saving acts in basketball who not coincidentally drinks Sprite and wears Nike products.[37] The mythic sports stars of corporate commercials portray the civil adulation for an elite group of personalities, individuals elevated to a nearly superhuman position in society.

Descriptions of the best players further disclose the American faith in the extraordinary abilities of a select few. Especially in baseball and basketball, the ball is "the pill" or "the rock," expressing a general association of activities by players with medical and other forms of special knowledge.[38] The people most gifted in the use of the ball often generate nicknames of medical or magical significance like "Doc Gooden," Doctor J," and "Magic" Johnson. Michael Jordan remains "Air Jordan," the unique one who defies the law of gravity through extended flights unlike the rest of humanity. According to a Hollywood-produced myth, Shaquille O'Neal possesses the wish-granting power of a "genie," supplementing self-proclaimed and powerful knowledge as "the Big Aristotle" in real life.[39] Fans trust in extraordinary players to accomplish seemingly miraculous feats, believing the greats can predict the future like the prophetic figures of old fashioned religion. In one legendary moment, Babe Ruth pointed in advance to the exact location of a home run at Wrigley Field in the 1932 World Series, while Magic Johnson and Joe Namath foretold things to come in championship

---

[37] The song about Garnet in the commercial remakes a traditional Sunday school hymn of devotion to Jesus.

[38] Traditionally, the leaders of indigenous religious are "medicine" people with magic-like powers, qualities also associated with leaders of "world religions" though to a lesser degree. See Karen Liptak, *North American Medicine People* (New York: F. Watts Publishers, 1990); David R. Kinsley, *Health, Healing, and Religion: a Cross-cultural Perspective* (Upper Saddle River NJ: Prentice Hall, 1996).

[39] The nickname comes from O'Neill, through association with the famous philosopher was mostly enjoyed rather than rejected by fans.

games, and then they "backed it up" to fulfill the prophesies. [40]
Similar to Ruthian acts of old, Albert Pujols of the St. Louis
Cardinals recently delivered on promises to a girl with Down
syndrome, believed by fans and the mother to improve the girl's
health dramatically.[41] The attribution of mysterious powers to the
stars of sports expresses the veneration in the United States for a
special constellation of individuals considered quite unordinary.

The American public gives the greatest amount of and longest
lasting reverence to those players inducted into a hall of fame,
specifically persons thereby memorialized. Each hall of fame requires
a difficult process for entry as a member, fostering a very distinctive
status for everyone "immortalized" there.[42] It demands that a player
clearly stand out from the crowd of candidates in performance and
character, even compared to "very good" players of the game. Voters
consider a "moral" standard, conveying transcendent meaning to the
induction beyond physical actions on a field or court. The "hit King,"
Pete Rose remains outside the Baseball Hall of Fame because he
committed the ultimate sin of gambling, an activity that detracts from
societal faith in the integrity of the game, a matter of great national
significance.[43] Fans save money and vacation time for many years to
visit a hall of fame at least once. Once present at the much-
anticipated place, they walk reverently past each shrine with a studied
and solemn manner, reflecting on the weighty importance of the
individuals honored. Acclaimed members of the professional football,

---

[40] Perhaps Muhammad Ali was the supreme prophet of athletic predictions, often
offering poetic declaration of events to come.

[41] For legendary stories about Base Ruth and healing of the terminally ill, see Jim
Reisler, *Babe Ruth: Launching the Legend* (New York: McGraw Hill, 2004); "Ruthian
Tales," Encarta Online Encyclopedia, http://www.encarta.msn.com/encyclopedia/
html/.

[42] The process is very much like that for saints in the Roman Catholic Church.
Players become eligible five years after retirement, while evidence of quite
extraordinary feats is required.

[43] Allen Barra, *Clearing the Bases: The Greatest Baseball Debates of the Last Century*
(New York: St. Martin's Press, 2002).

baseball, and basketball halls of fame join with other legendary individuals from politics, the military, and entertainment to constitute an elite group of the highly venerated in the United States, providing a personified example for how to interact with people outside and inside the nation.

Chapter Nine

The Experience of Football, Basketball, and Baseball

Each game of the sports trinity promotes a distinctive way to experience life, causing particular feelings and thoughts inside of the individual player, coach, or fan.[1] Football fosters an intense dissatisfaction with current circumstances, a numinous sense of great distance from ideal conditions. Difficult situations on the gridiron encourage the pursuit of dramatic self-change and a time of rebirth. Conversely, baseball cultivates mystical experiences, moments of inner peace and awareness of closeness to the ideal. It generates consistency in the individual, expressing an aspiration for a future end to the need for self-transformation. On the other hand, basketball conveys faith in a balance of experiences in lieu of a more perfect life to come. Frantic action on the hardwood produces personal discontentment and the striving for rebirth combined with internal comfort and steadiness.

Experiences of the Ideal

Generating grandiose expectations for the future, American civil religion inspires numinous experience of life and a personal

---

[1] For an overview of the experiential dimension of religion, see Ninian Smart, *Worldviews: Cross-cultural Explorations of Human Beliefs* (Englewood Cliffs NJ: Prentice Hall Publishers, 2000) 55–70.

awareness of the great distance from coming ideal conditions.[2] In early years, the nation preserved a Puritan sensibility of the sharp disparity between human realities and divine perfection, producing intense distress about the decided conflict between necessities of federal power and democratic goals. [3] The Civil War brought a more ominous feeling of transcendent judgment throughout the country and great discord concerning the contradictory character of current circumstances related to national hopes. Personal experiences of strong discomfort were pivotal to success of the civil rights movement a century later. Martin Luther King, Jr. persuaded the nation to adopt an inner state of "dissatisfaction" with the unjust present, fostering a weighty sense of guilt about the existing contradictions to constitutional ideals.[4] Today, persistent faith in "the American Dream" brings much discontentment with current situations, inwardly pushing each individual to "get out of the comfort zone" and to strive for something distant.

Football expresses the American dedication to numinous dissatisfaction with present circumstances. It upholds great importance for personal discomfort, generating a sacred dislike for conditions. Players become "angry with the world," even enraged in intensive self-agitation. In preparation for a game, they hit each other on side of the head to summon inner hostility. Coaches demand meanness in a player and encourage a "mean streak" of hatred for the opposition.[5] They frequently scream at team members in the hope of drawing angry responses, seeking to stir up harsh emotions inside of a player like a drill sergeant on the battlefield. Great players feature an

---

[2] For the classic description of the numinous element in religion, see Rudolph Otto, *The Idea of the Holy: An Inquiry into the Non-rational Factor in the Idea of the Divine and its Relation to the Rational* (London: Oxford University Press, 1955).

[3] Regarding the American penchant experiences of much fear or discomfort, see James A. Morone, *Hellfire Nation* (New Haven: Yale University Press, 2003).

[4] Martin Luther King, Jr. *The Speeches of Martin Luther King*, video (MPI Video, 1990).

[5] Brendan I. Koerner, "Why Some NFL Players Are Meaner than Others," *Slate Magazine, Washington Post*, 23 April 2004.

"edge" or "chip on their shoulder," internal animosity for the opponent. Running backs "hunger for the end zone," following strong feelings of unfulfillment, while the best receivers possess the insatiable desire to catch the ball, something never satisfied. Offensive and defensive linemen aspire to a nasty demeanor to fuel hard-hitting aggressions against the other team. Even fans take on personal dissatisfaction of the game, creating an emotionally explosive and potentially violent atmosphere in the stands. On and around the gridiron, powerful feelings of disdain convey the national devotion to numinous discontentment as motivation to overcome difficulties of life.

Commitment to personal dissatisfaction pervades football, enhanced by the experience of distant goals. The goal line remains barely visible to players during play, illustrating the American sense of disturbing distance between present situations and national goals. Nearby conditions at the violent line of scrimmage cause discomfort and an awareness of remoteness from the hoped-for end zone. The quarterback drops well behind the stressful line to throw the ball downfield in an effort to achieve the remote touchdown. Running backs begin at significant distance from the distressing area where a play begins to create momentum for overcoming the unsatisfactory divide to a score. Defensive players work to keep the opponent dissatisfied, eventually frustrated by the inability to satisfy demand for movement to the end zone. The far-off goal line expresses the civil sensibility of the troubling distance from ideal conditions. Similarly, the next game is distant in football, always at least a week away and sometimes most of a year at the end of a season, maintaining ill feelings of long-lasting character.

Though a source of self-agitation, the civil religion of the United States also encourages the aspiration for mystical experiences, moments of inner peace and a sense of closeness to the ideal.[6] From

[6] Jeremy Carrette, ed., *William James and the Varieties of Religious Experiences: A Centennial Celebration* (London: Routledge, 2005) 177–94; Nelson Pike, *Mystical*

the beginning, national life promoted the "pursuit of happiness," a coming time of personal contentment.[7] Pioneers pursued a more enjoyable state of existence, enduring adverse journeys and back-breaking work in search of a better experience to the west. The great disquiet of the Civil War produced a widespread and personal yearning for a peaceful life, national expectations regenerated by immense turmoil of twentieth-century wars.[8] The satisfying moments of success during the civil rights movement brought increased anticipation across the country for an enduring satisfaction to come.[9] At present, masses of people in the United States hurry to work, a new job and bigger house, ever in pursuit of a happier and more contented future.

Baseball portrays the American aspiration for mystical experiences, times of abundant personal peace and enjoyment to come. Game action generates concern for inner relaxation, a peaceful state of mind. Players prepare by talking calmly between each other, then in gradual "warm up" with leisurely throws of the ball to release anxious emotions. During play, hitters stroll to the plate in a slow walk to maintain the inner relaxation of thoughts and energies for quiet concentration on the next pitch. Similarly, the pitcher "settles into" a seemingly effortless rhythm of motion for undisturbed focus during a pitch. Great pitchers "cruise" through a game, "coasting" to successful results like easy-going accomplishments envisioned for the future. Fielders remain in calm preparation for each pitch, able to

---

Union: An Essay in the Phenomenology of Mysticism (Ithaca NY: Cornell University Press, 1992).

[7] Thomas Jefferson, *Light and Liberty: Reflections on the Pursuit of Happiness* (New York: Modern Library, 2004); Peggy Noonan, *Life, Liberty, and the Pursuit of Happiness* (New York: Random House, 1994).

[8] Tom Martinson, *American Dreamscape: The Pursuit of Happiness in Postwar Suburbia* (New York: Carroll and Graf, 2000).

[9] For example, the activities accomplished desegregation of bus transportation and lunch counters. However, Martin Luther King, Jr. and other civil rights leaders made sure that each celebration was brief since much remained to be dissatisfied with regarding race relations of the nation.

preserve the ease of private demeanor, while outfielders "camp out" in recreational fashion to field an airborne ball. Fans take on the relaxed mood, normally sitting in calm posture in the comfort of "box seats," a peaceful state that demands loud music and scoreboard commands to produce more intense support for the home team. The inner peace and relaxation facilitated by the game express the expectation in the United States for idyllic calmness within every individual in a much happier future life.

Experiences of closeness to goals permeate baseball, illustrating the American hope for a coming time of personal intimacy with ideal conditions. As the destination of efforts on offense, home plate is nearby, only inches from the batter. Its proximity generates a sense of great familiarity with goal of the action, warm feelings like those associated with a family "dish" at home. Hitters consistently feel near to winning a game, even when well behind in the score, ever just a "bloop and a blast" away from overcoming the deficit. According to the mindset, one swing of the bat can quickly turn the momentum to achieve a victory, expressing the awareness of existence on the brink of success. Oftentimes, a pitcher is "just one pitch away" from successful results despite several runners on base, close to the hoped-for result in thought and emotion before an external turn of events. After good outcomes, pitchers achieve an "at home" feel, gaining contentment with their present position on the mound. Because of the daily occurrence of the competition, the next game remains just ahead with fresh opportunity after a string of losses. Frequently, players get "hot" in hitting streaks of great personal harmony with something ideal for many days, one time lasting for fifty-six straight games. Spectators sit near the action and to each other in "friendly confines," an intimate setting that inspires personal conversation. Many fans listen to daily broadcasts of games, experiencing the action by way of description from a very familiar and almost family-like voice. Similarly, players are individuals of great familiarity, expressed by abundant nicknames with family or neighborly feel (e.g., "Big Pappy," "Mick"). The sense of closeness to others and the achievement of aspirations convey the anticipation in the United States for a future of remarkable intimacy.

Representative of the third ingredient in the American experience of life, basketball generates both personal agitation and internal relaxation, a blend of the numinous and the mystical. The intensity of a game produces numinous dissatisfaction with threatening conditions of "attacking" opponents, a heightened dislike within to motivate strenuous efforts. Teammates "get in the face of each other" and internalize high energy music in preparation for the action, seeking "an edge" of personal discontentment for maximum performance. The greats stir up an attitude or air of superiority, self-agitated contempt for the opposition.[10] Inner disquiet and insatiable desire drive them to make the opponent look silly, inwardly disturbed unless a scoring play "fakes [the opposing player] out of his jock" or "posterizes" the rival in a photographed moment of dunking dominance. Internal animosity also moves a player on defense, pushing for the "rejection" of a shot or for the "steal" of a pass. Fans exhibit self-agitation of the game in show of contempt and even hatred for the visiting team, especially in Philadelphia and Boston. Personal dissatisfaction on the hardwood portrays the American belief in intense internal distress to motivate effort for overcoming adversity.

Symbolizing the purpose of basketball, the field goals reside far from the start of a play, conveying a numinous sense of great distance from ideal conditions. Teams begin from one end of the court with an unfulfilled feeling about the well-removed hoop like the nation's pursuit of distant goals. Contentious opponents disturb the advancement up court, making the pursued rim seem more remote. Even free throws occur fifteen feet away from the basket, a significant distance that grows distressfully greater in perception with approaching the end of a game. Produced by the not-close hoops,

---

[10] Related to this attitude, Michael Jordan became known as "his Highness," condescending in demeanor and on court status.

experiences of dissatisfaction express the dedication in the United States to personal agitation about the present distance from national ideals.

In complement to the numinous qualities of self-discontent, basketball fosters a concern for inner control and the relaxation of unsettling energies, portraying the American aspiration for mystical experiences of personal peace. Game action demands the moderation of internal anxiousness and dissatisfaction to avoid committing a foul or mishandling the ball in an overly aggressive action.[11] Players quiet their distressful emotions to "see the whole court" calmly and to deliver a precisely thrown pass. Proficient shooters remain composed despite the menacing presence of an opponent. In a show of exceptional coolness inside, they sink free throws even when rival fans wave neon streamers and scream in opposition. On defense, individuals relax the agitated feel about the threatening actions of the other team to achieve a controlled focus on the mid-section of an opponent, maintaining prime posture. Similar to the internal peacefulness expressed on the court, fans sit in a calm fashion most of the time, rising to a more intense and agitated mood at select moments of a game. Exhibited on and around the hardwood, the calming of inner dissatisfaction illustrates the expectation of coming peacefulness inside each person, communicating the civil belief in the progressive movement of history to a more satisfying life.

Though at times distant, the field goals of basketball often reside not far from the ball handler to moderate distress about the difficulty of scoring. Routinely, teams run a "set offense" within a comfortable shooting distance of the hoop. Good shooters stay "within range" from two feet or more, relaxing the internal concern about the physical separation from the basket. "Inside" players "post up" near the bucket, able to flick or lay the ball in for a score. Even when losing by a large margin on the scoreboard, a team is "not out of it,"

---

[11] "The Chalkboard," National Collegiate Athletic Association, http://www.ncaa.org/bbp/ basketball/ html/.

oftentimes generating a feeling of closeness to a rapid run of points for a revolution in the score. The accessible goals of basketball depict the American trust in historical progression ever closer to an ideal existence.

The Experience of Personal Change

Beyond inner feelings and sensibilities, the civil religion of the United States upholds strong expectations for dramatic moments of change for each individual, moments of personal rebirth.[12] After the Revolution, the founding fathers encouraged every individual to dedicate themselves to constitutional ideals to facilitate times of personal and societal change.[13] Abraham Lincoln helped inspire a "new birth" of collective freedom during the Civil War, persuading many people to internal shifts in attitude and perspective regarding the emancipation of slaves.[14] Economic expansion in the late nineteenth century brought the renewal of national aspirations for revolutionary turns in personal fate, a "rags to riches" transformation of the individual. Decades later, civil rights activists sparked a "new beginning" of fresh dedication to founding ideals, resulting in transformed individuals and who led a revolution in race relations of the nation.[15] Recently, the tragedy of 9/11 produced almost immediate and marked changes inside of individual citizens, moments of quite personal rededication to national convictions.[16]

Football portrays the American dedication to the rebirth experiences of the individual. Players undergo a dramatic shift in personality during each play of a game, expressing the civil devotion

---

[12] See John W. Tebbel, *From Rags to Riches: Horation Alger, Jr. and the American Dream* (New York: Macmillan, 1964). Protestant faith in the "born again" experience had a strong impact on the broader civil faith.

[13] Harold Hellenbrand, *The Unfinished Revolution: Education and Politics in the Thought of Thomas Jefferson* (Newark: University of Delaware Press, 1990).

[14] Abraham Lincoln, *The Speeches and Addresses of Abraham Lincoln* (New York: Little Leather Library Company, 1911).

[15] King, *Speeches of Martin Luther King, Jr.*

[16] Immediately, individuals displayed flags and other forms of civil devotion.

to the remaking of individuals.[17] Every snap of the ball brings a transformation of slow-moving and stationary persons into fiercely aggressive people. On offense, teams start in stillness, except for one or two individuals "in motion," and then they move sharply to intense action with the start of a play. Linemen charge forward in a decided change to "drive blocking" like "road graders" that shift through powerful gear changes to transform the country's landscape. "Skill players" explode forward from a motionless position in a burst of new energy, resembling the transformed individuals of American mythology who rise from rags to riches.[18] Defenders change in an equally dramatic manner to match the shifts by the opposing offense. Like their offensive counterparts, defensive linemen thrust forward in a marked alteration from the low and stationary four-point stance to become upright agents of aggression. Similarly on special teams, players line up in still positioning and are quickly changed into sprinting, leaping, and lunging blockers or tacklers. Dramatic shifts in behavior on the gridiron illustrate a civil belief in dramatic moments of personal change, rebirth experiences of the individual to overcome life's hardships.

The rebirth action of football extends well beyond the start to each play. Ball carriers strive for a sharp change of personal condition through a radical shift in movement to the distant end zone. A kick returner takes the ball from great danger "deep inside" his own territory all the way to the other goal line in a spectacular change of circumstances, covering 100 or more yards. Quarterbacks and receivers seek a similar turn of individual fate through a pass from behind the line of scrimmage to a high scoring touchdown far downfield. On defense, players experience a dramatic alteration by taking the ball away from opponents in a "turnovers" of revolutionary proportions. Quick shifts of possession instantaneously transform a defender into an empowered offensive force, suddenly able to score

---

[17] The United States is a "make-over" culture, dedicated to radical self-changes.

[18] Tebbel, *From Rags to Riches*.

many points. Fans also exhibit the self-transformation of the game, moving in a rapid and radical swing from relatively composed individuals to raging enthusiasts with snap of the ball. Like the striking shifts of "rags to riches" by legendary citizens, players and fans experience sharp alterations of character. Football illustrates the American faith in dramatic changes of personality, moments of individual rebirth to overcome life's hardships.

Though a source of dedication to personal transformation, the civil religion in the United States inspires the aspiration for rest from the struggle to change oneself, generating a vision for a future of great consistency. After achievement of victory in the Revolution, the nation envisioned a more relaxed life, a coming time for enjoyment of great accomplishments.[19] In subsequent decades, settlers into the West increased the nation's anticipation of a settled life to come through pursuit of an end to strenuous efforts of the present.[20] By the late nineteenth century, industrialization produced a richer imagination for an ideal future of leisure, forseeing a tomorrow when people will routinely remain at home in the blissful steadiness of great prosperity. In the twentieth century, immense disruptions by world wars further cultivated the national hope for a lifestyle of constancy associated with the familiar surroundings of a stable home and hometown.[21] Today, individuals across the country strive for retirement someday to more consistent and restful living, searching for a conclusion to the frenzy of an ever-changing society.

Baseball expresses the American aspiration for a future of personal restfulness. Stops and starts of game action are moments of

---

[19] Benjamin Rush, *The Writings of Benjamin Rush* (New York: Philosophical Library, 1947).

[20] The American ritual of barbequing expresses this expectation associated with outdoor life past and present. See Vernon Parrington, *The Beginnings of Critical Realism in American Literature, 1860–1920* (New York: Harcourt and Brace, 1958).

[21] For example, classic film of the thirties, *The Wizard of Oz* delivered the conclusion: "There is no place like home." In the wake of World War II, the fifties brought idealized expectations for home life, portrayed in television by *Leave it to Beaver*, *Dennis the Menace*, and a host of other sitcoms.

subtle change, highly measured shifts in behavior. For long periods of time, players remain in a stationary or slow-moving posture, conveying the national expectation of an end to the need for dramatic self-change. They routinely move in steady and slight motions, only infrequently becoming more intense in activity. Before each half inning, teams "warm up" in a gradual increase to the pace of action. Consistently, each player begins a play in an upright and prime position without need of drastic change in personal makeup. Hitters maintain a controlled "stance" with much stability, balanced and poised to smack the next pitch. They launch the ball through a level swing with minimal movement of the body. Pitchers start motionless on the mound, and then they deliver the baseball with a "smooth" and controlled "motion," avoiding "rushed" or "herky-jerky" action. Catchers "slide" from side to side to block a wild pitch without a drastic shift in location. Infielders approach a ground ball with gradual steps of refined footwork, while outfielders run in smooth strides to maintain a steadiness of vision or move with the greatest of ease to make a "basket catch." Similar to endings to play, the conclusion of a game brings a smooth transition from a relaxed pace of action to a leisurely walk off the field. Displayed on a diamond of play, easy-going and steady movements convey the imagination in the United States for a time when individuals will act with great consistency, coming freedom from need for personal transformation.

The personal constancy of baseball reaches into every element of the game. Changes of possession produce subtle moments of transition, not traumatic turnovers. After recording the final out of a half inning, players softly drop the ball to rest on the ground for the opposing pitcher to pick up in an easy motion, portraying the civil aspiration for gentle changes and accommodating circumstances to come. Influenced by the smooth flow of a game, managers show a continuity of behavior, normally sitting or standing in a consistent manner, only rarely shifting to intense gestures and shouts.[22] Individual players remain "hot" or "on a roll" for extended period of success, bringing consistency even to times of extraordinary accomplishment. The great teams steadily win two out of three games in glorious constancy. Fans too exhibit the steadiness of the game, infrequently changing to active movements, and then typically in deliberate clapping or cheering.[23] The steadiness of baseball depicts the hope for a future of personal rest, a time to come of the end to the frenzied strivings of today.

Complement to football and baseball, basketball portrays the American dedication to rebirth experiences, moments of dramatic personal change in pursuit of a more consistent life. Routinely, players make sharp changes of direction, conveying the civil faith in decided shifts by individuals to meet the demands of unsettled circumstances.[24] Each player moves with great variance of pace, in deliberate speed at start to a play, only to abruptly shift into intense "drives" and "cuts" to the basket. Frequently, the ball handler dribbles rhythmically toward the hoop and then suddenly leaps upward for a ferocious slam of the ball through the rim in a moment of explosive self-transformation. The great leapers of the game jump from a striking low to high action that resembles the remarkable "rags to riches" changes of national heroes.[25] Defenders respond with personal alterations of a similar magnitude to match the intensity of attacking opponents. Oftentimes, the head coach quickly overflows with energy in a marked change of demeanor to shout out and gesture instructions after standing relatively still with folded arms in studied concentration on play of the team. Fans undergo a similarly striking metamorphosis of personality. Most of the time, they sit

---

[22] As a Baltimore Orioles fan, I grew up watching many heated motions of Earl Weaver, though still only at certain moments in a game.

[23] At a game, the playing of music or sound effects leads the fans in rhythmic, steady chants like "let's go Mets."

[24] Trebbel, *Rags to Riches*.

[25] Ibid.

calmly in a cushioned seat, and yet they periodically take on animated postures with much yelling. On and around the hardwood, sharp shifts in behavior express the devotion in the United States to dramatic alteration of personal character for overcoming current difficulties.

Along with the transformations of personality, the end-to-end action of basketball illustrates the American belief in far-ranging change of individuals to succeed in spite of life's hardships. Players move in full-court transitions like legendary pioneers who accomplished sweeping changes in thoughts and feelings to match expansive physical journeys. Similar to fast-rising entrepreneurs of the country, they achieve rapid self-advancement, generating success through the frenzy of a fast break score. Frequently, teams experience a pronounced swing from a defensive state to an aggressive offensive role, suddenly able to "take it to the opponent." Routinely, changes of possession are turnovers with a stunning revolution of conditions by way of a "steal" or "rejected" shot, instantaneously overturning the status of players. Sudden and far-reaching alterations in game action convey the civil faith in sharp turnarounds of personal makeup to meet the challenges of adversities.

Complementing the dedication to individual rebirth, basketball illustrates the aspiration in the United States for a future of self-consistency. Oftentimes, players move across the court in the constant pace of a jog or steady dribbles of the ball, portraying the national trust in advancement of events to a steadier mode of action. Even when shifting to intense effort, they "take the ball strong to the hole" in pursuit of a more relaxed future at the free throw line or victorious in the post-game shower. Similarly, defenders exert energy for the future award of the ball by a referee, at times drawing an offensive foul. Individual players enact dramatic changes of personality in the anticipation of a steady and calm time to come, produced by accolades from the media. Before the end to a game, teams remain in a relaxed posture during timeless moments of free throws, expressing a hope for a more consistent existence to arrive beyond time. Not pressured by the clock, the foul shooters move to flick the ball in a rhythmic motion of personal constancy. Steady movements and the pursuit of more restful moments in the game depict the American belief in historical progress to consistency for the individual person.

Hope for a more constant life echoes from many areas of basketball. Most changes of possession in a game are smooth and unremarkable. For example, the ball routinely bounces up from the floor after a score for easy handling by the other team without much delay or effort to start the next play. On a missed shot, the defensive rebounder gives a change of status and the basketball to the best ball handler in an easy-going transit with a soft and short pass, sometimes even by way of a gentle handoff. After a time-out or turnover, referees hand the ball in an almost effortless exchange with players to initiate inbounding action. Like the subtle changes of possession, the head coach often sits or stands in a composed manner while fans rest in soft theater seats for extended time, expressing the aspiration for a relaxed pattern of events. The smooth and sweet flow of action on the hardwood portrays American faith in the advancement of history to a steadier life of personal continuity, ever the goal for more dramatic moments of self-transformation.

Game time

The sports trinity creates highly meaningful moments of "game time" in the United States. Anthropologist Victor Turner provides an analysis to help explain why the act of watching or playing a game has such exalted status.[26] Turner delineates a "ritual process" of "separation, seclusion, and return," describing how ritualized actions lead believers through a sequence of life-shaping experiences. First, the practitioner undergoes "separation" from common conditions of life, a clarification of the distinction between the profane aspects of

---

[26] Victor Turner, *The Ritual Process* (Chicago: University of Chicago Press, 1968).

the world and the sacred.[27] Second, he or she enters a state of "seclusion," a sense of immersion in surroundings symbolic of the most revered beliefs.[28] Finally, the ritual participant "returns" to ordinary activities at home and work, having a revitalized sense of priorities.[29] To further illuminate the significance of religious rituals, Turner highlights pivotal moments of "liminality" and "communitas" that are reached during time of "seclusion." Initially, the experience of separation from the everyday brings a personal awareness of passing beyond the boundaries or limits of commonplace life.[30] This moment of "liminality" generates a strong perception of freedom from restrictions of ordinary living, a sense of open-ended possibilities.[31] Eventually, the liminal situation gives way to "communitas," an experience of intense closeness to truths and others of shared belief.[32] Human beings depend on ritual actions of ultimate meaning, guiding participants through a process of defining moments.

For the sports fan, game time produces a personal "separation" from aspects of life deemed more ordinary. In expectation of a scheduled contest, fans perform acts of preparation to begin the inner movement away from the commonplace. They take off the clothing of work, symbolic of the daily grind, and put on the garb of great devotion (e.g., hats, shirts, and other objects of dedication associated with a favorite team). During the change of clothes, he or she initiates a shift within, concentrating less on stressful thoughts of earlier hours and ever more on the highly anticipated activities of the upcoming game. Oftentimes, this inner journey starts much earlier in the practice of daydreaming about envisioned events to come on a playing field or court. Players undergo a similar transformation inside

---

[27] Ibid., 94–130.
[28] Ibid.
[29] Ibid.
[30] Ibid.
[31] Turner describes this sense of liberation as experience of "anti-structure."
[32] Turner, *The Ritual Process*, 131–65.

while dressing in the locker room. They experience a separation from ordinary living by way of putting on the uniform, achieving a heightened sense of competitiveness and attentiveness with the change in appearance. Entry onto the playing surface escalates the internal separation from more commonplace sensibilities associated with even greater concentration on the all-important contest at hand. Likewise, a fan experiences an increased shift away from everyday concerns with the movement into the stadium, arena, or sports bar. A personal sense of separation from the mundane in life reveals the weighty significance of the games, causing internal changes.

In the United States, a game of football, baseball, or basketball generates awareness inside individuals of nearly total separation from ordinary affairs, an experience of seclusion within surroundings considered of ultimate importance. Fans enter an inner state of immersion, completely dedicated to the present moment of game action like religious believers in state of worship or meditation. They give play-by-play attention to every detail, agitated by others not so supremely concerned. A fan engages in running commentary, internal and sometimes externalized, about each act of a game, totally invested in thought and emotion. Resembling the devoted followers of traditional religions, he or she will "live or die" with every twist and turn of the competition, offering their every capacity to find abundant meaning in the games. Record-breaking situations produce even greater awareness of unlimited significance, a sensibility of total dedication to the unfolding event. With Hank Aaron at 714 home runs and at the plate, the crack of the bat pushed the true fan into a realm impossible to reproduce, a spell-bound time to be witnessed, not questioned or analyzed in the withholding of something personal. Occurring at a playing field or court, individual experiences of total engagement disclose the belief in the presence of something considered sacred.

Exhibiting the life-shaping power of religious rituals, games of the sports trinity produce inner awareness of increased ability for the "return" to the ordinary aspects of life, a perceived result of seclusion in overwhelmingly meaningful game time. Fans gain perspective, clarified point of view, which lessen the significance and stress of the daily routine. Post-game, he or she feels "recreated" with a renewed feel for priorities centered on enjoyment of life and core American convictions. Many become too attached to the exhilarating effect of the contest, spending most of their time in thought about the last or next game rather than more important matters of vocation and family. Such fanaticism profanes the game time. It makes reflection and meditation on the games commonplace, routine rather than special acts of personal regeneration.[33] Ideally, moments of game-watching enable a fan to function better at work and home, providing a sense of purpose relevant to everyday efforts. At its best, devotion to games of the sports trinity motivates greater commitment to family, local community, the nation, and human beings in general.

Like the fans, players gain an increased capacity for return to common living through complete engagement in game time. Oftentimes, they find inspiration for devotion to become more devoted to others through playing a game, expressed by unique gestures at the free throw line, home plate, or line of scrimmage in thoughtfulness of loved ones. Frequently, the difficulty of competition brings to mind special love for family, friends, and country. Some individuals do not become more dedicated to other people as a result of participation in game time, nurturing a highly individualistic purpose nevertheless associated with the national way of life. Though of diverse experiences, players and fans achieve a sense of clarified meaning through personal commitment to the playing of a game, empowered for the return to more common circumstances by way of increased understanding. Ideally, they regain ultimate concern for others and a set of shared convictions nationwide. At worst, faith in the game action produces self-absorbed individuals of narrowly defined interests and beliefs.

---

[33] Undoubtedly, the potential for this unhealthy and extreme approach continues to grow, especially with the "twenty four hours a day, seven days a week for fifty-two weeks a year" culture of ESPN and other media venues.

Through power to separate the public from ordinary life, game time generates liberating experiences of dramatic movement beyond the limits of commonplace conditions, producing exhilarating moments of "liminality." While watching a game, fans experience freedom from restrictions of everyday affairs, bringing a personal sense of open-ended possibilities. With this internal shift to a more hopeful and imaginative state, a fan exhibits dramatic changes in external behavior, often in action well beyond the boundaries of his or her normal personality. Though subdued at work and home, he or she "goes nuts" in wild exuberance during games, propelled by the limit-breaking force of the action. Otherwise reserved individuals become quite demonstrative, at times jumping up and down in shouts of joy or stomping and groaning in disappointment. After a routine day of obeying orders from an overbearing boss, sports fans act as demanding dictators of players during game action at night, liminal and liberating moments of role reversal. Game time produces a belief in freedom from the limitations of social position in the outside world, pushing the believer in another realm with the power to command others, especially highly visible players on the field or court.

Players also enter a "liminal" state inside a game. Frequently, they transition into intense and even mean individuals during play, though easy-going and friendly "off the field," pushed beyond their normal persona by the competition. Each play of game time causes liminality, unpredictable and never quite like any other, triggering a player to forget about previous boundaries of action while expecting an unprecedented level of performance. Especially in the postseason, the intensity of games brings the best out of the greatest performers since it inspires new heights of offensive and defensive achievement. Regardless of the timing, players and fans marvel at record-breaking times in a game, moments that shatter longstanding limits of accomplishment. Game time generates a perception of power to transcend well-established boundaries, fostering faith in the capability for remarkable achievements.

In complement to heightened sense of ability to cross limits of everyday living, the playing of a game produces an experience of close connection with others, times of "communitas." Fans achieve an awareness of intimacy with other supporters of their favorite team, finding community in the mutual suffering of a loss or the enjoyment of a victory. Strangers before the start of a contest easily engage in friendly conversation about play action and are quickly brought together by the common cause of a game. Oftentimes, they act in remarkable togetherness, rising as one at special moments in the competition. Previously distant to each other, crowds of fans chant, move, and sing in unison to create a collective "roar" of support for the same team. Similarly, players sense strong unity within the time of a game, a harmony otherwise nonexistent or much less intense. Even when at odds before the game, teammates root for each other in a connected feeling. Great teams follow the forces of game time to overcome differences between members, gaining an incredible synergy of abilities and efforts in an unshakeable chemistry.

Through the force of a game, fans and players develop imagination for a common purpose with each other, causing mutual celebration at moments of success or shared concern with each failure. The achievement of a championship provides a dramatic expression of this inner bond, pushing fans out of the area for spectators and onto the playing surface in nearness to the players. Record-breaking feats bring similar intimacy between performers and supporters. After transcending the longstanding record for consecutive games played, Cal Ripken of the Baltimore Orioles took a victory lap around the stadium to slap and shake hands with hundreds of fans in a show of incredible unity. The crack of the bat, the pop of pads on the gridiron, and the squeak of sneakers on the hardwood draw the fan ever nearer to the players of games, generating a perception of shared purpose. Events of national importance and the playing of football, baseball, and basketball cause a remarkable connection between masses of individuals who have abundant reasons to remain separate. With great power to create community, game time draws the devoted attention of many millions, generation after generation, reaching into every inch of American life.

Chapter Ten

Revelations of the Sports Trinity

Football, baseball, and basketball are yearly rituals of civil religion in the United States, leading the nation through three seasons each year. Football brings a season of self-sacrifice, a time for the expression of personal dedication to the collective good of society. Baseball generates an extended period of festive celebration, culminating with two weeks of World Series fanfare. Situated between football and baseball in the calendar, basketball provides a transitional season and mindfulness of fast-paced advancement from sacrificial efforts to accomplishment of great festivity. Together, the three sports produce a daily way of life, a never-ending connection to the national worldview, pivoting on acts of devotion to the spoken and written word. At special points of the week, game action inspires the gathering of individuals at a stadium, arena, sports bar, or home in a show of common faith in a team. Of guiding influence for a lifetime, the sports trinity produces rites of passage that mark maturation at pivotal times of birth, adolescence, mid-life, and death. They present a comprehensive set of ritual actions, giving guidance of the American belief system from daily to once-in-a-lifetime situations.

Through their ritualized dramas on a field or court, football, baseball, and basketball illustrate three core stories of American civil religion. Football portrays a story about the realities of life within history, conveying the national mythology about hostile conditions and a dedication to sharp departures in pursuit of fulfillment somewhere else. Baseball depicts the mythic vision a perfect world to come, a national imagination for a coming time of unprecedented freedom, synergy, and a life-cycle of perpetual return to ideal circumstances. Basketball presents the story of irreversible progress, presenting a belief in the rapid advancement of the country from harsh realities of history to a much better future. The fast-paced action of a game communicates confidence in the movement of human beings away from hardships, contentiousness, and the need for abrupt departures to pursue a freer, more unified, and rhythmic life. The sports trinity represents three foundational myths of civil religion in the United States, generating interplay between the understanding of realities, ideals, and progress from the real to the ideal.

Through mythic accounts of life, the three major sports disclose core doctrines of the country and beliefs about truth. First, they present the unified conception of the source for truths, upholding faith in a higher power, one supreme being with three-fold character. Second, the three games reveal the triune thinking of the nation about how to gain ultimate knowledge and solve problems. Football portrays the mindset for the worst of circumstances, directing attention well beyond ordinary or nearby conditions to a transcendent means of truth. To resolve difficulties, it upholds belief in the self-help efforts by human beings. Conversely, baseball expresses the expectation for the immanence of truths in an ideal life to come, illustrating the national aspiration for guidance from study of the familiar and reception of abundant help from greater forces of divinity. Basketball presents the reasoning in the United States for most situations. Conveying the commitment to a balance of beliefs, it displays a conviction that truths are becoming immanent in common conditions, progressively realized, while more advanced knowledge remains transcendent to be discovered through a look beyond the easy to find. Hoops action highlights trust in self help works by humanity, supplemented by the perception of growing aid from higher forces. Collectively, the trinity of sports reveals the American structure for belief on broad matters of truth.

Alongside the themes of doctrine, ethical convictions mark the lessons of football, baseball, and basketball, expressing directives for how to make moral decisions and understand issues of special concern. Football illustrates morality in the United States for times of crisis (e.g., war). It portrays devotion to obeying commands, just use of violence, collective action, and the acquisition of much property. Baseball depicts ethical ideals of the country, which are envisioned for an ideal future. Game action on a diamond discloses the supreme virtues of self-motivated effort, nonviolent competition, individuality, and achievement of generous prosperity. The third element to the national equation, basketball conveys moral reasoning for commonplace circumstances, encouraging balance of adjustment to realities and aspiration for ideals. It upholds national commitment to following commands, disciplined use of physical force, cooperative work, and acquisitiveness combined with pursuit of self-directed action, nonviolent competition, individuality, and the sharing of personal possessions. Together, the three games provide comprehensive guidance in morality, representing American values for the worst, best, and most typical of situations.

Collectively, the sports trinity communicates the dedication in the United States to certain social arrangements, directives for interactions with people outside and inside the nation. Especially relevant to times of emergency, football exhibits national devotion to strict separation from outsiders and a hierarchy for domestic relations. Depicting an ideal future, baseball reveals the aspiration for integration with other nations and equality of individuals inside the country. Ever the complement to football and baseball, basketball expresses commitments for common circumstances, upholding the importance of both independence from and integration with foreign countries. For relations within the nation, hoops action encourages a balance of hierarchy and a push for equality. Functioning as a unit, the three sports produce a constellation of stars, idols of personified example for how to interact with outsiders and insiders.

Reaching into every facet of life, football, baseball, and basketball inspire life-shaping experiences inside individuals. Football generates numinous moments of intense dissatisfaction and aspiration for dramatic change, disclosing the national sense of great distance from ideals and pursuit of personal rebirth. Baseball brings mystical experiences of inner peace with awareness of closeness to the ideal. Play on a diamond expresses the national anticipation for remarkable self-consistency in a much more comfortable future. Basketball prompts a blend of the numinous and the mystical. It produces an inner dissatisfaction about distant goals alongside self-control, while encouraging personal search for both dramatic change and steadiness. Of great significance in the United States, the sports trinity creates highly influential experiences of "game time." Offering distinction of beliefs held sacred from the profane, games generate inspirational power of inspiration for individuals to move beyond the established limits of personal demeanor, an achievement of something new and seemingly unlimited with possibility. For better or worse, experiences of football, baseball, and basketball shape the lives of many millions, generation after generation, providing guidance for diverse dimensions of life.

Race and Ethnicity:
Grand Potential of the Sports Trinity

Historically, the trinity of American sports has been an inspirational force for the advancement in racial and ethnic relations.[1] Early on, baseball presented moving illustrations of celebrated accomplishments through teamwork between individuals of Anglo, Irish, Italian, German, and Jewish descent. In 1947, it provided the dramatic story of Jackie Robinson, generating imagination for racial integration of society a decade before the civil rights movement. By the 1960s, each team featured several African Americans, including most of the game's stars. Football presented Jim Brown, Gale Sayers, and Bubba

---

[1] See John Bloom and Michael Willard, eds., *Sports Matters: Race, Revelation, and Culture* (New York: New York University Press, 2002).

Smith, while basketball highlighted Bill Russell and Wilt Chamberlain, joining with Hank Aaron, Willie Mays, and Frank Robinson of baseball to form a set of highly revered characters. In the 1970s, basketball became a sport of prolific achievement by African Americans. During subsequent decades, it drew increasingly diverse support from across the globe, inspiring people in Europe, Africa, Latin America, and all the way to China.[2] Similarly, baseball receives ever more international attention. Today, major league teams feature players from the Caribbean, Central America, South America, Asia, and Australia. Football, baseball, and basketball possess a mighty capacity to gather people across ethnic and racial lines in shared dedication to a team, offering a public example of sophisticated cooperation among individuals from diverse parts of the world.

Illustrating the American concern with the real conditions of society, football presents the current situation in race relations, displaying significant progress achieved since the civil rights era, improvement evident in the prominence of African Americans on the field. Blacks represent 70 percent of players in the NFL and 50 percent in college football, reflecting increased inclusion in recent decades. Scores of black quarterbacks, team captains, and coaches disclose growing acceptance as persons of authority in national life. Black and white fans intermingle like extended family members, while many African American analysts indicate greater importance given to the thoughts of non-white people. Increasingly in positions of importance on the gridiron, African Americans portray the advancement of the United States from the more exclusionary past not so long ago.

Along with the progress achieved, football reveals much unfulfilled in racial concerns. Blacks predominate as players but not in roles of authority (i.e., quarterback, head coach, management, owner). The position of greatest power—quarterback—features the

---

[2] For the increasingly international appeal of basketball, see Walter LaFeber, *Michael Jordan and the New Global Capitalism* (New York: W. W. Norton and Company, 1999); John Hareas, *Ultimate Basketball* (London: DK Publishers, 2004).

smallest percentage of black players. As quarterbacks, African Americans often receive quicker and more intense criticism from fans than white counterparts.[3] Few head coaches are black, 15 percent in the NFL, well below the percentage of African American players. Major college football includes just four African Americans in the role of head coach, only one ever in the Southeastern Conference.[4] Even fewer blacks function as administrators of university or professional teams, while the NFL has not had an African American owner. Expressing the American recognition of the harsh realities in life, football gives quite an accurate portrayal of African Americans in society, showing significant improvement but without much effect on key positions of decision-making. The scarcity of Native Americans and Latinos conveys the national focus on inclusion of African Americans since the civil rights movement, further disclosing the limited character of advancements in race relations.

Portraying the American vision for the future, baseball expresses an aspiration for ideal relations of the races. Not coincidentally, it became the sport of integration for African Americans, featuring the brightest stars during pivotal years for the civil rights struggle.[5] Before Jackie Robinson broke "the color line," the game offered venue for blacks to exhibit exceptional capabilities through play in

---

[3] Wisdom T. Martin, *Intentional Grounding: The History of Black Quarterbacks in the NFL* (Bloomington: Indiana University Press, 2002); Jeffrey Jufto, "Progression of Black Quarterbacks in the NFL, 1950–2000," diss., 2002.

[4] See Gary A. Sales, *African-Americans in Sports: Contemporary Themes* (New Brunswick NJ: Transaction Publishers, 1998); Mike Licker, *Orange Daily*, 30 October 2003.

[5] Pollack played in the NFL during the 1920s but with little social impact, especially compared to the national significance of Jackie Robinson in 1947. See Karen M. Coombs, *Jackie Robinson: Baseball's Civil Rights Legend* (Springfield NJ: Enslow Publishers,1997); David Falkner, *Great Time Coming: The Life of Jackie Robinson, From Baseball to Birmingham* (New York: Simon and Schuster, 1996); Joseph Dorinson and Joram Warmund, *Jackie Robinson: Race, Sports, and the American Dream* (Armonk NY: M.E. Sharpe, 1998).

the legendary Negro Leagues.[6] Soon after integration, African Americans dominated the Major Leagues in an even more public display of abilities, generating imagination for similar accomplishments in other areas of national life if given the chance. From coast to coast, people developed the expectation of great things to come from African Americans. They were witnesses to the prolific success of Hank Aaron, the spectacular grace of Willie Mays, and unstoppable excellence from Bob Gibson.[7] Soon, the Baseball Hall of Fame featured many blacks, integrating the nation's most enduring cast of heroic figures. The story of African Americans in baseball reveals the abundant powers of inspiration in the games, great potential for motivation of close and productive relations between the races.

Beyond the celebrated years of racial integration, baseball continues to provide a rich example of an idealistic state for racial and ethnic matters.[8] Every year, it becomes more diversified in continental and national affiliation, encouraging anticipation in the United States for a much more international future. In 2005, the rotation of starting pitchers for the Baltimore Orioles of 2005 featured individuals from Panama, Aruba, Canada, Mexico, and the

---

[6] Periodically, "Negro" teams played against "white" major leaguers in well-publicized exhibitions. See Neil Lanctot, *Negro League Baseball: The Rise and Ruin of a Black Institution* (Philadelphia: University of Pennsylvania Press, 2004); Mark Ribowsky, *A Complete History of the Negro Leagues, 1884–1955* (Secaucus NJ: Carol Publishing Group, 1995).

[7] For the connection between sports and the civil rights movement, see Patrick B. Miller and David K. Wiggins, *Sport and the Color Line: Black Athletes and Race Relations in Twentieth-century America* (New York: Routlege, 2004). Hall of Fame journalist, Peter Gammons describes baseball as "the sport of social conscience" in the United States. "Baseball Tonight," ESPN Television, 11 July 2005).

[8] Alongside the increasingly international character of baseball, decline in participation represents failure to maintain interest of a group pivotal to history of the game. In 1980, African Americans represented 30 percent of Major League players but only 5 percent in 2005.

Dominican Republic.[9] Currently, Major League Baseball includes players from eighteen countries, including those of Latin American heritage and an increasing number of stars from Asia.[10] Several members of the Baseball Hall of Fame originate from outside the United States, generating a greater appreciation for people who speak a language other than English. Each year, the World Series becomes more global in scope with audiences and players from more parts of the world. Ethnic and racial diversity in baseball nurtures the American expectation for greater integration of nations.

The complement to football and baseball, basketball expresses the national trust in the existence of rapid progress to ideal relations of the races. More than any other area of professional life in the United States, the NBA displays remarkable success by African Americans, revealing a dramatic improvement from the harsh discrimination of the past. Incredibly, the color line excluded colored players just over fifty years ago.[11] Today, African Americans make up the vast majority of NBA and major college teams.[12] Many blacks are head coaches and general managers, making pivotal decisions for institutions worth hundreds of millions of dollars, while the NBA features the first black owner of a major sports franchise in the country. Every professional and major college team includes several African American players, giving blacks a pivotal place in the intellectual constellation of each fan, a fact of significant development from the severe prejudice of earlier times. Displayed on courts of hardwood, the prolific achievements by African Americans portray

---

[9] For most of 2005, Bruce Chen, Sidney Ponson, Eric Bedard, Rodrigo Lopez, and Daniel Cabrerra were the starters.

[10] Peter C. Bjarkman, *Diamonds across the Globe: The Encyclopedia of International Baseball* (Westport CT: Greenwood Press, 2005); W. P. Kinsella, *A Series for the World: Baseball's First International Classic* (San Francisco: Woodford Press, 1992).

[11] Miller and Wiggins, *Sport and the Color Line*; Amy Bass, *In the Game: Race, Identity, and Sports in the Twentieth Century* (New York: Pelgrave Macmillan, 2005). Earl Lloyd was the first African-American player in 1950, playing for Syracuse.

[12] Charles K. Ross, *Outside the Lines: African Americans and the Integration of the National Football League* (New York: New York University Press, 1999).

the American sense of dramatic advancement since the civil rights era.

Though revelatory of improvements in race relations, basketball also discloses much still to be accomplished. Too many African American youths aspire to play the game as a profession when only a very small percentage succeeds. Because of special abilities with a basketball, thousands of black teenagers receive scholarships for higher education, but many fail to graduate, unable to adequately take advantage of the educational opportunity.[13] Though prominent as players, African Americans make up a relatively small number of coaches and management officials at the higher levels of competition.[14] African American stars dominate play, and yet they often draw the public perception of being "just athletes," not considered capable of similar achievements in other professions. Frequently, fans and commentators label African-American players as "natural athletes," born to be exceptional by some greater force, while they deem many white players like Larry Bird or Steve Nash "hard workers" and "intelligent," apparently the agents of more self-determined success.[15] Enacted for the watching nation, the story of African Americans in basketball reveals both decided progress and much unachieved in American race relations.

Beyond the drama of African American participation, basketball generates the involvement of an increasingly international population, encouraging confidence in improving relations between nations of the world. At present, NBA teams feature players from more than a dozen countries, hard evidence of an increasingly global game. Like legendary the immigrants to the United States of years past, stars arrive from Europe, Africa, and even China in increasing

---

[13] Christopher M. Spence, *The Skin I'm In: Racism, Sports, and Education* (London: Fernwood Publishers, 1999); Richard E. Lapchick, *Sport in Society: Equal Opportunity or Business as Usual?* (Thousand Oaks CA: Sage Publications, 1996).

[14] Consequently, Ice Cube recently described the NBA as "still blacks working for whites." "Outside the Lines," ESPN Television, 4 May 2005.

[15] Harry Edwards, *Sociology of Sport* (Homewood IL: Dorsey Press, 1973).

numbers, bringing a sense of movement to more diverse and worldwide relations in life outside game action. Recently, international competition discloses several countries with a nearly equal chance to win. Well-publicized victories by nations against "dream teams" of Americans results in openness to the abilities of players from across the globe, producing the imagination for similar inclusion in the larger society. Basketball portrays the national dedication to the fast-paced advancement of social conditions from harsh realities—illustrated by football—in pursuit of a much more integrated and international future—envisioned especially through baseball. For the interaction of diverse ethnic and racial groups, the trinity of sports offers the potential from the three-way philosophy of American civil religion, generating concern for realities, the ideal life to come, and rapid progress from the real to the ideal.

Gender Relations:
The Limited Meaning of Football, Baseball, and Basketball

In contrast to matters of race and ethnicity, gender relations reveal the limits of significance for the sports trinity. The three games do not accurately portray social realities or ideals for the female population, failing to disclose the progress achieved during the twentieth century. Women are not players, coaches, or management officials at the highest levels of play.[16] Today, they thrive as corporate executives, judges, lawyers, doctors, politicians, and professors, but they are not present in football, baseball, and basketball. The scarcity of females in prominent places shows the limited nature of meaning associated with the three major sports.

Expressing the American concern for the recognition of realities, football provides the restrictive roles for women. Recently, it gives opportunity to female reporters at a game, however, only for brief moments from the limited perspective of the sidelines, contrasted to the "play-by-play" and "color" commentators who talk for three

---

[16] Wilbert M. Leonard, *Sociological Perspective on Sport* (New York: Macmillan, 1993).

hours from a prime position above the action.[17] Mostly, sideline reporters simply report factual information about injuries or personal situations of players, refraining from broader and more critical analysis. Beyond presence on the sidelines, women act as cheerleaders in the traditional role of giving inspirational support to the men who play and coach. Though not well heard during college and NFL competition, cheerleading squads remain quite visible, often the focus for split-second shots of television, though infrequent compared to hours of attention on the masculine actors in a game. Increasingly, female spectators populate the stands and sports bars in dedication to a professional team, long true of college loyalties, and yet their role is more supportive, like that of the cheerleaders. One woman, Georgia Frontiere, is the owner of the St. Louis Rams, very much the exception to the many sideline reporters, cheerleaders, fans, and the uninterested. The overwhelmingly secondary functions for women near the gridiron fail to disclose a realistic presentation of life in the United States.

To fulfill its civil purpose as purveyor of real conditions, football would have to include female players and coaches, presenting a more direct account of gender relations. Currently, women play featured roles in the larger society during times of crisis, moments of adversity like those illustrated by the game. Female officers are prominent during emergencies as members of the police, military, and government, though they hold positions far from equal with the men.[18] The physical demands of the sport probably inhibit women from participation on the field in numbers to match the current status in the nation, resulting in a similar exclusion from higher ranks

---

[17] Tamara McElroy, *From Then to Now: The Evolving Role of Women Sports Reporters* (Frederick MD: Hood College, 2005).

[18] Judith Stiem, *Its Our Military Too: Women and the U.S. Military* (Philadelphia: Temple University, 1995); Laurie L. Weinstein and Christie C. White, *Wives and Warriors: Women and the Military in the United States and Canada* (Westport CT: Bergin and Garvey, 1997).

of coaches, team officials, and analysts.[19] Football has more room for female spectators, commentators, and perhaps even coaches, but not enough to offer places of leadership near the social standards of today. In all likelihood, it cannot provide a realistic presentation of gender relations. Unable to provide a prominent role for the female population, the game expresses the core beliefs of American civil religion, but in a limited fashion, demanding clarification of the significance for women.

In line with of its visionary purpose, baseball presents more diverse opportunities for women. Girls play the sport at an early age, while many adult leagues feature female players, building on tradition of the All-American Girls League, made famous during World War II.[20] A variation of baseball, softball is a prominent sport for females in high school, college, and beyond. Through increasing coverage on television, it produces female stars with presence in the national consciousness. Though played by men, professional and college baseball lack formal cheerleaders, highlighting women more directly in personal roles as mother, wife, daughter, or friend, often in public view by way of televised close-ups. The San Francisco Giants employ a woman announcer, giving a female tone to the well-publicized action at SBC Park. Several women have been owners of Major League teams, the boss for multi-million-dollar organizations at the most advanced level of play.[21] The game draws attention from a large number of female fans, revealing the meaning of events on the field that transcend the thinking of the male population.

Despite offering some opportunity and significant appeal to women, baseball produces highly restrictive gender roles, far from

---

[19] A few women have been kickers on the college level but not players of other positions.

[20] David Finoli, *For the Good of the Country: World War II Baseball* (Jefferson NC: MacFarland and Company, 2002); Gai Berlage, *Women in Baseball: The Forgotten History* (Westport CT: Praeger, 1994).

[21] For example, Marge Schott was long-time owner of the Cincinnati Reds. See Mike Bass, *Marge Schott: Unleashed* (Champaign IL: Sagamore Publishers, 1994).

the ideals otherwise represented. Professional and college competition confine females to spectatorship and sideline reporting, distant to game action. Only men present "play-by-play" or "color" commentary, rarely including a female point of view. At the highest levels of play, mothers, wives, daughters, and girlfriends receive attention in supportive rather than leading roles, the focus for brief looks of television away from players on the field. Played most prominently by women, fast-pitch softball grows in popularity but not approaching dedication to Major League Baseball. It takes place inside of diminished dimensions, almost miniature in scale compared to the more highly esteemed "hardball."[22] A "softball" is softer, bigger, and easier to see than the harder, faster-moving, and farther-traveling ball for the men, images difficult to reconcile with the goals of equality in gender relations. Portraying the American imagination for an ideal life to come, baseball fails to illustrate improved conditions for half the population.

Within the sports trinity, basketball gives the most and best opportunities for women, exemplifying its civil function to represent social progress. Many thousands of girls play in organized competitions with a large number who continue to play into high school and college. The Women's National Basketball Association (WNBA) features women as professional players, contributing a set of feminine stars to the national culture. In the NBA, teams employ squads of dancers, female performers with a more sophisticated role than football's cheerleaders, while referees for the league include a woman, a female authority figure for the teams of men. Large numbers of women attend NBA and college games, providing a feminine perspective on the male activities on court. Each contest begins with the singing of the national anthem, often by a female vocalist, revealing civil meaning in the upcoming action relevant for both women and men.

---

[22] The bases are just sixty feet apart, and the pitcher is only forty-six feet from the home plate.

Though disclosing advances for women, basketball does not adequately express progress toward equality in gender relations. Especially on the college and professional levels, women's basketball receives far less attention than its male counterpart. Women are not players at the highest level of competition (i.e., the NBA), while the WNBA and college women draw small audiences live or on television. Female reporters provide sideline coverage of well-publicized games but never in play-by-play or color commentary. NBA team dancers offer more than traditional cheerleading yet move off court during game action, becoming leading supporters of the male players. Periodically, beloved mothers, wives, and girlfriends appear in televised moments but only for seconds during time-outs from the competition on court. In contrast to its otherwise strong message of irreversible progress for social conditions, basketball lacks the portrayal of fast improving conditions for women.

In matters of gender, the sports trinity illustrates the three-way perspective of American civil religion. Football presents the reality of severe restriction in roles for women. Baseball provides a more ideal scenario for female involvement, particularly by way of fast-pitch softball, while basketball gives the most opportunities for women, representing significant improvement from decades past. However, the highly restrictive conditions of football are not a realistic portrayal of current conditions for women in the country, and baseball fails to offer detailed illustration of the ideal future for females, at least in any direct way. Basketball discloses advancement for women but well short of equality. Gender relations reveal the limited significance of football, baseball, and basketball, demanding the recognition of the games as flawed expressions of national beliefs. Nevertheless, the three modes of thinking depicted by the three sports can be productively applied to male-female relations. Football generates concern for recognition of harsh realities, heightened awareness to face inequities for women. Baseball produces rich imagination for greater freedom and equality, an idealistic vision for inspiration of the genders. Basketball encourages confidence in the fast-paced progression of conditions to an ideal future, progress not to be withheld from the female population. Football, baseball, and basketball express representational meaning, offering symbolic and not an exact presentation of civil precepts.

The Power of Interpretation

Gender issues reveal the sports trinity as imperfect manifestations of the American belief system. Football, baseball, and basketball were not created in a mistake-free laboratory, nor were they produced to meet a preconceived design. On the contrary, each sport emerged in a natural development from the nation's worldview, more like the growth of fruit from a tree than the chiseled work of a sculptor. Civil religion in the United States planted seeds of thought that eventually produced particular games, an unintended consequence. Like other forms of culture, the three sports represent the creative effort to express purpose in life, the result of inventive work by flawed people. Over a process of decades, they achieved exalted status by way of public recognition, drawing acknowledgement of great significance to be found in the sporting competition. Ultimately, the trinity of sports developed into a less-than-perfect, yet exceptional, illustration of national convictions.

Given the limited nature of meaning associated with football, baseball, and basketball, the nation possesses access to diverse venues for supplementing the influence of sports. For gender relations, fans benefit from the example of institutions for education, business, and politics where females thrive in leading roles. Even the most fanatical fan interacts with women as authority figures in the larger public, while players encounter female professors, school administrators, government officials, and corporate executives on the way to a professional career. Television programs, movies, and popular music communicate a more direct message of equality for women than the three major sports, establishing a rhythm of idealistic thoughts that lingers in the consciousness of the country during the viewing of sporting contests. The sports trinity presents a flawed portrayal of civil religion in the United States, requiring supplementary input from other elements of national culture.

Football, baseball, and basketball provide one among many expressions of the American worldview, not the exclusive means agents of truths. Politics, business, music, performing arts, and food also communicate pivotal beliefs of the nation. Activities of Congress, the Supreme Court, and the presidency convey core convictions of the United States, featuring dedication to balance of power by way of competition and the guidance of constitutional documents. From the workings of the stock market, the country receives an illustration of special commitment to competitiveness in the pursuit of wealth and of competing philosophies that uphold realistic assessment, idealistic vision, and pragmatic decision-making. Diverse styles of music present devotion to individuality, free expression of individual thoughts regardless of the philosophy; whereas, television and movies depict highly influential stories about the origins, history, and future of the nation, generating some version of faith in special status of the United States. The perfect complement to the national way of life, fast food delivers quick energy to a society in hurried pursuit of future bliss and advancement, expected somewhere well beyond the drive through exit. The manifestations of civil religion are prolific. However, only a select group of representations possess an established position at the center of national attention, a special set of institutions including the games of football, baseball, and basketball.

Though established with privileged place, the sports trinity does not exercise a predestined manner of influence, revealing the power of human beings to interpret meaning. Through thoughtful analysis, people in the United States can distinguish the supremely important from the more secondary in the games, similar to the interpretive efforts generated by the stories of conventional religions. Football, baseball, and basketball exert incredible power in the thoughts and feelings of many millions within the nation, demanding increased effort to analyze their significance on the level of worldview. The struggle to understand public significance of the games more fully will facilitate a more voluntary embrace of selected concepts and rejection of others. The trinity of American sports possesses abundant potential yet to be determined, much possibility for thoughtful development, though the future could also bring unfulfilling neglect.

Like the yearly rituals of traditional religion, football, baseball, and basketball portray stories of rich importance, open-ended in meaning rather than a strict definition of belief. A game offers storied accounts of life through nondescript events on a field or court. Together, they illustrate national perceptions of realities, ideals, and progress from real to ideal conditions, not a clearly defined list of faith claims. They present concepts open to discovery, leaving much to the imagination, undoubtedly a source of far-reaching appeal. Each sport provides a distinct type of narrative with certain boundaries of belief but without exact determination of thoughts. Like the mythology of Islam or Christianity that informs diverse subgroups, football, baseball, and basketball inspire diverse communities (e.g., Republicans, Democrats, apolitical people, individuals from thousands of local cultures) as a result of story-like power to guide in expansive ways.

Functioning like the enduring stories of well-established religions, the games football, baseball, and basketball possess much long-term promise by way of thoughtful and symbolic interpretation, not through a literal mode of understanding that leaves the details of contests undistinguished. The three sports should not be considered revelatory of play-by-play detail but helpful for broad thinking, expressing the supreme importance of select ideas.[23] The violent action of football does not command violence by fans, nor is baseball revelation that life literally is a nonviolent competition. On the contrary, the games reveal symbolic portrayal of core convictions, providing precepts of guiding knowledge without precise or exacting

---

[23] For example, the three sports offer ethical guidance of dedication to collective effort, individuality, and gradual progress to more individuality in lifestyle.

directions. Football, baseball, and basketball fail to deliver a script of how to see the world. However, they depict patterns of belief, capable of directing people in many dimensions of life.

After close examination, the sports trinity discloses three streams of thought foundational to the American worldview. Football portrays the element of realism in the national culture, generating concern for the recognition of harsh realities. Baseball illustrates idealism of the United States. It expresses strong imagination for an ideal life to come. while basketball presents the pragmatic philosophy of the country, considered relevant for the most common situations.[24] Hoops action conveys dedication to a balance between adjustment to realities and aspiration for ideals, commitment to fast-paced yet gradual movement from current difficulties to a much better future. Passion for the three sports reveals the American faith in three modes of reasoning, promoting the checks and balances of triune perspective to overcome the dangers of one unchallenged point of view.

Devotion to football, baseball, and basketball discloses the dedication in the United States to diversity of thinking. Football depicts dedication to "just the facts," knowing the "bottom line" reality of situations, while baseball expresses optimism about the future. The third element to the interactive equation, basketball communicates belief in a practical effort to move one step at a time, increasingly closer to idealistic goals. As a unit, the three games represent commitment to exchange of divergent viewpoints, symbolizing three checkpoints of understanding in search for balanced thought. Each year, the interplay of the sports trinity generates concern for the relational mindset of the country, faith in the interaction of competing perspectives and avoidance of uniformity in mind or sport. Revealed by the dedication to three sports, American civil religion

---

[24] Because of intimate association with the ideal life, baseball generates concern for purity of how to play not present in football and basketball. For example, the recent steroids controversy in baseball has not brought similar focus on football or basketball.

pivots on a three-way convergence of thoughts, producing creative tension between the view of realities, ideals, and progress to the ideal.

Expressed by a fanatical concern for the three types of games, devotion to diversity of perspective in the United States creates wide-ranging possibilities. In the best of moments, it inspires commitment to expanding plurality of people, historically leading to greater inclusion of Catholics, Jews, African Americans, and women. At its worst, however, the creed of dedication to plural ideas inhibits openness and brings exclusion in an ironic twist of circumstances. At such times, the highly publicized belief in diverse perspectives provides justification for not giving serious consideration to the grievances of a minority group, using the statement of faith in diversity as a claim to special status in denial of responsibility to be more inclusive. For many decades, the nation tolerated enslavement for millions and the exclusion of most adults from the right to vote despite civil proclamations of universal rights for human beings. Similarly, the sports trinity does not guarantee respect for plurality in society. Through the ritual enactment of dedication to diversity of thought, it may function simply to support the mindset that the country has achieved ideal state of inclusiveness, undercutting the sense of much still to accomplish. On the other hand, the yearly cycle of the three sports can motivate and guide advancement toward greater pluralism, functioning as a call to responsibility rather than as a claim to power. Then, the games will encourage expansion of the mainstream to society in the tradition of abolitionists, suffragettes, and civil rights activists. Empowered with special status, football, baseball, and basketball generate potential for inspiration of a more diverse nation, the product of historical commitment to democratic ideals. For better or worse, they are ever-present resources, offering the possibility of great improvement in conditions but also for delusion and stagnation. Through the power of interpretation, the people of the United States possess the capability to determine the fate of three beloved sports.

Bibliography

Albanese, Catherine. *America: Religions and Religion*. Belmont CA: Wadsworth Publishing, 1981.

Alexander, Charles C. *Our Game: An American Baseball History*. New York: Holt Publishing, 1991.

Andrew, David L. *Michael Jordan, Inc.: Corporate Sport, Media Culture, and Late Modern America* (Albany: State University of New York Press, 2001.

Bak, Richard. *Lou Gehrig*. Dallas: Taylor Publishing, 1995.

Barber, Phil. *The NFL Experience: Twelve Months with America's Favorite Game* (New York: DK Publishing, 2001.

Bass, Amy. *In the Game: Race, Identity, and Sports in the Twentieth Century*. New York: Pellgrave Macmillan, 2005.

Bausum, Ann. *With Courage and Cloth: Winning the Fight for the Women's Right to Vote*. Washington DC: National Geographic, 2004.

Bellah, Robert. *The Broken Covenant: American Civil Religion in Time of Trial*. New York: Seabury Press, 1975.

———. *Habits of the Heart: Individualism and Commitment in American Life*. New York: Perennial Library, 1986.

Berlage, Gae. *Women in Baseball: The Forgotten History*. Westport CT: Praeger Publishers, 1994.

Bernstein, Richard. *Are We to become a Nation? The Making of the Constitution*. Cambridge: Harvard University, 1987.

Blum, John M. *V was for Victory*. New York: Harcourt Brace Publishers, 1976.

Boswell, Thomas. *How Life Imitates the World Series*. Garden City NY: Penguin Books, 1983.

———. *Why Time Begins on Opening Day*. Garden City NY: Doubleday, 1984.

Bryant, Darrol, and Donald Dayton, editors. *The Coming Kingdom: Essays in American Millennialism and Eschatology*. Barrytown NY: International Religious Foundation, 1983.

Bryson, Michael A. *Visions of the Land: Science, Literature, and the American Environment* (Fort Worth: Harcourt & Brace, 1998).

Bjarkman, Peter C. *Diamonds across the Globe: The Encyclopedia of International Baseball*. Westport CT: Greenwood Press, 2005.

Campbell, Joseph. *The Hero of a Thousand Faces*. New York: Pantheon Books, 1949.

Carleton, James, and Mike Schatzkin, *The Baseball Fan's Guide to Spring Training*. Reading MA: Addison-Weseley, 1998.

Carnegie, Andrew. *The Gospel of Wealth and Other Timely Essays*. Cambridge: Harvard University Press, 1962.

Carrette, Jeremy, editor. *William James and the Varieties of Religious Experiences: A Centennial Celebration*. London: Routledge, 2005.

Crawford, S. Cromwell. *World Religions and Global Ethics*. New York: Paragon House, 1989.

Deloria, Vine. *God Is Red: A Native View of Religion*. Golden CO: Fulcrum Publishers, 2003.

Doubleday, Abner. *My Life in the Old Army: Reminiscences of Abner Doubleday*. Fort Worth: Texas Christian University, 1998.

Doubleday, Russels. *Stories of Inventors*. New York: Doublepage and Company, 1904.

Douglass, Mary. *Natural Symbols: Explorations in Cosmology*. New York: Pantheon Books, 1970.

Dowidoff, Nicholas. *Baseball: A Literary Anthology*. New York: Library of America, 2002.

Edwards, Harry. *Sociology of Sport*. Homewood IL: Dorsey Press, 1973.

Eliade, Mircae. *The Sacred and Profane*. New York: Harcourt Brace, 1959.

———. *Myth of the Eternal Return*. Princeton: Princeton University, 1971.

————. *Rites and Symbols of Initiation: The Mysteries of Birth and Rebirth*. New York: Harper and Row, 1965.

Evans, Christopher H., and William R. Herzog II. *The Faith of Fifty Million: Baseball, Religion, and American Culture*. Louisville: John Knox Press, 2003.

Falk, Gerhard. *Football and American Identity*. New York: Hayworth Press, 2005.

Falkner, David. *Great Time Coming: The Life of Jackie Robinson, from Baseball to Birmingham*. New York: Simon and Schuster, 1996.

Foner, Eric. *Slavery and Freedom in Nineteenth Century America*. New York: Oxford University, 1994.

————. *Nothing But Freedom: Emancipation and its Legacy*. Baton Rouge: Louisiana State University, 1983.

Fox, Larry. *Illustrated History of Basketball*. New York: Grosset and Dunlap, 1974.

Fulop, Timothy E., and Albert J. Raboteau, editors. *African American Religion: Interpretive Essays in History and Culture*. New York: Routledge, 1997.

Giamatti, A. Bartlett. *A Great and Glorious Game: Baseball Writings of A. Bartlett Giamatti*. Chapel Hill NC: Algonquin Books, 1998.

Gilbert, Thomas W. *The Soaring Twenties: Babe Ruth and the Home Run Decade*. New York: Franklin Watts, 1996.

Golden, Mark. *Sport in the Ancient World from A to Z*. London: Routledge, 2003.

Gossett, Thomas. *Race: The History of an Idea in America*. New York: Schocken Books, 1965.

Green, Michael S. *Freedom, Union, and Power: Lincoln and His Party during the Civil War*. New York: Fordham University, 2004.

Haesley, Richard, editor. *Woman's Suffrage*. San Diego: Greenhaven Press, 2003.

Horwitz, Robert H. *The Moral Foundations of the American Republic*. Charlottesville: University of Virginia, 1986.

Hovde, Ellen, director. *Liberty!: the American Revolution*. Video. Hollywood: PBS Video, 2004.Howlett, Charles F. *The American Peace Movement*. Boston: G. K. Hall, 1991.

Hunt, A. D. *Ethics of World Religions*. San Diego: Greenhaven Press, 1991.

James, William. *Varieties of Religious Experience*. Cambridge: Harvard University, 1986.

———. *Essays in Pragmatism*. New York: Hafner, 1948.

Jefferson, Thomas. *Light and Liberty: Reflections on the Pursuit of Happiness*. New York: Modern Library Books, 2004.

Kildea, Gary, director. *Trobriand Cricket: An Ingenious Response to Colonialism*. Berkeley: University of California, 1975.

King, Martin Luther, Jr. *The Speeches of Martin Luther King, Jr.* Video. Oak Forest, Illinois: MPI Video, 1988.———. *Where Do We Go from Here: Chaos or Community?* New York: Harper and Row, 1967.

———. *Why We Can't Wait*. New York: New American Library, 1968.

Kinsella, W. P. *A Series for the World: Baseball's First International Classic*. San Francisco: Woodford Press, 1992.

Knock, Thomas J. *To End All Wars: Woodrow Wilson and the Quest for a New World Order*. New York: Oxford University Press, 1992.

LaFeber, Walter. *Michael Jordan and the New Global Capitalism*. New York: W. W. Norton and Company, 1999.

Lanctot, Neil. *Negro League Baseball: The Rise and Ruin of a Black Institution*. Philadelphia: University of Pennsylvania Press, 2004.

Lincoln, Abraham. *The Speeches of Abraham Lincoln*. Video. Oak Forest IL: MPI Video, 1992.———. *The Speeches and Addresses of Abraham Lincoln*. New York: Little Feather Library Corporation, 1911.

———. *The Gettysburg Address*. Boston: Houghton Mifflin, 1995.

Mandelbaum, Michael. *The Meaning of Sports: Why Americans Watch Baseball, Football, and Basketball and What They See When They Do*. New York: Public Affairs, 2004.

Marone, James A. *Hellfire Nation*. New Haven: Yale University Press, 2003.

Martin, Wisdom T. *Intentional Grounding: The History of Black Quarterbacks in the NFL*. Bloomington: University of Indiana, 2002.

Martinson, Tom. *American Dreamscape: The Pursuit of Happiness in Postwar Suburbia*. New York: Carrol and Graf, 2000.

Marty, E. Martin. *Religion and Republic: The American Circumstance*. Boston: Beacon Press, 1987.

Mead, Sidney. *The Nation with the Soul of a Church*. New York: Harper and Row, 1975.

———. *The Lively Experiment: The Shaping of Christianity in America*. New York: Harper and Row, 1963.

Miller, Patrick. *The Sporting World of the Modern South*. Urbana: University of Illinois, 2002.

———, and David K. Wiggins. *Sport and the Color Line: Black Athletes And Race Relations in Twentieth-century America*. New York: Routledge, 2004.

Miller, Perry. *Errand into the Wilderness*. Cambridge: Harvard University, 1956.

Muir, John K. *The Encyclopedia of Superheroes*. Jefferson NC: McFarland And Company, 2004.

Namias, June. *First Generation: In the Words of Twentieth-Century American Immigrants*. Urbana: University of Illinois, 1992.

Nash, Roderick. *Wilderness and the American Mind* (New Haven: Yale University Press, 2001).

Novak, Michael. *The Joy of Sports: Endzones, Bases, Baskets, Balls, and Consecration of the American Spirit*. New York: Basic Books, 1976.

Otto, Rudolph. *The Idea of the Holy: An Inquiry into the Non-Rational Factor in the Idea of the Divine and its Relation to the Rational*. London: Oxford University Press, 1955.

Perret, Geoffrey. *Lincoln's War: The Untold Story of America's Greatest President as Commander in Chief*. New York: Random House, 2004.

Powell, Harfold. *Walter Camp: The Father of American Football.* Boston: Little, Brown, and Company, 1926.

Price, Joseph L. editor. *From Season to Season: Sports as American Religion.* Macon GA: Mercer University Press, 2001.

Roosevelt, Franklin. *Rendezvous with Destiny.* New York: Krauss Reprint, 1995.

Rowland, Della. *Martin Luther King, Jr.: The Dream of Peaceful Revolution.* Englewood Cliffs NJ: Prentice Hall, 1990.

Rush, Benjamin. *The Selected Writings of Benjamin Rush.* New York: PhilosophicalLibrary, 1947.

Schulte, Nordholdt J. W. *Woodrow Wilson: A Life for World Peace.* Berkeley: University of California, 1991.

Segal, Howard P. *Technological Utopianism in American Culture* (Chicago: University of Chicago Press, 1985).

Smart, Ninian. *Worldviews: Cross-Cultural Examination of Human Beliefs.* Englewood Cliffs NJ: Prentice Hall, 2000.

———. *Dimensions of the Sacred: An Anatomy of the World's Beliefs.* London: Harper Collins, 1996.

Stewart, Wayne. *Fathers, Sons, and Baseball: Our National Pastime and the Ties that Bind* (Guilford: Lyons Press, 2002).

Swanson, Wayne. *Why the West Was Wild.* Toronto: Arnick Press, 2004.

Taylor, Dale. *Simpler Times: Baseball Stories from a Small Town.* Waverly OH:, Dale Taylor, 1997.

Tebbel, John W. *From Rags to Riches: Horatio Alger, Jr. and the American Dream.* New York: Macmillan, 1964.

Tierney, Thomas F. *The Value of Convenience: A Genealogy of Technical Culture.* Albany: State University of New York Press, 1993.

Tillich, Paul. *The Protestant Era.* Chicago: University of Chicago, 1948.

Tobin, James. *To Conquer the Air: The Wright Brothers and the Great Race for Flight.* New York: Free Press, 2003.

Toma, J. Douglas. *Football U: Spectator Sports in the Life of the American University* (Ann Arbor: University of Michigan Press, 2001).

Turner, Victor. *Ritual Process: Structure and Anti-Structure*. Chicago: University of Chicago, 1969.

Van Deusen, Gyndon D. *The Rise and Decline of Jacksonian Democracy*. Huntington NY: R. E. Krieger Publishing, 1979.

Ward, John W. *Red, White, and Blue: Men, Books, and Ideas in American Culture*. New York: Oxford University, 1969.

Webb, Bernice. *The Basketball Man, James Naismith*. Lawrence: University of Kansas, 1973.

Weinstein, Laurie L., and Christine C. White. *Wives and Warriors: Women and the Military in the United States and Canada*. Westport CT: Bergin and Garvey, 1997.

Wells, Ronald A, editor. *Liberty and Law: Reflections on the Constitution in American Life and Thought*. Grand Rapids MI: Erdmann's Publishing Company, 1987.

Wentz, Richard E. *American Religious Traditions: The Shaping of Religion in the United States*. Minneapolis: Fortress Press, 2003.

Wenzel, Frank and Rita C. *The Fanatic's Guide to SEC Football*. Pensacola: Light Side Publishers, 1993.

White, Richard. *The Frontier in American Culture*. Berkeley: University of California, 1994.

Whiting, Robert. *You Gotta Have Wa*. New York: Macmillan Press, 1989.

Williams, Juan. *Eyes on the Prize: America's Civil Rights Years, 1954–1965*. New York: Viking Press, 1987.

Young, Jeffrey. *Forbes Greatest Technology Stories: Inspiring Tales of Entrepreneurs and Inventors who Revolutionized Modern Business*. New York: Wiley and Sons, 1998.

Zuckerman, Paul. *Invitation to Sociology of Religion*. New York: Routledge, 2003.

Index